APPRENTICE IN WONDERLAND

ALSO BY RAMIN SETOODEH

Ladies Who Punch: The Explosive Inside Story of "The View"

APPRENTICE IN WONDERLAND

HOW DONALD TRUMP AND MARK BURNETT TOOK AMERICA THROUGH THE LOOKING GLASS

RAMIN SETOODEH

HARPER

An Imprint of HarperCollins*Publishers*

HarperCollins books may be purchased for educational, business, or sales promotional use. For information, please email the Special Markets Department at SPsales@harpercollins.com.

FIRST EDITION

Library of Congress Cataloging-in-Publication Data has been applied for.

ISBN 978-0-06-313990-9

24 25 26 27 28 LBC 5 4 3 2 1

To my dad, who is voting for him

"But I don't want to go among mad people," Alice remarked.
"Oh, you can't help that," said the Cat: "we're all mad here."

—Lewis Carroll

Don't forget, when it first went on, everybody said, "No way. Who's going to watch Trump on television? It's not going to work." And, you know, it worked. And they want to renew me as long as I live, I guess.

—Donald Trump on Fox News, February 2015

Contents

APPRENTICE IN WONDERLAND

Into the Boardroom

Donald Trump is back in the boardroom. But as reality TV's ultimate boss slumps in his chair twenty-five floors above Manhattan, the cameras are nowhere to be found. It's August 2021, the summer after Trump was voted out of the White House. This president in exile's most adoring fans, and his most ardent detractors, probably think he's at Mar-a-Lago or Bedminster. Yet Trump has covertly made his way back to the city he loves, and he's agreed to meet me here at Trump Tower to relive his TV glory days. Clad in his familiar armor of a boxy suit and too-long necktie that became his trademark as "The Donald," he's going to travel back in time with me to 2004. That's when his reality TV series *The Apprentice* became a national phenomenon, transforming Trump into an unlikely blue-collar folk hero with swagger, comedic timing, and world-class negotiating chops. Trump, until then a New York celebrity who was pushing his way forward with the help of the tabloids, suddenly blew up as America's most famous businessman.

Trump's four-year presidency was a kaleidoscope of distortions and "fake news," ending with an attempted coup. The country has moved on—or so it seems—from Trump. And Trump seems, for the moment, to have moved on as well. He lost his Twitter privileges because of his role in inciting the insurrection on January 6, 2021. Without a platform on which to rant, in 280-character bursts, about the injustices he's facing, Trump essentially disappeared. But on this afternoon, he has reason to crack a smile. He's about to do something that's going to remind him just how powerful he used to be. He's going to revisit some of his best exchanges as NBC's top reality TV moneymaker, to remember a simpler time when he knew exactly what to say and when everybody, not just his partisan loyalists, looked up to him.

"There are a lot of big moments!" Trump says. I press play on an eleven-minute video that I've edited together of key scenes from *The Apprentice*. The clips range from the three times he axed the troublemaker contestant Omarosa Manigault (he could never stay mad at her, and later made her a top aide in his White House) to crowning Joan Rivers the winner of the second celebrity edition of the series. "It is true, isn't it?" he asks, boasting about his unique perch in popular culture. I assure the former leader of the free world that yes, his reality TV series changed history.

The conference room that we're in today has the generic feeling of a workspace that could exist anywhere, with a scuffed-up long wooden table, a TV projection screen, and rolling chairs. Only if you squint, though, does it resemble the boardroom from *The Apprentice*. In a way, we're on a working set: the NBC series was shot in Trump Tower, and Trump charged the show's creator, Mark Burnett, hundreds of thousands of dollars to lease office space. "Okay, so we had two floors of this building—big floors!—taken up by *The Apprentice*," Trump says after we watch the scene in which he first uttered the words "You're fired!" on TV. "Down below, we had the boardroom. There were hundreds of people that worked on the show. You know, this television stuff is great. You'll think they'll have, like, two cameras." He pauses for effect. "They had two cameras on every person, especially after it became a big hit, actually."

Trump goes on to say that he improvised the catchphrase that helped propel the series into the ratings stratosphere. The show cast Trump as a no-nonsense CEO tasked with gleefully firing mediocre job candidates (and later celebrities) who couldn't cut it in his version of the high-stakes world of corporate America. "When I said, 'You're fired!' the whole building shook," Trump says of that first episode. "Everybody, because they have so many screens, they saw what was going on in the boardroom. The place just reverberated. People were screaming. They were shouting. The crew! The makeup people! Everyone was watching it. There were hundreds of them, and they went crazy." He sounds like a retired high school football coach, lounging in a diner in the middle of the day, rewinding the clock on his favorite plays.

As a storyteller, Trump can struggle with facts, the chronology of events, and what exactly he accomplished as president, but the details of that day from more than seventeen years ago flow freely. "In fact," he says, "they had to stop the tape. They had to get them to shut up, because you can't have that. Although"—Trump seems to imagine the sound of a crew cheering for him again, right now—"they could have left it; it would have been interesting. But the people in their homes went crazy too! Because that first night, when it aired, that first show, I got calls from people that I hadn't spoken to in years. They said, 'That was the most unbelievable show!'"

As he crisscrosses through time, his brain misfires. Even he can't accept that a version of himself existed that was once broadly uncontroversial and popular. "So, it actually got very good reviews, which is hard for me, because they hate to give me good reviews," Trump says. "I got unbelievable reviews. Now, that was before my political days, okay? You know."

Trump makes a face like a toddler being forced to eat his vegetables. If this were a scene from a reality show, and not real life, the producers might cut to a confessional booth where Trump would look into the camera and admit that he regretted running for president and that starring in *The Apprentice* was the best job he'd ever had. Of course, on *The Apprentice*, Trump, unlike the contestants, never gave confessional interviews. By issuing commands and beheading the unworthy, he was simply the voice of God.

He squints at me from across the room.

"Go ahead. Show me another one." And so I play another clip, and another one, and another one.

CHAPTER 1

Keeping Up with the Trumps

Throughout his career as a real estate mogul, Donald Trump agreed to practically every interview request that came his way, because he believed there was no such thing as bad publicity. He followed this same strategy as a reality TV star. That's how I first started talking to him in 2004 as a twenty-two-year-old reporter at *Newsweek* covering *The Apprentice*. Most celebrities employ a publicist to field their interview requests, but such a system proved too bureaucratic—and perhaps too costly—for Trump. Instead of going through a PR flack, I'd call his office at Trump Tower, and his secretary Norma Foerderer would patch me through to his desk (or cell phone) so quickly that Trump wouldn't even stop to ask which publication was on the other line. "I love *Newsday!*" was a regular salutation. After I'd then tell him that I was actually calling from *Newsweek*, he'd restart our conversation by listing off new superlatives—leaving the poor reporters at *Newsday* in a ditch.

Nearly twenty years later, when I announce in the press I'm writing this book, Trump reaches out to me through his office, offering to be the first person I interview. Given the circumstances—that he's not only the central figure of my book but a former U.S. president engulfed in scandal—I expected that I'd need to work much harder to track him down. Once we get started, he keeps extending our time together, which would spill over into follow-up appointments. "Okay, so why don't we do another meeting?" is how he'd usually end our sessions. Sitting across from him with my prepared list of questions, I have no way to contain our conversations just to *The Apprentice*. He haphazardly swings from one monologue to the next.

A question about a contestant cascades into a defense of his leadership as POTUS, and then he swings back to the 2000s again. On some days, I have the feeling he has no idea whom he's even talking to; at our second meeting, he tells me he couldn't remember sitting down with me, even though it was only a few months earlier, a startling admission about his short-term memory. "That was a long time ago," he says. But each time we meet is another chance to drum up press for himself, to prove that he still matters. And there is something about talking about *The Apprentice* that soothes him, like a calming chest balm applied to a patient with pneumonia. "If this comes out right, it's such a great thing," Trump explains. "The true story has never been told."

Even though I'd witnessed how untethered Trump had become during his press conferences from the White House and other public appearances, meeting him in person means experiencing the former president on another level. In the spring and summer of 2021, he looks lonely, a shadow of a famous person. He seeks validation from even the tiniest groups of humans, assembled in his office on any given day, badgering his adviser Jason Miller or deputy communications chief Margo Martin to voice their approval aloud as he tells stories about how much better he'd be than "Sleepy Joe" or how unfairly the media treats him. In other ways, for all that he's visibly aged, the presidency hasn't fundamentally changed him, not as a man, nor as an interview subject who'd never learned how to listen in a conversation. He pivots to his vendettas and lashes out about his many enemies, from Dr. Anthony Fauci to the MSNBC host Lawrence O'Donnell to the *Will & Grace* star Debra Messing. "She's brutal," Trump hisses, admitting that he'd spent time in the White House closely monitoring the Twitter account of a sitcom actress.

Here is the forty-fifth president of the United States of America, trapped behind a desk in a corner office inside his own glass tower, with a bare-bones staff, an empty calendar, and hours of unfilled time. I never know when our afternoons together will end. There is always the possibility that if things went extremely well, Trump could keep talking at me through dinner, and maybe I'd have to excuse myself to escape from *him*.

For my first interview in May 2021, I take a car to Trump Tower. The stillness on Fifth Avenue reflects the widely held belief by most New Yorkers that Trump has permanently fled their city. There are no crowds to mark his presence, in the form of MAGA fans or curious tourists. The skyscraper that shields him from a Manhattan that no longer wants to be associated with him has its own history—most notably as the recurring co-star of *The Apprentice* and the site of the escalator that he famously rode down in 2015 to announce his first run for president. Now, all these years later, Trump Tower feels like Grey Gardens without the cats.

Within these walls, there are ghosts of Trump's past. When I enter the lobby on my first visit for this book, a security guard waves me upstairs after checking my name off a list, but he doesn't wand me or pat me down for weapons; this is exactly how I entered the building years ago as a reporter with an appointment to see "The Donald." I'm surprised just how easy it is to physically access him. I'd gone through heavier security at concerts and museums.

Inside the elevator, someone has stuck a faded "Make America Great Again" sticker next to the buttons. Twenty-six floors up, I encounter Trump via a papier-mâché bust of his head—sitting on top of a cabinet in a hall. I'm reminded of the faded billboard in *The Great Gatsby*, featuring the vacant eyes of the optometrist Dr. T. J. Eckleburg. There is something about the quiet inside Trump Tower that feels like a department store past its prime. The reception area, often featured on the show, has lost its sheen: Rhona Graff, an assistant, who shot to fame on *The Apprentice* for telling the contestants when Trump was ready for them in the board-room, has left her position. (She was subpoenaed in 2022 by the New York attorney general during a probe of the Trump Organization's finances.) The only reading material within sight are old copies of *Trump* magazine, a vanity publication that folded years ago.

On this afternoon, a longtime Trump associate, Meredith McIver—the former ballerina and a professional ghostwriter who took the blame for Melania Trump's plagiarized speech at the 2016 Republican National Convention—is manning the desk, dressed like Cruella de Vil in a white dalmatian-spotted jacket and leopard flats. A secretary assists her with answering phones. Eavesdropping on her conversation with a young Secret Service agent offers a window into the lives of Trump's staff: they sound as if they were being held against their will inside their ruler's bunker.

"We've seen a lot of action in these halls over the years," the secretary says. "Things were always changing. It's very exciting!" she cries out, trying to convince herself as much as her conversation partner.

Then she picks up the phone and puts on a chirpy voice: "*Trump Organization.*" As soon as she hears who is on the other line, she quickly hangs up. "This guy is screaming in Russian, not an English word," she says. "There's always a crank caller you can just count on." (Somehow the Russians are always finding a way to crash into Trump's orbit.) The phone starts to ring again. "There he is." She switches over to her secretary voice: "*Trump Organization.*" And then she hangs up again.

The Secret Service agent shuffles his feet.

"Were you able to go outside today?" she asks him. "It's really pretty."

"I worked in the motorcade, so I rode in," he says.

The agent scoffs as he glances down at his suit. "I don't think people like me because I look like a detective."

"I didn't think about that," she says. "You're suspicious?"

"The last thing I want to do is get in a fistfight. I want to grunge down a little bit so I don't attract attention."

"It's hard to blend." The phone keeps ringing, but now she's ignoring it.

"He's still calling?" the agent asks, and the secretary nods. He goes on: "Do you get a lot of protesters?"

"Not that much. They are pretty minor. That would cause too much consternation." She holds on to the last word, raising her eyebrows long enough to suggest that Trump wouldn't tolerate such a thing. Suddenly the room gets quiet, and even the phone calls from Russia stop.

"You have a rough job," the Secret Service agent says.

"Fortunately, I'm only in for an hour when he's here," the secretary says, blinking a few times to show that she hasn't surrendered to a hostage situation. "It doesn't wear me down."

"I always got the biggest ratings—to this day!" Trump says. He's referring to millions of people who tuned in to *The Apprentice*, but that gives him an opening to hype himself up about the audience he captivated from the White House. "Did you see where I had 49.9 million people watching my State of the Union address?" Trump says, neglecting to pinpoint a year, though he's likely referring to the 47.7 million viewers who watched his first address to Congress as president in 2017, according to Nielsen. "And Biden had 11 million," Trump declares. (Biden's numbers in 2021 were smaller, at 26.9 million, but not as small as Trump suggests.) "And you say, 'So how does he win!?' Everybody says the same thing: He didn't win. It was a rigged election, that was a totally rigged election!"

Since Trump's conspicuous ascent in American politics, *The Apprentice* has been endlessly analyzed, debated, referenced, and credited as a major factor in his 2016 victory. But what's been lost in most of the conversations about the show is the show itself—not just a symbol, but a seminal moment in the history of popular culture.

Before social media gave everybody a chance to be famous, the early years of reality TV offered America a new form of entertainment. When fifty-two million Americans tuned in to the season finale of *Survivor* in 2000 to watch Richard Hatch outwit his competitors on a desert island to win $1 million, it marked an inflection point. No longer were the networks dependent on stars or even writers. They just needed to come up with an outlandish premise, cast reasonably attractive or out-of-control people, and find a story through the magic of editing. Some of the big early reality TV series involved strangers living together (*The Real World*, which kicked off reality TV as we know it in 1992, and *Big Brother*, which premiered shortly after *Survivor*), trying to hook up (*The Bachelor* and its many copycats), or facing off in disgusting dares (*Fear Factor*). In 2002, *American Idol* built to the coronation of Kelly Clarkson as a new pop star, but along the way the real fun had been watching the judge Simon Cowell tear the lesser singers to shreds.

The Apprentice, which was created by Mark Burnett, also the genius behind *Survivor*, took a different path. It was *aspirational*. It premiered as a mid-season replacement on NBC in January 2004 as uncertainty reigned over how long the post-9/11 economic recovery would last. The city of New York had come back after the terrorist attacks in 2001, and the show was a love letter to Manhattan as the cameras swooped in on skyscrapers (especially Trump Tower) and the contestants scampered around Wall Street and Times Square, completing tasks. Rather than require its heroes to eat worms on an island in Malaysia, or pretend to fall in love on TV, *The Apprentice* was framed as "the ultimate job interview"—with sixteen professionals vying for the chance to climb to the top as the president of a company in the Trump Organization, with a salary of $250,000 a year.

"If you think about the reality TV shows that were successful, you had *Idol*, you had *Survivor*, you had *Fear Factor*," recalls Jeff Gaspin, who became the chairman of NBC Universal Television Entertainment during *The Apprentice*. In Gaspin's opinion, most Americans couldn't really picture themselves on the other shows: "Well, I don't want to participate in *Fear Factor*, and I don't necessarily want to go to a desert island and starve, and I can't sing. But do you know what? I have a job, and here's a show where if you have a job, you might be able to succeed."

Gaspin wasn't initially sure Burnett's pitch would lead to a TV phenomenon. "Honestly, as a buyer, that felt a little too common," he says. "It felt a little too average. But it turned out to be one of its greatest strengths: the masses could see themselves participating."

Unlike most reality shows, which cast for good looks or for shamelessness, the early seasons of *The Apprentice* were packed with professionals who'd gone to top colleges and already established themselves in fast-paced careers such as real estate, marketing, consulting, and law. The show positioned Trump as the ultimate taskmaster, a symbol of success who judged the performance of his wannabe minions in tasks that required both business school smarts and street savvy. Each week brought a new challenge for the cast, originally divided up into men versus women. Many of the competitions were pure skills tests that had little to do, practically speaking, with the work of running a corporation: The very first episode, titled "Meet the Billionaire," saw the teams get a $250 "investment" to sell lemonade in the streets of New York. Later first-season challenges had more to do with Trump's line of work as a real estate developer, as when the cast had to take over a Planet Hollywood restaurant for a night to boost its profits or renovate an apartment on the cheap and find the highest-paying renter. At the end of each episode, the winning team collected a prize, often a cross-promotion involving a Trump property, such as one of his golf courses or casinos. The weakest performer got the boot in the boardroom.

In New York City, Trump was a huge star, and *The Apprentice* treated him as such. But as its ratings soared in the first season, drawing an average of twenty-eight million viewers during its two-hour finale, it managed to accomplish what no amount of calls to the press and attention-grabbing stunts had done: it made him into a towering national figure. By mentoring so many young aspiring businesspeople, Trump was portrayed as an all-knowing leader who was generous enough to share his Midas touch with the viewers at home. He even spoke directly to the camera each week, dishing out his own secret business tips printed on the screen like *Sesame Street* lessons: "Location, Location, Location"; "It's Easier to Think Big"; and "The Art of the Deal." Burnett knew he needed to build his series around Trump as a hulking personality. The show's first scene featured him riding in a helicopter over the Manhattan skyline; the episode ends with him granting the winning team a tour of his penthouse apartment plated in gold. "This is like rich—like really, really rich," one of the contestants stammers in disbelief.

The Apprentice allowed Trump to enshrine the mythic scale of his own wealth. The premier episode had him addressing viewers at home, listing off his résumé. "I'm the largest real estate developer in New York. I own buildings all over the place, model agencies, the Miss Universe pageant, jetliners, golf courses, casinos, and private resorts like Mar-a-Lago, one of the most spectacular estates anywhere in the world." On the show, Trump came across as a tough-talking mogul who didn't back down from anybody. He even acknowledged his own corporate bankruptcies, however vaguely: "About thirteen years ago, I was seriously in trouble. I was billions of dollars in debt. But I fought back and won—big league!"

Trump's previous self-mythologizing—covered daily by the New York tabloids, where he'd show up Mayor Ed Koch every chance he got and spin the details of his ugly divorce from Ivana—went supersonic. He was suddenly a star whose charisma made anything possible for him, the avatar of a businessman par excellence.

In truth, on the set of *The Apprentice*, Trump was notable not as a brilliant business mind but as an insecure actor. He sulked when he wasn't the center of attention, leered at attractive women, and hijacked the production with his own ego and inability to read a teleprompter. He didn't take directions and surrounded himself with a team tasked with making him look good. He wasn't interested in reading briefs about what had happened that day. Instead, he was purely focused on maximizing his screen time. It was in the hunt for audience attention—a skill he'd honed by playing off the competing *New York Post* and *Daily News* against each other, but perfected before the cameras on the set of *The Apprentice*—that Trump discovered the formula that would take him to the White House.

"Did you have your vaccine?" It's thirty-one minutes into our first conversation when Trump poses this question to me. *Of course I've been vac-
cinated!* I almost blurt out, but instead I simply nod—to match his own
apparent ambivalence. In addition to lax security measures, vaccine pro-
tocols are lacking at Trump Tower. During this time, restaurants in New
York won't let you inside without an Excelsior Pass, but these rules didn't
carry over to spending time with a seventy-four-year-old germophobic
senior citizen who until recently had access to our nuclear codes. In the
car ride over, I'd wondered whether anyone would be wearing a mask: no
one was. I consider leaving my mask on when I sit down, until I realize
that won't be practical in the company of the person who caused daily
national confusion about their effectiveness. Trump is so animated as he
leaps into a conversation about the vastness of *The Apprentice*'s ratings it
becomes clear that I'll need the full use of my facial muscles to meet him
halfway. Now, deep into our talk, suddenly the emotional tide is turning,
and Trump is seething with rage.

His question about my vaccination status turns out to have nothing to
do with his—or my—safety. It follows a tangent about how COVID-19 is
working its way through Asia. "Remember when they used to say how well
India is doing?" Trump says, without waiting for an affirmation. "India is
being ravaged. It's all over. Forget the hospitals. Do you know what the
health care is? They lie down in the streets, and they're dying in the streets!
It almost seems like a stronger strain. It's killing hundreds of thousands of
people." He seems to take some kind of solace in this horrific depiction of
suffering. So many people had questioned him when he was in the White
House about why the United States' COVID mortality rates were higher
than India's. "It just wasn't their turn," he says. "We did unbelievable, and
then I came up with a vaccine. Then I bought $12 billion of the vaccine
before we knew it was going to work."

The webs he's spinning hang in the air. "It was the greatest bet ever
made in the history of the world," Trump says. "You wouldn't have had
the vaccines till October had I not bought it early. And if I didn't do that,
you wouldn't have had yours. This would have been another Spanish flu."

Now he's spiraling, debating with himself. "These two vaccines would have taken another president five years, but you probably wouldn't have had it," he says. "Fauci said, 'You can't do it, 'cause it'll take too long.' Fauci was wrong on everything, when you think about it. He said, 'Don't wear masks!' Now he wants about three of them. 'Don't close up China!' I closed up China. Then I closed up Europe. He said that won't be necessary. Five months later, he said, 'Trump did an amazing thing by doing that.'"

He's all juiced up now. I half expect him to declare that Fauci is fired. But, of course, Trump lacks that power—lacks the ability to do much but look back, at the time he was a president, and before that, a TV star. "They love Fauci! The whole thing is so crazy when you think about it . . . . So . . . back to *The Apprentice* . . ."

If you've ever said a negative word about Donald Trump, chances are you're on his enemies list. The Clintons, Obamas, and Bidens of course haunt Trump's thoughts every day; the intensity of the hatred is unusual, but at least it can be explained by their being his political adversaries.

On one of my visits to Trump Tower, I cued up a clip of Kim Kardashian making a cameo on *The Apprentice* in 2010, in order to promote her signature fragrance line. In the scene, Kim mentions that her sister Khloé sends her best, even though Trump had fired her from *The Celebrity Apprentice* the year before. This early meeting of members of reality TV dynasties led to friction for all involved. And while at first Trump seems nonchalant while talking about the Kardashians, he grows increasingly frustrated thinking about the only family in American celebrity culture that rivals his own.

"Yeah, I never got along great with Khloé," Trump says, immediately attacking her looks and character. "There was little chemistry." (Women who did well on *The Apprentice* often fawned over Trump, even on the celebrity version; Khloé never seemed that impressed by him.) "Khloé was arrested"—in 2007—"for drunk driving. Did you know that?" Trump flashes a smug look at his ability to recall this piece of compromising information. "I think it's a terrible thing—so many people die with drunk driving. You don't hear about it, but they do."

Trump is once again claiming, as he did on *The Apprentice*, that he fired Khloé because she'd been arrested for drunken driving one year before filming his reality show. But this excuse contradicts a *Huffington Post* story from 2016, alleging that he actually axed her because of her weight. According to the story, published just a few weeks before he was elected president, anonymous sources on the show (who also spoke to me) recall that Trump referred to Khloé in derogatory language such as "piglet" and called her "the ugly Kardashian." The story ran after a presidential debate in which Hillary Clinton had reminded America that Trump, as owner of the Miss Universe pageant, mocked the 1996 winner as "Miss Piggy" when she gained weight.

Even now, Trump can't stop himself from commenting on Khloé's appearance. "She looks so much different today," Trump says. "I saw her fairly recently." He searches for the right word. "Better! She looks *better*. It was just her time to be fired. It's hard to be on a show like that. You're with other people who are very smart. I mean, some of these contestants are vicious. I'd watch it go on, and they were ferocious."

Trump zeroes back in on his target. "And some weren't. Some were eaten alive. Khloé was quiet." He asks to go off the record, but rather than offer some Kardashian tea, he simply mumbles.

Then the conversation turns to Kim, who, in 2018, visited him in the Oval Office and persuaded him to grant clemency to a woman named Alice Marie Johnson, who was serving life in prison for a 1996 arrest for cocaine trafficking. The trip was, of course, chronicled for the cameras on her hit E! reality series *Keeping Up with the Kardashians*. For a made-for-TV president, being merciful—something not in Trump's nature—was a small price to pay for the reward of the spotlight (Jared Kushner brokered the meeting, in an attempt to give his father-in-law some good publicity).

Kim returned to Washington, D.C., for another gathering with Trump in early March 2020, bringing along Johnson and other women whom she'd help free from prison as part of her criminal justice efforts. Kardashian had the good luck of coming into her activism at a moment when the White House was occupied by a president who was obsessed with celebrity culture and was happy to receive her. Because of the access Trump gave her, and the success of her passion projects, she walked a fine line in avoiding criticizing him. "I have nothing bad to say about the president," Kardashian said to Jimmy Kimmel in 2018. "I'm very grateful. I'm very hopeful more good things will come out of our meeting."

But Trump now believes that Kim betrayed him by celebrating Joe Biden's 2020 win on Twitter and posting three blue heart emojis next to a picture of Biden and Kamala Harris. "I was disappointed in Kim," Trump says. "I get along with her fine. I got along with her then husband"; infamously, he'd struck up a bromance with Kanye West. "In fact, he endorsed me"—in 2016, even though West later said he didn't vote—"and all that stuff. But with Kim, I did a lot of prison reform that she couldn't get done with anyone else. Then, in order to be accepted by Hollywood, she didn't endorse me. I heard . . ." He corrects himself. "Somebody told me she did not endorse me."

He starts to mope. "She went for Sleepy Joe! Which is incredible to me. Incredible, because I did something that was perhaps important to her." Trump, whose suspicious nature is always at its most acute when he's feeling hurt, can't help implying that Kim was insincere in her commitment to prison reform. "Maybe it was just publicity for her," he says. "I don't know. But she came to the White House. I saw her. She told me the story, and I let people out of prison that I thought were deserving to be let out."

He shifts back in his chair. "Now, I'm a very strict person when it comes to drugs." Trump says of Johnson, "I don't think these were really hard drugs, and there was a question as to whether or not she was using. I did a very good thing. People liked it very much."

Trump's ties to the Calabasas mother ship run deeper than Kim and Khloé. Caitlyn Jenner, an outspoken Republican and vanity candidate in the 2021 election to recall Governor Gavin Newsom, has long agonized in public over Trump. She's stumped for him as a presidential candidate while also expressing disappointment over his transphobic policies. When asked about his relationship with Jenner, Trump offers a blank stare. "I don't know her," he says. Trump's stance on LGBTQ rights is one of the areas in which he has been most inconsistent, and his forgetfulness about Jenner—with whom he's appeared in photographs even after she transitioned—feels too convenient to be an innocent mistake. "I knew Bruce," he says. "But I don't know Caitlyn." He's now trolling, stoking something.

Similarly, he pleads ignorance about *Keeping Up with the Kardashians*. "I don't watch it," he says. "I never watched it." Yes, it's hard to engage with the competition, besides keeping track of their missteps and betrayals in articles. But Trump concedes that whatever they're doing as a business-oriented, attention-seeking family is working. "There must be something, right?"

It's more than something—as Trump should know—it's *everything*. Like the Trumps of the West Coast, the Kardashians sought endless press coverage to make their fame and fortune and found a path to stardom on reality TV. Trump invited America into a family business, but the Kardashians brought the cameras inside their homes, building their brands and raking in hundreds of millions of dollars as moguls—selling everything from skin care to swimwear. The approach is the same; what separates Trump from Kim are some three thousand miles of American landscape and, of course, the presidency.

"So do you think I would have been president without *The Apprentice*?" It's a question that Trump asks me in every conversation we have. He offers a different answer depending on the day. "I say yes," Trump announces in our first meeting, after a dramatic pause. "But some people say no. Many smart people say no." He hedges, considering how much to acknowledge that he had some assistance in his rise to power. "It helped me a little bit, probably."

Trump compares himself to Marlon Brando and Clint Eastwood and notes that the latter star, whom he calls a friend, moves with the same macho swagger in real life that he did as Dirty Harry. "It's sort of not acting," Trump says. "It is what it is." Eastwood, of course, never achieved office higher than the mayoralty of Carmel-by-the-Sea, California, but the organizing principle remains the same: what makes a celebrity, to Trump, is charisma, which can't be taught. "Look," he concludes, "you either have it or you don't have it for television." No wonder Khloé's reluctance to play ball annoyed him.

When we discuss this topic again a few months later, Trump is stuck on coming up with an answer. "I guess it was great for my brand," he says about the show. "The theory is they"—millions of Americans—"got to know me, because they didn't really know me. Mark Burnett and Jeff Zucker, those two main characters, they either get praised or blamed for me becoming president. Mark Burnett says without *The Apprentice*, I wouldn't have been president. I never spoke to Zucker about it."

As the president of NBC Universal, Zucker coddled Trump and treated him like a TV star as big as Jennifer Aniston. Later, as the boss of CNN, Zucker pumped him up as a Republican candidate in the early days of his run, airing his rallies live as "breaking news" events before the two had an ugly falling-out. As for Burnett, Trump was an important cog in his reality TV empire, and the two operated as one entity, splitting profits from the show. Even now, it's hard to know where the mirage of him began and where it ended: Was Trump a self-creation, or made for TV by Mark Burnett?

Trump suddenly gets quiet, revealing something that he's never said before. "Maybe I wouldn't have run if I didn't do *The Apprentice*," Trump says. "You know, that's a little bit of a different thing. I might not have run."

In January 2024, well after my first meeting with Trump—as the man gears up to run for office once more—his son Eric greets me with a firm handshake. Unlike his always-in-uniform dad, he's dressed down in khakis and a sweater with the words "Trump Scotland" over his chest. But when he sees me in a suit, he apologizes twice for his casualness. "Sorry, I was traveling today," he says, even though his assistant had told me he'd been in New York the day before. "That's the only reason I'm not in a suit."

Eric's office is on the same floor of Trump Tower where I watched *Apprentice* clips with his father in a conference room; it's one floor below Donald's corner CEO office. It's less than half the size of his father's lair, a more modest workspace, but still high enough above the ground to offer a breathtaking view of the Manhattan skyline.

"I got to pull up all the *Apprentice* memorabilia for you," Eric says. He remembers how he used to work all day on real estate dealings and then film scenes for *The Apprentice* in the boardroom on the fourteenth floor of Trump Tower at dinnertime. Eric stored a bag of Trump-branded neckties, part of his father's clothing line at Macy's, near his desk so that he could vary his look from episode to episode. As he revisits this memory, Eric opens a locker-style closet in his office, reaching past a photograph of him posing on a golf course with Tiger Woods. "I have one right here," he says, pointing to a necktie. "We'd keep a hundred ties and we'd literally go there and grab. How many ties do you wear on an active basis?" he asks me. "Five, six, seven? I think the last season had eighteen episodes." Suddenly Eric is doling out fashion advice to his younger self. "Is there a yellow that doesn't look hideous that is different?"

In person, he's relaxed, less rigid than the political surrogate on TV representing his father's campaign. "That was the first entry into show business for us and the family outside of news," Eric says. "If you have ratings, they will double down on you. You don't have ratings, and they will throw you to the curb faster than anybody. I got my sea legs on that show, to tell you the truth." In the press, Eric—Trump's younger son from his marriage to Ivana—has often been portrayed as the Khloé of the family. And wandering through Trump Tower, the Kardashian connection isn't all too far off. (To extend the metaphor, Ivanka would be Kim, Don Jr. is Rob, Tiffany is Kendall, and Barron is also Rob.)

Portraits of Trump's three grown-up kids from his first marriage—
Ivanka, Don Jr., and Eric, who all got their first real taste of fame by
joining *The Apprentice* as judges—are plastered in the entryway to the elevator, in high-definition sheen. Eric takes me for a tour of the rest of the
floor, where in a back hallway he stashes framed posters from four seasons
of *The Celebrity Apprentice*, signed by every member of the cast. "All our
stuff is pretty current to the properties we have," he says, as we walk past
pictures of buildings. "Our hotels, golf courses, but this is my little *Apprentice* wall! It was amazing, and these are some of my seasons."

If his father is always finding reasons to hold a grudge, Eric seems
to think highly of every celebrity who competed on *The Apprentice*, describing them in glowing language. "The characters were amazing," he
says. "Bret Michaels was amazing. John Rich is a phenomenal guy. Lisa
Lampanelli, I'm not sure if that comedy could exist today, meaning how
canceled she'd be." Lampanelli, an insult comic, got along so well with
the Trumps that she appeared onstage at the 2011 Comedy Central
roast of the future president along with Larry King and Snoop Dogg;
perhaps the man who coined "Crooked Hillary" saw her as a peer, or an
aspirational figure.

"I got to know her outside; she had a heart of gold," Eric says. "If you
see her up onstage, she's an absolute killer! Vicious."

He looks at the autograph from Joan Rivers, who died in 2014. "She
guest judged with me a bunch of times," Eric says. "The Eric and Joan
combo happened a lot for some reason." He thinks the network liked
their chemistry together. "She was awesome. You want to talk about
funny, witty, don't give a damn, would say anything at any time, let it all
out." Eric's voice gets softer. "My mom had Joan's personality," he says of
Ivana, who passed away in 2022. "She had a very direct, no-nonsense personality in a beautiful way, who is so elegant. They were so sharp in terms
of the tongue. Joan was awesome. What a remarkable lady."

On the day after we meet, Eric will fly back to Iowa for his father's
2024 campaign. He reveals that in 2016 he had no idea what a caucus
was until his plane landed in the state. "I did stump speech after stump

speech," Eric says. "There were probably twenty thousand people at this school, and I felt at complete ease on a completely unknown topic. Reality TV was an unknown topic for us. Real estate was the one thing we truly knew and could speak to. And there's no question a lot of comfort came from being in front of a camera. When those lights came on, and you know a couple weeks later you're going to be speaking to fifteen million people." His assistant brings us two bottles of iced tea as we spend the next ninety minutes reliving the glory of *The Apprentice*. Eric agrees with Burnett: *The Apprentice* is to be credited (or, depending on one's perspective, blamed) for his father's political success.

"I could argue *The Apprentice* paved the way for the entire presidency," Eric says. "It's a lot more meaningful of a show than people realize. My family was obviously out there in the media, but sitting in front of a camera, hours upon hours. Sitting in the boardroom, connecting with these people, and playing to a national audience, where you have to create drama—at the same time, you have to come across as the voice of reason. You have to be perceived as fair. You always have to be entertaining."

Eric believes this unique combination of traits helped his father succeed in politics. "What's the common denominator with every president who has ever won? They've had a level of star power. I don't know how you define that—he certainly had it on the show. There's no question about it. My father had great fame and notoriety before *The Apprentice*, but *The Apprentice* made him into a true household name."

And it made Trump's three oldest kids stars of their own. Eric says that his father's years of practice in the boardroom, responding to stubborn contestants, translated to destroying his adversaries on a different stage. "You look at the debates, and you look at the quickness. Look at the Megyn Kelly answer," Eric says, referring to a famous confrontation at the first Republican primary debate in August 2015, where the then Fox News host tried to corner Trump on his misogynistic treatment of women (and he countered with a punch line about Rosie O'Donnell). "That was a pure sabotage question," Eric says. "There was somebody who wanted to take him out of politics, and he fired back with the same wit he exhibited in every episode. I think if 99 percent of traditional political candidates got that question, it's 'Pack your bags—go home!'"

Eric chuckles, comparing his dad's savvy to another billionaire who attempted to run for president in 2020. "Bloomberg would have absolutely turned to mush and thrown another billion dollars into his campaign and gotten one delegate in Guam," he says. "You can quote me on all that." (Like father, like son.)

Contestants from *The Apprentice*, who had a front-row seat to how the real Trump transformed in the public eye, agree with Eric's assessment about the influence of the show. "I do believe *The Apprentice* is the reason he became president, because I don't think any of the other chapters in his life on their own would have enabled him to get there," says Sam Solovey, a real estate agent who appeared on the show's first season. (Considered the show's class clown, Solovey tried to sell lemonade for $1,000 a glass and relentlessly flattered his would-be boss. Trump told *The Washington Post* that Solovey "is great television, no doubt about that.")

"*The Apprentice* normalized him," Solovey says. "It made him almost like the personification of the American dream. He was an aspirational character for Middle America. And it was just perfectly packaged on television in a very black-and-white way; he was the judge, the jury, and the executioner. And then you've got these younger people, looking at this godlike character, elevating him."

On election night 2016, Heidi Bressler—a feisty sales rep who became a fan favorite from the first season—wasn't surprised that Trump defeated Hillary Clinton. "People just liked him," she says. "They thought, at the time, he was a breath of fresh air. And I'm like, oh my God, look at what we created."

CHAPTER 2

Donald on Thin Ice

Donald Trump has long had a fascination with Hollywood. In his early twenties, he flirted with a career as a film and stage producer. "I wanted to be a moviemaker," he says. "I didn't want to go into real estate." Trump says that one day he struck up a conversation with the New York artist David Black, who produced a series of Broadway shows from *George M!* to *A Funny Thing Happened on the Way to the Forum*. Black wanted to buy a house, and Trump gave him advice on how to make the most out of his down payment.

"He asked my opinion, and I gave him an hour-long dissertation on how to do it," Trump says. "He said, 'You shouldn't be in the entertainment business; you should stay in the real estate business,' which was easier because my father had a real estate business in Brooklyn and Queens." That's putting it mildly. Fred Trump, one of the city's most aggressive postwar real estate barons, had built more than twenty-seven thousand apartments in "the neighborhoods of Coney Island, Bensonhurst, Sheepshead Bay, Flatbush, and Brighton Beach in Brooklyn and Flushing and Jamaica Estates in Queens," according to his 1999 obituary in *The New*

York Times. Donald joined the family business in 1968, after receiving a degree from Wharton, the business school at the University of Pennsylvania. Rather than making his son climb his way up the corporate ladder, Fred appointed Donald president of the family company after only three years of working there.

Looking back, Trump says he has no regrets about not giving the film business a real shot. "No matter how good you are, no matter who you are, it's luck," Trump says. "What hits? Why did *The Apprentice* hit? You see movies where every star is perfect, everything is perfect, they have unlimited financing, they have everything going on—it bombs!" Even after his much-publicized ups and downs in real estate, he still sees it as a safer business. "If I have a great location, Fifty-Seventh and Fifth," he says, naming the cross streets of Trump Tower, "generally your odds are a hell of a lot better."

And the odds were in Trump's favor in real estate because Fred could protect him. "Donald and I first met through his father," says George Ross, a seasoned Manhattan real estate lawyer who later served as a boardroom adviser on *The Apprentice*, adding that Fred was a client at his firm Dreyer and Traub. "He said he had a young son who wanted to do real estate. Would I speak to him? And I did. Donald was twenty-seven years old. His father wanted to know whether I would be his mentor. The answer was, 'Sure—if you pay the fee, I'll do that.'"

Ross saw a spark in the young Trump, not necessarily related to his aptitude for property values, but in his confidence. "Right away, I recognized Donald had characteristics that would make him successful in real estate," Ross says. "He was very charismatic. He could be very convincing. If he wanted to convince you white was black, when he got through the discussion, it was. He had a tremendous ability to convince people to think along the lines he wants."

Trump didn't give up on Hollywood completely, though. As he built casinos and bought and renovated the Plaza hotel, Trump still managed to find time for the cameras. No matter how busy he was on construction projects, he'd agree to pop up in cameos on-screen, starting with a

1989 turn where he negotiated a deal with Bo Derek in the sex comedy *Ghosts Can't Do It*. The role won Trump the Razzie for worst supporting actor. But that didn't discourage him, and he spent the next decade sharing scenes with Macaulay Culkin (with seven words of dialogue in 1992's *Home Alone 2: Lost in New York*), Will Smith (in a 1994 episode of *The Fresh Prince of Bel-Air*), Whoopi Goldberg (in the 1996 basketball comedy *Eddie*), Fran Drescher (that same year, in *The Nanny*), Michael J. Fox (in 1998's *Spin City*), and Kim Cattrall (in a 1999 episode of *Sex and the City* called "The Man, the Myth, the Viagra"). This last appearance brought Trump into the universe of the turn of the century's most fabulous Manhattanites. "Samantha, a Cosmopolitan, and Donald Trump," Sarah Jessica Parker's Carrie Bradshaw intones. "You just don't get more New York than that."

Trump also showed his flair for showmanship and competition through his purchase of the Miss Universe Organization in 1996, which includes the Miss USA pageant. "I really ran that thing good!" Trump says. "I'll tell you, that thing was hot. I made it hot. I bought it for $2 million. I sold half to CBS, and then I bought it back from CBS for nothing, because they played games with the location of the show. They put it on the real dead days. Then they said, 'It's not doing that well in the ratings.' And so I took it back for nothing." This was in 2002. "And I sold it to NBC for a fortune." (After he bought Miss USA, it was broadcast from cities such as Branson, Missouri, and Gary, Indiana, on CBS; on NBC, it often aired from Las Vegas or Los Angeles, cities more in line with Trumpian glitz.)

Trump then fast-forwards to 2015, when NBC officially cut ties with him, after he launched his presidential campaign and began making racist comments about Mexican immigrants. "And then I took it back and sold it to IMG for a fortune. It's a hell of a crazy business deal, actually."

Trump says he couldn't run a beauty contest as an active candidate for president of the United States, but that's because no network wanted to do business with him at the time. ("I said, 'This doesn't politically work.'") Evidently, after he got into the White House, he was still monitoring the pageant. "The COVID thing was not good," he says. "They tried to put it on with the girls wearing masks on the runway. It's tough when you have to cancel shows, but I sold it before the COVID situation."

Trump boasts that his approach to Miss Universe was showing more skin, not less. "Miss America went to no bathing suits," he says about the retirement of the so-called swimsuit competition, a change pushed by the organization's chair, Gretchen Carlson, the former Fox News anchor and Miss America 1989, when she briefly took over in 2018. "First, they went to one-piece, meaning the big one," Trump explains. "And I said, 'I'm going to make our bathing suits smaller.' They made theirs big. And I'm going to make it smaller!" (In 1997, a year after Trump acquired Miss Universe, Miss America allowed bikinis in its swimsuit competition, reversing a ban from 1949.) Trump laughs as he reminisces about one of his favorite business enterprises. "It gave me good press. I had a lot of fun with the whole Miss Universe thing."

To maximize his public profile, Trump infiltrated the talk show circuit. Since he lived in New York and could swoop in whenever a guest bailed or there was otherwise an empty spot on the schedule, he'd regularly sit down with Phil Donahue, Regis Philbin and Kathie Lee Gifford, Larry King, David Letterman, and the ladies of *The View*. His close friendship with Barbara Walters eventually led to a public conflagration when in 2006 he picked a fight with her daytime co-star Rosie O'Donnell. But generally in those years, when cameras were involved, Trump was willing to play nice.

If it weren't for Mark Burnett, his talk show appearances and movie cameo ubiquity might have been as far as Trump got on the national stage.

In the spring of 2002, Burnett was looking for a venue to film the finale of *Survivor*'s fourth season, which was to air on live television. It was a challenging time, because events from the real world had crashed into his make-believe civilization. Burnett had originally planned to send the next batch of castaways to Jordan for *Survivor: Arabia* before the 9/11 attacks and George W. Bush's "war on terror" in the Middle East forced him to change his plans. "Nothing would ever make us feel safe, and we'd never get the necessary insurance coverage," Burnett writes in his memoir, *Jump In! Even if You Don't Know How to Swim*, published in 2005. "It would be impossible to film *Survivor: Arabia*. That part of the world was simply too dangerous, especially for a group as conspicuous as an American television show."

Burnett thought that after September 11, 2001, CBS would surely allow him a delay in filming to scout for a new location. But with more than $100 million in advertising on the line, CBS's president, Leslie Moonves, ordered Burnett to crash-land in a different part of the world. The network needed new episodes of *Survivor* for the spring TV season. ("Sometimes, it's fun doing the impossible," Burnett writes in his book, misquoting a famous saying from Walt Disney: "It's kind of fun to do the impossible.")

With no time to spare, Burnett boarded a plane four days later, at a time when most Americans were so traumatized by fear that they couldn't imagine flying again. Burnett scrambled to move that season of *Survivor* to French Polynesia, a destination that was as far as he could imagine from the Middle East. As an added bonus, the new setting was far less likely to ring alarm bells for jingoistic viewers. Burnett called Moonves back, getting him to approve the $5 million in extra budget costs required for the newly titled *Survivor: Marquesas*. Months later, when it came time to crown Vecepia Towery as the series' first Black winner, Burnett chose to broadcast from New York to demonstrate solidarity with a city in the midst of healing. And that's how Mark Burnett came to meet Donald Trump.

On May 19, *Survivor* set up its final tribal council in Central Park's Wollman Rink. As part of his real estate portfolio, Trump had negotiated a deal to renovate and operate the ice rink on and off, starting in the mid-1980s. "Mark Burnett called up," Trump says. "I didn't know Mark at all. And CBS called, because they had *Survivor* and they wanted to use Wollman Rink and build a jungle set in the middle of Central Park. I said, 'What a unique idea—that's great!' They asked whether or not I'd go." Not surprisingly, Trump accepted the invitation and agreed to appear on TV, even in a crowd shot. So he and his girlfriend at the time, Melania

Knauss, attended the finale, which was hosted by none other than Rosie O'Donnell. "I got to know Mark Burnett," Trump says. "He was a great guy."

Mark Burnett always seemed to be keenly aware of the dangers associated with reality TV. In his book, he writes about creating *Survivor*, which aired its first season in 2000, after every network in Hollywood passed, including CBS on his first pitch. Burnett envisioned a *Lord of the Flies* society with a ritualized method of kicking off outcasts, and it wouldn't come cheap. He didn't sell *Survivor* on a pilot; he needed CBS to cough up millions to order a full season based solely on his vision. (This was before deep-pocketed streamers such as Netflix changed the business by green-lighting shows without a proof of concept.) "The logistics were incredible," Burnett writes in his book. "Was I good enough to pull it off? Would America embrace my quirky little show or would they laugh at my surreal Tribal Councils, native 'art direction,' and overly serious confessionals? Beyond my dramatic intentions, what if someone died?"

Burnett had always liked living dangerously. Part of his self-mythology is how he came to the United States in 1982, at the age of twenty-two, having been raised in a blue-collar London family, with no connections and only $600 in his pocket. In his first two years in America, he worked as a nanny for three families in or around Beverly Hills, convincing them that a man from a foreign country could do the job without any experience, based on the regimented work ethic he learned during his four years as a paratrooper in the British army. He'd made it, somehow, in America.

Burnett would eventually become one of the most prolific producers of reality TV in Hollywood, and he took inspiration from his own upbringing. His greatest projects often involved pushing people to unlock their competitive drive for a shot at a better life, revealing grit under impossible pressure. That's one of the through lines in the shows he's created, from *The Apprentice* to *Shark Tank* and even *Are You Smarter Than a 5th*

Grader? (This last no-frills quiz show, on which regular people tested their intelligence against grade-schoolers, offered a $1 million prize.)

Burnett's first TV credit, *Eco-Challenge*, isn't as well remembered, but it set the prototype for the kinds of highbrow theatrics he could perfect on TV. He'd read a 1991 *Los Angeles Times* article about a French competition, called Raid Gauloises, where teams of five raced through the jungle to win a one-of-a-kind contest. Burnett, interested in launching the American version, decided the only way he could do that was to compete himself. So he packed his bags for Oman, where he embarked on a "race nonstop across the mountains and deserts for almost four hundred miles." After ten days, he arrived at the last checkpoint—unruly camels failed to get him to the official finish line.

With a broadcast partnership at MTV and sponsorship money, in 1995, Burnett had a $1 million budget to stage *Eco-Challenge* in Utah. He ended the first race hundreds of thousands of dollars in debt, but he eventually scored a deal with Discovery.

As a young producer, Burnett dug in, rolled up his sleeves, and worked hard, often against improbable odds. His book is peppered with sappy self-help tips to inspire leadership, such as "Do not fear rejection," "Choose teammates who possess greater skills than you," and "Negativity drains energy" (which is comical coming from someone who partnered with Donald Trump). As he arrived in Hollywood, Burnett had one goal—to become as rich as humanly possible—and he banked on his own wily instincts. For *Survivor*, Burnett brokered an astonishing deal with CBS, guaranteeing him half of all advertising dollars from the show, including any product placement. At the time, during the nascent days of reality TV, the network didn't think product placement would become a meaningful source of revenue. But after *Survivor* became the hottest show on TV, brands such as Doritos (which in season 2 rewarded the starving contestants with chips) were lining up to feature their products, and Burnett pocketed tens of millions of dollars.

"Mark Burnett has got a wonderful flair for entertainment, for creating a scenario that people would find interesting," says Ross, the attorney who'd serve as Trump's right-hand man on air and who was perhaps the only person on *The Apprentice* allergic to hyperbolic compliments. But for Burnett, he makes an exception: "To me, he's a creative genius."

Yet as much as Burnett wanted to rule Hollywood, he didn't crave the spotlight. Among his colleagues, he was known for having a mean, needling sense of humor, but it's a side of himself that he kept away from the press. In interviews, Burnett carried himself as though he were wearing a freshly tailored suit (the whimsical British designer Paul Smith was among his favorite fashion labels), because he believed in keeping the attention solely on the projects he was producing. And while Trump loved to make friends with journalists, Burnett preferred to keep them at a distance. After *The New Yorker* published an exposé about *The Apprentice* in 2018, detailing how the reality series had manufactured a fictional public persona for Trump, Burnett loved to repeat a story about how a fact-checker at the publication supposedly told his publicist that the magazine was knowingly printing lies to make Burnett look bad. He was, it seems, a conspiratorial disciple of the school of "fake news."

I first talked to Burnett in 2011, on the eve of the launch of *The Voice*, which he produced with Christina Aguilera, Adam Levine, CeeLo Green, and Blake Shelton as celebrity mentors training aspirant singers in competition with one another. At the time, Burnett understood the politics of Hollywood: He wouldn't even take a swipe at the new judge that his rivals at *American Idol* had hired that season. "People love Jennifer Lopez," he said about the A-list judge, who was coming to a ratings-hobbled *Idol* after her own series of career setbacks.

Burnett always had a knack for handling the famous. As a nanny trying to teach grade-school boys how to play basketball, he'd charmed the actor James Caan, one of the fathers watching. On *Survivor*, he'd dine with world leaders as he personally decided which region he'd journey to next. And indeed, Burnett had the advantage, because his cameras would always bring exposure and tourism. Burnett even managed to land a girlfriend in the industry, dating the *Touched by an Angel* actress Roma Downey, whom he saw at a beauty salon in 2004. "He was having a haircut, and I was having a pedicure," Downey would later say in an interview. "Our eyes met in the mirror, you know, once, twice. And then I thought, 'I can't look over again,' and I did."

After they got married in 2007, Burnett changed shape again. He started talking about Christianity, believing there was an underserved market for faith-based projects in the industry. He'd never been particularly religious before, but now it became a selling point for his brand as he was producing the 2013 miniseries *The Bible* with Downey. (She'd convinced him that, in his personal life, he'd been too materialistic.) By 2015, when he appeared on the cover of *Adweek* touting his continued power as a producer, Burnett had grown out a scraggly beard. The executives who worked with him couldn't help but snicker at his makeover. "He convinced himself he was Jesus," one of his high-ranking former colleagues told me. "He grew his hair. He grew his beard. This guy is fucking nuts."

Upon first meeting Trump, Burnett showed his hypnotizing charm for getting what he wanted. Burnett, who at that time didn't speak much about his faith, told Trump about his strong devotion to Trump's business strategy, as outlined in his 1987 book, *The Art of the Deal*. Trump recalls Burnett claiming to have used the guide for inspiration during his darkest days, just after he'd moved from England to California as a young man. "He was a nanny," Trump says. "He was selling T-shirts on Venice Beach. Can you believe it? He said, 'I read your book *The Art of the Deal*.' He said, 'It's the most important book I ever read.' That was then, so I don't know." Does Trump think there's a chance that the book's been displaced as Burnett's favorite, given his conversion to evangelical Christianity? "Maybe it still is, probably is," Trump says. "He said, 'I got so many ideas from that.'"

Trump is famously susceptible to flattery, and hearing from one of TV's most successful producers that he'd been key to Burnett's career origin story was irresistible. "He liked me," Trump says. "I liked him. We got along well. It was a tremendous chemistry."

This instant spark provided an opening for Burnett to contact Trump a few months later with a pitch. After *Survivor*, Burnett was having trouble finding another show with broad appeal. His next series, NBC's *The Restaurant*, which debuted in 2003, followed the up-and-coming chef Rocco DiSpirito as he tried to open a successful new eatery in Manhattan's Flatiron District, putting out a casting call for waitstaff on *Today*. But the premise proved to be too inside baseball, and perhaps was ahead of its time, before food culture had entered the mainstream. Worse, it lacked the competitive heft for which Burnett had become known; DiSpirito was competing only with himself. He lost his restaurant (and his credibility in the food world) when the series was canceled after two seasons.

Still, Burnett had a much better idea brewing. He was tinkering with a pitch for a show that he envisioned as *Survivor* set against the backdrop of corporate America. "It was clear that my new show would need to be about people wanting the American dream, wanting to get rich, wanting recognition," Burnett writes in his book. "It would need to focus on aspiring moguls looking to be hired and mentored by a true leader in the industry." He believed that the premise would succeed or fail based on the charisma of a central Svengali figure, who could sift through the young applicants and decide who had what it took to make it—humiliating the rest on national TV for our entertainment. He thought his show, which he wanted to call *The Protégé* or *The Apprentice* (which he'd cribbed from *The Sorcerer's Apprentice*) could rotate between business leaders. That would give each season a new perspective and guarantee longevity—just as *Survivor*, in its early going, added flavor and spark from its shifting locations. Besides, what business leader would have the extra time for multiple seasons of filming? *The Apprentice* would need to find a business genius—or to invent one.

In February 2003, Burnett landed in Manhattan, ready to cast the star of his next hit show. When he called Trump's office to set up a meeting on his way into the city, Trump got on the phone with him directly and invited him to come over to Trump Tower. Twenty minutes later, Burnett found himself sitting face-to-face with Trump, pitching his idea.

Trump says that at the time, Hollywood had come knocking with "many offers." But most of the concepts for reality TV were too trashy even for him. After *The Osbournes* became a hit for MTV in 2002, Trump was soft-pitched a docuseries centered on his family. The idea of playing dad to his three adult kids, though, didn't appeal to him. Burnett offered something flashier—the chance for New York's brashest real estate mogul to flex his business chops to America. Trump shook Burnett's hand after the pitch, committing to the project on the spot.

This proved to be an alarming revelation for Trump's representation, who tried to shut it all down. Trump's then agent at William Morris, Jim Griffin, told him not to do *The Apprentice* because it was bound to fail. "He said, 'You could have a big embarrassment,'" Trump recalls. "I said, 'Why?' He said, 'Very few shows succeed, and if you don't succeed, because it's you, they'll make a big deal out of it.'"

But Burnett had Trump hooked. To sweeten the deal, the show's creator offered Trump a credit as executive producer of *The Apprentice* and even went as far as agreeing to split the profits with him from any product placement they'd generate. (Otherwise, Trump wouldn't do the heavy lifting as the spokesperson for these brands.) Trump might not have understood exactly how much richer Burnett's offerings would make him, but he decided to ignore his agent and move forward as they took the pitch around town.

Both men were wary of CBS. Trump was still feeling stung by Moonves for dropping the ball on Miss Universe, and Burnett was in a secret dispute with the network, because Moonves was trying to yank back the advertising dollars he'd foolishly given him. As Burnett saw it, there was no way that he could get CBS to agree to such a deal on *The Apprentice*.

At ABC, executives showed interest in the project. But according to Trump, Michael Eisner, then CEO of Disney, balked at the high production budget that would be required for the series to shoot all over New York. "Eisner ended the deal," Trump recalls. "He said, 'Nope! I'm going to want it for a lower price.' He wanted to chisel. I said, 'I'm not surprised.' I knew him a little bit. Then NBC heard about it."

As he thinks about what happened next, Trump starts to chuckle. "It's funny, because now I have to deal with a lot of the same characters," he says about his long entanglement with Zucker. The ratings-hungry programmer, who made a name for himself as a young executive producer on NBC's *Today*, had been appointed president of NBC Entertainment in 2000, and he was desperate to replicate Burnett's magic with *Survivor* on NBC—which, he'd soon learn, wouldn't happen with *The Restaurant*.

"Jeff called Mark and I, begging us to come over," Trump says. This wasn't exactly true. "Mark was one of the hottest producers in town back then," recalls Jeff Gaspin, the NBC executive. "Burnett came in to pitch both Zucker and me"—without Trump in the meeting, according to Gaspin. "He said, 'This is *Survivor* in the toughest jungle of all, Manhattan.' He said he had Donald Trump in his first season. And Jeff Zucker said to him before he left, 'We're buying it.'"

"He gave us everything we wanted," Trump says of Zucker. "He said, 'You're not leaving the room until we have a deal.' We signed a deal. That was great for NBC, because they had no Top 10 shows. They were dying." Even though Trump might not have been present, in his version of events he was driving the negotiations. Burnett was able to get Zucker to agree to allow Burnett and Trump to share all of the product placement revenue. For a show that hadn't even started filming yet, it didn't seem like that big of a deal.

Burnett had leverage; though NBC wasn't dying, it was showing signs of weakness, with the long-running sitcoms *Friends* and *Frasier* drawing to a close and the Aaron Sorkin drama *The West Wing* slowing down with age. Yet Trump didn't get *everything*. "They were paying me $25,000 an episode," Trump says. "That's it! But they had no option," which meant that Trump could exit the show after one season. This was, after all, supposed to be a temporary gig. "I did a one-season contract, because they figured we'd go on, go off, and that would be it," Trump says. "It was going to be a quickie."

CHAPTER 3

The Tao of Mark Burnett

Mark Burnett needs my help. It's after midnight when he sends me a text. "Make sure that I get in," it reads. "Please." On this Saturday night, Burnett has turned his full attention to gaining admission into a hot nightclub at the Sundance Film Festival. Sundance is hazardous—high up in the snowy mountains of Park City, the altitude goes to your head, and drinks hit harder than they do at home. The twenty- and thirtysomething crowd of Hollywood types and hangers-on hardly mind, of course. Burnett, at sixty-two then, was outside the typical demographic, which made it all the more surprising he was blowing up my phone to see if I could sneak him into a pop-up rave at Tao.

Burnett and his wife, Roma Downey, had been making the rounds at Sundance that weekend—not as producers or as talent: just for show. They owned a vacation home in Park City, a pricey resort area famous for skiing that also happens to be where Sundance plays out every January. In 2023, crowds were lining up for blocks to see the A24 indie darling *Past Lives* and the psychological thriller *Fair Play*, but Burnett wasn't interested in spending time in a theater as an anonymous pass holder. When you're there to be seen, there's little point sitting in the dark, and Burnett's preferred form of entertainment was parties, not movies.

It was pure chance that I'd bumped into him after months of trying to interview him for this book. Earlier in the week, we'd both been guests at a charity dinner, called "A Taste of Sundance," held at a fancy eighty-seven-thousand-square-foot gym that felt like a set from *Survivor*. Here, in the company of industry heavyweights like the *Black Panther* director, Ryan Coogler, and the *Fifty Shades of Grey* star Dakota Johnson, Burnett might have felt lucky to be in the room at all. For the first time in years, he was no longer a VIP. His once endlessly ascendant career trajectory had started moving in the wrong direction—fast.

He'd just stepped down from his job as chairman of MGM's TV division, after the company had been acquired by Amazon in 2022 for $8.5 billion. Even as Burnett added to his considerable wealth as the deal closed, he'd lost the lustrous power of running a studio. And, as the man responsible for crafting the forty-fifth president's image through *The Apprentice*, he had spent the Trump years receiving some of the worst press of his career. It wasn't just for helping Trump get elected; among his embarrassing falters, he and Downey produced a 2016 remake of *Ben-Hur* that bombed at the box office, and insiders accused him of intense meddling in scripted TV projects, a genre that he didn't know much about.

In all my conversations with Trump, we spent much of our time talking about his closeness to Burnett, but the two had drifted apart after Trump left the White House. In discussing their present lives, Trump sounds like he has FOMO that Burnett got so far in Hollywood without him. "We have a very good relationship," Trump says. "I don't speak to him much. There are so many other people to speak to, it's like crazy." Trump tries to sell himself on the notion that his schedule is too packed to make time for Burnett, even though the former president is free enough to spend hours reminiscing with me. For example, on the day I brought my *Apprentice* reel for him to watch, no one in Trump tech support could figure out how to connect my laptop to his TV projector. (Didn't they have Apple TV at Trump Tower? It seemed as if nothing invented after 2004 had entered these walls.) But as we scrambled to figure things out, Trump's calendar was apparently so wide open he simply delayed our meeting until we were ready.

Trump may or may not have had time to call Burnett, but he had time to gossip about him with me, picking my brain as the editor in chief of *Variety*. In one of our first meetings, Trump asks me about the MGM sale to Amazon. "I guess he scored big on that one, didn't he? What did he make on that one, do you know? Over a billion?" I inform Trump that the terms of Burnett's payout weren't public, but it wouldn't be that much. "Isn't that fantastic?" he says, sounding hollow in his praise. On the surface, he compliments Burnett's success, but Trump takes pleasure in knowing that his wingman hadn't caught up to his own image as a billionaire businessman. It's like a classic maneuver from the *Apprentice* boardroom—in which Trump cast himself in the role of player, trying to present the case that his was the superior business mind. And he regularly quizzes me about the ratings for *Survivor*, as if he's imagining a face-off with *The Apprentice* if it were still on TV. "How's *Survivor* doing now? That's still considered successful?" Trump asks me a version of this question repeatedly.

But at least Burnett can still rub shoulders with Hollywood. At Sundance that Saturday night, he starts out with his wife at our *Variety* party, where he's eager to pose for photos as a happy couple. He then drops off Downey at their home as he makes his way to the United Talent Agency party, with a buttoned-up crowd of agents. Most executives of his stature, and his age, would be content to wind down after two rounds of networking. But now Burnett is ready to really turn up.

"Heading to TAO in 10," reads the next text from him. I chase down the party's publicist so that Burnett, a fabulously wealthy man by Trump's or anyone else's estimation, can get into this club without buying a table for $10,000. "You are THE MAN," he writes, firing off a Bitmoji meant to represent him. In this avatar of Burnett, he re-created himself in the form of a college fraternity president decked out in a green-and-white pledge jacket with the letter *B* emblazoned over his heart. This youthful cartoon

Mark Burnett, looking less like the producer than Zac Efron with a five-o'clock shadow, had his arms up next to two words in pink: "Let's Party!"

"Two minutes," he texts as his car pulls up. It's just after 1:00 a.m. as I stand next to the publicist on the red carpet, where a stream of influencers and then Tiffany Haddish in rainbow-colored sweats rush in to escape the freezing Utah cold. I look down at my phone. "OK. We are here." But as he and his small crew hover outside, the Tao publicist stops the arrivals line. In the rules of the red carpet, Burnett and his friends are just suits, and I'm just a journalist, but on-camera talent is coming through. Adam Lambert, who came in second place in the eighth season of *American Idol*, makes a grand entrance. It's a collision that says it all about celebrity, and about the long hangover from the pop culture of the 2000s: even with all he's accomplished since his days selling T-shirts on the beach, Burnett is displaced in the perverse pecking order of reality TV fame.

During my first run-in with Burnett at the charity dinner, when someone introduced us, he extended his right hand to shake my hand while his left hand sharply pinched my nipple. It was an uncomfortable greeting, not how I customarily say hello to a stranger. He then squeezed both of my arms. The display of physical dominance actually brought to mind Trump, for a moment, but I tried to shake the thought away. For one thing, Burnett looked far more casual than the box-suited former president. He wore a T-shirt with a Malibu logo and faded jeans, giving off a California vibe.

Burnett spent two nights in a row clubbing at Tao during Sundance. Before he hit me up on Saturday, he'd been on someone else's guest list. I first saw him from a distance there on Friday night, flanked by a group of people half his age. He climbed over a blue suede couch to enter his VIP area. He wore a gray trench coat over his green T-shirt with the word "practice" on it. His jeans were ripped by design and covered in patches—a rainbow on his leg, a firefly on the rear pocket where he'd stuffed his iPhone. But this look was true to Burnett: he'd always had eccentric taste in fashion, dressing somewhere between an executive and a bro.

The first night at Tao, he swayed to a set list that felt more like an edgy warehouse party than a film-festival event for media titans. The celebrity DJ, the music producer Diplo, spun his favorite bangers under strobe lights. The room got down to everything from the EDM superstar Tiësto's "The Business" to the 1990s hip-house classic "Short Dick Man." Burnett seemed content simply to hang out, behind the velvet rope; he was subdued enough, in his kooky getup, that maybe he wondered whether the cost of a table was really worth it.

On the second night, freed from the stuffy barrier of the VIP section, he really let loose. He even danced with members of the *Variety* staff, grinning the whole time, between frequent trips to the bathroom. By this point in the festival, I'd gotten used to seeing Burnett as the life of the party. It was easy to forget that his image, to the nation that knew him as Mr. Roma Downey, was that of a Christian family man. But anything was possible in Burnettland: he'd help convince half of America that Donald Trump was the only person who could fix the country.

I lost track of him at some point; we'd gotten separated on the dance floor. The night ended with one final text. "Thanks for handling that," Burnett wrote to me on his way home at 4:27 a.m. "You have a fun team."

We were supposed to talk for this book, but he ended up ghosting me for a few months, never agreeing to a real interview. The next time we texted, we were both at the Cannes Film Festival. "I was in Monaco and ended up til super late at Café Sass"—an exclusive restaurant and club that serves five hundred grams of caviar for $2,000—"with friends from London, Paris and Tel Aviv," he texts me after I'd asked if he was in town. "It was wild." Now that I knew his love for a good party, I suggest he might enjoy one I was attending for work, held at a magnificent castle on a hilltop with views of Cannes. If Burnett accepts my invitation, he'll be part of a circle of guests that include Naomi Campbell, Brie Larson, Michelle Yeoh, and Leonardo DiCaprio. The star of *Titanic*, who'd traveled to Cannes for the premiere of the Martin Scorsese film *Killers of the Flower Moon*, is bringing his mom as his date.

But I'm surprised at the size of Burnett's squad. "I've got a super fun fashionable crew with me," Burnett writes back. "How many can I bring?? Ideally me plus 7. We are moored off Eden Roc," sitting in a yacht off the Mediterranean Sea. I tell him I'm not sure I can get everyone in. "Ok, zero pressure," he texts me. "We will just hang here on the boat. We are a big group. Let's rain check it." To change the subject, I respond that Cannes is my favorite film festival, because it's always such a good time. Burnett's reply perfectly capped off my five months of knowing him. "Yes too much fun," he writes back. "Hahaha."

Burnett's love for partying wasn't just about bottle service and electronic music. Over several interactions with him, it became clear to me that what charged him was the idea of being at the center of the action, in the most important room. In this, he resembled the man he took from a tabloid star, locally famous for his love life and bankruptcies, to reality TV leading man.

Donald Trump and Mark Burnett were made for each other. What really tied them together was a similar thirst for success and a similar thirst to be seen as successful. "They are very similar in personality from what I could see—just always wanting more, more, more," says Jeff Gaspin of NBC. "I think they had similar goals. They looked at this as part of the

American dream, this capitalism. Winning was all that mattered to both of them, and I saw infinite ambition in both Mark and Donald." Gaspin clarifies: "Mark more than Donald. Mark was so driven by money and success. He just had this drive like I'd not really seen in anybody. He saw America and Hollywood as just this open playing field that he wanted to conquer."

That sense of conquest would end up making Burnett a shockingly consequential figure; after all, he helped shape the image that changed modern American history. But it expressed itself at every level of production. Burnett's style of micromanaging meant learning intimate details about the players he was putting on TV. When it came to casting the first season of *The Apprentice*, Trump was in the backseat, and Burnett took the lead. He vetted the contestants through a series of tests that amounted to psychological torture.

The Apprentice found its stars through a nationwide search that stopped in a dozen cities, traversing both red and blue states. Around the country, people traveled for hours, standing in large crowds for the sliver of a chance to be on Burnett's next TV show. Back then, *Survivor* was a national obsession, and the contestants had a chance to parlay that fame into endorsement deals and other TV appearances. Ironically, the selling point for most of the *Apprentice* auditioners wasn't Trump, although he was mentioned in the ads that aired on TV and the radio. "I was a big Mark Burnett fan," says Bowie Hogg, then a twenty-five-year-old salesman for FedEx who quit his job when he was offered a spot on the show. "And honestly, at the time, down here in Texas, I can't say we totally knew who Trump was."

On a scorching-hot June day in 2003, Hogg waited in line for four hours in Dallas for a chance to talk for only a few minutes with a casting director. "People always say, 'How did you catch her attention?'" Hogg says. "I said, 'My name is Bowie Hogg, and yes, that's my real name.'" He proceeded to tell quick, witty stories about his family as a "fifth-generation Texan." He briefly talked about his professional success, saying that he was ranked No. 1 in sales in his region. But it was his charm and southern twang that made him stand out. "I just caught her attention right then," Hogg says. "And the next day, they invited me back, and we did a full interview."

Sam Solovey took a different—and admittedly more annoying—approach. On a July day in sweltering Washington, D.C., Solovey's mom called to inform him that she'd just heard about a business-themed reality show starring Trump. "Well, anyway, it turns out I'm only five minutes away from where they're doing these auditions at this former nightclub in Georgetown," Solovey says. "And it's daytime. So I drove by, and I see a line wrapped around the block of these very good-looking women and guys, all in suits with briefcases and résumés. And here I am, in flip-flops and a Hawaiian shirt and shorts. I'm dressed like a slob."

Solovey would not give up. After he learned the wait to get inside was at least four hours, he decided to find a way to cut the line. He greased someone at the front $50 in cash, and the ploy worked in more ways than one. As he made it inside in no time, crunching on a cup of ice to cool down, he found himself at a table in a group interview with other aspiring contestants and a casting director. "And she says, 'Business ethics. Discuss!' So I throw my hands up. I say, 'Well, I got one for all of you. You've been waiting for hours to get in here. I've been here for only ten minutes.'" When Solovey explained how exactly he cut the line, the others were outraged. But the stunt got him to the next round, and it became the fabric of his story to producers. "We left and forty-five minutes later, I got a call to be back a couple of days later at the Embassy Suites in Dupont Circle for a callback," he says.

There would be more questions and more tests to explore the personalities of these budding TV competitors. The hundreds who made it to the next round were asked to put themselves on camera. And then it was time for the last hurdle: a trip to Los Angeles to go head-to-head with reality TV's reigning king. Over several days, the contestants lived in the same hotel, but they weren't allowed to leave their rooms much or talk to each other. They had marathon rounds of interviews with the group of final decision makers, including network executives, with Burnett leading the charge. He relished putting people on the spot, pushing their buttons, even bullying them to see how they'd react. He believed that was how he would find the best contestants. A good reality TV contestant, to Burnett, was one who would fight back; anything else would be too boring for the cameras.

When Heidi Bressler walked into the final round of interviews, she recalls Burnett hurling a shocking—to a professional woman in the dawning era of the status handbag—insult at her. He asked if the purse that she was carrying was a fake. "And I'm like, 'My fucking Gucci is not a fake!' I go, 'Look at the fucking *hat* that you're wearing.'" (Even indoors, Burnett liked to don a wide-brimmed outback hat that was one of his favorite accessories on *Survivor*.) "And he was like, 'Would you talk to Donald Trump like that?' And I said, 'Damn right I would!' and he laughed." Her brashness, which came in convenient soundbites, made her an immediate favorite.

Burnett would "mess with you," recalls Kristi Frank, then a cheery, thirty-year-old restaurant owner from the Bel-Air neighborhood of Los Angeles. "I remember one time getting all dressed up. And he makes you sit in your hotel room, like three or four hours. And then another time, he pulled me out of the gym when I was working out, and then we had to do my interview." They wouldn't even let her change back into the business wear she'd packed. When she gave a long answer to a question, Burnett feigned boredom, shouting, "Cut the shit, Kristi!" Trump, while absent from the auditions, came to feel like a presence in the room, as Frank found herself referring to him casually as "Donald." It had a nice ring to it, as if, even before the show launched, he were a familiar figure. "It kept coming out of my mouth," she recalls.

The line of questioning would be intimate, ranging from past romantic relationships to work experience. Psychologists screened the finalists to make sure that they could all handle the stress associated with the show. But what really mattered was the way each applicant was able to make their time with Burnett count. It was important to be memorable, to be authentic, while also making clear that your personality fell into one of the sets of stock characters that could fuel a full season of TV. "The research they did on us was wild: they knew about our parking tickets," Solovey says. "But it was all done to see how you'd react."

In Frank's last interview with Burnett, he fired three tough questions at her. "And I rattled off really direct, professional answers. And he said, 'Those were the best answers we've heard all day.'" But even after Burnett had made his selections, choosing sixteen finalists to compete on *The Apprentice*, he kept torturing his contestants. "When they actually called us to say who was on the show, they kept me for last," Frank says. "And they told me it was because they knew I had the personality that would, like, just freak out." As she received the good news, she had a feeling that being on *The Apprentice*—moving to New York in the fall to compete in front of Trump—would be a defining moment in her life.

In fact, all the contestants felt that way. "I remember going back to my hotel after they told me," Hogg says with a laugh. "I could not believe it. And the worst part was the next day." One by one, the contestants were brought in for one last appointment—with Burnett's personal doctor. "The doctor says you need to grab a wall or a pillow or something," Hogg recalls, as part of the screening, which included invasive STD testing. While it's common practice to do these checks for *The Bachelor*, it wasn't necessary for *The Apprentice*. But since the contestants would be living together, Burnett wanted to make sure he wouldn't be held legally liable for anything that was shared after the boardroom closed for the night.

This mandatory physical exam is a memory that still makes many of the men from the show wince. "It was a funnel that they stick in there," Hogg says. "Not to be crude, but they inserted it in your penis and they turned it and scraped it and pulled it out. And it was the most painful thing I've experienced in my whole life."

This wasn't the last time the contestants would be turned inside out. The fun was just about to start.

CHAPTER 4

George, Carolyn— and Omarosa

Almost from the beginning, *The Apprentice* wasn't just a job for Donald Trump. It became his life. His chemistry with the contestants and magic as host were things that came naturally to him, and he couldn't disassociate the character he played on TV from his own identity. Trump was a more effective CEO on TV than he could ever be in reality, and so his hard-charging image on the show did what endless movie and TV cameos never could: it cemented his idea of himself as pop culture's main character.

And he traded on it. Soon enough, there was a line of *Apprentice* board games. There were talking Trump dolls, saying his famous catchphrase, "You're fired!" There was even a clothing line at Macy's. For a man whose baggy-suit wardrobe didn't seem particularly enviable, Trump had suddenly become a trendsetter and a tastemaker, and it all came back to him in profits. "He was doing it for the money," George Ross says. "He said it would help his career."

Ironically enough, Trump's endeavors in television, which some might have considered a distraction, seemed to make him more present at work day to day. "I think the real version merged with the performing version, and I don't think he could tell the difference," says Jeff Gaspin, who compares Trump to a Method actor who starts to adopt the traits of a character: think Austin Butler mumbling as Elvis for months after playing him in the 2022 movie. "You look at stories like Madonna, who moved to the U.K., married Guy Ritchie, and spoke with the English accent. The real persona merges with their public persona, and they lose perspective." Gaspin believes that's what happened to Trump. "Obviously, the guy who likes to sit in his house, watch Fox News, and eat McDonald's is not a great public figure," Gaspin says. "He's a loner who knows how to perform in public."

Even so, Trump's performance leaned heavily on his co-stars. And of all the contestants who appeared on *The Apprentice*, no one had a more long-lasting—or messier—relationship with Trump than Omarosa Manigault, who would later take her husband's surname and serve in Trump's presidential administration under the name Omarosa Manigault Newman. Back in the late 1990s, Manigault was already a White House veteran, albeit in a low-profile way: she'd cycled through four different jobs during the Clinton years, including a brief stint as an assistant in Al Gore's office. "That's a very difficult environment, because they don't believe in training," she later said in an interview. "They just kind of throw you in the fire."

She needed a place where she could burn brighter. At twenty-nine, in between work as a political consultant, Manigault joined the first season of *The Apprentice*. She wouldn't score points as the most likable contestant, but she was arguably the one person besides Trump who made the show a ratings phenomenon.

By the time she was fired in March 2004, Manigault had become a one-name celebrity, one that served as a TV trope going forward. The "Omarosa" persona on a reality competition was that of a contestant who understood, somehow, that viewers would love to hate her. Her style on

The Apprentice was a kind of weaponized incompetence. She bumbled through challenges, all the while observing the chinks in her opponents' armor so that she could suddenly go into attack mode in the boardroom. And Trump—who respects an adversarial spirit, and who knows what works on camera—seemed impressed. "Omarosa was a major hit in her first year," Trump says. "Her anger, her craziness, it just worked so incredibly well."

This was before the age of social media; viewers weren't able to register their discontent with Manigault in real time. But she was clearly a sensation, nevertheless, with perhaps the most sympathetic take on her coming from *The New York Times*, where the TV critic Alessandra Stanley wrote that Omarosa was depicted as "a corporate version of Glenn Close in 'Fatal Attraction.'" Stanley blamed the editing, not Manigault herself. However much the editors were at fault for her character assassination, the optics were ugly—the series' lone Black woman was portrayed as a serial liar and manipulator.

And yet Manigault became a Trump favorite. Perhaps it was her slight remove from reality, her ability to spin every situation in her favor. After her elimination, which came at the end of an episode in which she claimed that her poor performance was due to a concussion incurred after getting hit in the head by a small chunk of plaster on the set, Manigault told the MSNBC host Chris Matthews, "The first reason I got fired was very simple. I was truly the strongest player."

Eric Trump laughs when he recalls that episode. "Listen, Omarosa played the villain," Eric says. "We as a company know plaster extremely well. We're builders. A little drop of plaster landed on her shoulder, and she's walking around with ice packs, as if a high beam had dropped off the top of a building and hit her. Do I think she was hurt? No. But that was great entertainment."

Manigault was a magnet for the audience, just as the naked corporate trainer Richard Hatch had been on *Survivor* four years earlier. The difference between them was their competence; Hatch won the game with his secret dealmaking and greasy alliances, whereas Manigault was destined to be eliminated because of her inability to execute. (Indeed, many viewers felt she was kept around longer than her performance seemed to merit.) It certainly appeared that Burnett knew well enough to exploit a train-wreck contestant for ratings, having realized as the first season filmed what Manigault was bringing to the competition.

But something bigger was going on. Trump had found a kindred spirit of sorts in Manigault. After firing her in the middle of season 1, he and Burnett brought her back to *The Apprentice* for two more rounds—the first celebrity edition in 2008, and then an all-stars edition in 2013. Was she truly a celebrity? In 2008, she competed against the actor Stephen Baldwin, the Kiss singer Gene Simmons, the boxer Lennox Lewis, and the eventual winner, Piers Morgan; among them, she was the only person whose fame originated from *The Apprentice* itself. To Trump, she was the best kind of star—one who existed entirely in his shadow, able to shine only when he allowed it.

On her seasons of *The Celebrity Apprentice*, she delivered, picking fights with everyone from Morgan to La Toya Jackson. She made head-lines and generated talk show fodder. Trump repeated this playbook as president. Manigault's tenure as director of communications for the Office of Public Liaison ended in her fourth firing by Trump, and the most explosive yet: she was escorted off the White House grounds. This was followed by her 2018 tell-all book, *Unhinged: An Insider's Account of the Trump White House*, in which she portrayed her boss as a deranged, racist bully.

"She had nothing going, and I gave her three chances at show busi-ness," Trump says. "So she sold out. And in a truest sense of the word, I made her."

As Trump and I watch a clip of the first two times he fired Manigault from *The Apprentice*, his eyes flicker with excitement.

"She was a great television personality the first time," he says. "And then I put her on a second time, and she bombed. She wasn't the same. And I put her on a third time, she bombed. And then I helped her get a job in the White House because she was begging me to help restore her.

So I figured, why not? I put her in." He exhales. "She was just hated by everybody."

But when it comes to innate reality TV stardom, he might have learned a few things from her. Trump blames what he deems Manigault's diminishing returns as a TV personality on her playing a part instead of simply being herself. When she was on *The Apprentice* during the first season, he says, she didn't know just how big her arc was going to be—as the villain who tried to get others to do work for her and then undermined them if things didn't go her way. She was just, in his telling, doing what came naturally. "The first time she was evil," Trump says. "The second time, she *tried* to be evil. And the third time, she tried even harder. And when you try, it doesn't work. Does that make sense?"

Trump's made-for-TV problem child learned how to perform for the cameras and give viewers the villain she thought they wanted, and he came to do the same thing as the 2016 campaign wore on. When the only positive reinforcement Trump got came from the more extreme corners of the Republican Party, he transformed from the pro-choice moderate he'd been during his *Apprentice* years to a hard-line conservative who appointed Supreme Court justices who would eventually overturn *Roe v. Wade*. For fans of *The Apprentice*, it's sometimes hard to see the please-everyone showman in the radically right-wing president. But Trump had learned from Burnett that keeping people guessing was the only recipe for success. And his years on reality TV had taught him that the good guys went home early. A villain edit would, at least, ensure that people talked about you.

And Trump wasn't always aware of just how big of an audience he was playing to. In *Unhinged*, Manigault reveals that she made secret recordings of Trump and his staff during her time at the White House. Reflecting on that betrayal now, Trump says he's not surprised by her actions. "I told people when we hired her, I said, 'When we fire her, we'll have nothing but trouble,'" Trump says. "But that's okay. That's the way life goes."

He tries to explain, for the first time, why he brought Manigault with him to the White House, even though he says he knew he couldn't trust her. "A lot of things I do in life, I do as an experiment," Trump says. "I mean, I do it out of human interest—just to see who's loyal, who's not loyal." Abraham Lincoln stacked his cabinet with a "team of rivals," because he believed dissent among the most intelligent men would help him govern the country more wisely. Trump's White House—from his revolving-door chiefs of staff to political novices such as Ivanka and his son-in-law, Jared Kushner, as well as Manigault—at times felt cast out of a Burnett reality show.

"She was actually great to me, until she left," Trump says. "And then after she left, she got a book deal, and she made some money. They could all do that. But they are scumbags when they do it." Manigault's book is one of countless volumes about the chaos of the Trump era, a genre that has generated huge sales for the publishing industry. "They don't pay, I guess, if you say nice things." And, as often when Trump feels wounded, he goes on: "I hear she lost that money," he says, not offering any proof of this claim. "I don't know—something happened. She had the whole thing with the husband too," Trump says, suggesting that she needed to financially support her spouse. "And the family. It was always drama."

Drama, of course, has always been Trump's specialty. And Manigault's infamous televised antics didn't disqualify her later from having a direct line to the president; in fact, they strengthened her ties to the one commander in chief in living memory who saw histrionics as proof of character. After her betrayal, Manigault—who has claimed she had constant access to Trump's Oval Office—is, at last, on the outs with him. "I saw her very little in the White House," Trump insists. "The White House is a very big place! It's buildings, actually. But the people hated her in Washington." He turns to a handler who is babysitting him today, sitting in on our interview. "Didn't they? Were you there at all when she was there?"

"I was," says the twentysomething man, dressed in a plain Washington, D.C., Brooks Brothers knockoff suit, who has been dragged into the boardroom to watch these clips with us. He looks aggrieved, like a student sitting in the back of a college lecture, trying not to get called on.

"Do you agree with me?" Trump asks.

"Yes, I do," he says, obediently, as if he were auditioning for *The Apprentice*.

"They hated her," Trump says.

"Yes," repeats the young man, completing his one task—offering reassurance.

"Her personality—she was late all the time!" Trump says. "She wouldn't show up. Look, I tried to rehabilitate her reputation as an experiment. And when I did, I said, 'This probably won't work out, but let's see what happens.' And I also said"—he doesn't specify to whom, but it sounds as if he were talking to a voice in his head—"when she gets fired, you always have to pay a price. It's too bad. In the White House, she didn't cut the mustard."

Trump takes a short pause. "By the way," he says, "there are no tapes!"

I was wondering how I'd bring this up, but I guess I shouldn't have been surprised that Trump—often eager to discuss all the scandals associated with him—would just blurt it out. By now, the whole world knows about the *Apprentice* tapes, an ugly rumor that has followed Trump like his own Watergate. The legend has it that Trump was caught using the n-word on a hot mic during a boardroom taping. The origins of this story trace back to the final stretch of Trump's first presidential campaign. On October 8, 2016, the day after the leaked *Access Hollywood* audio recording, in which Trump was heard boasting to the host Billy Bush that being famous meant he could "grab 'em by the pussy," a former *Apprentice* producer, Bill Pruitt, took to Twitter with this cryptic message: "When it comes to the #trumptapes there are far worse." In the media circus that followed, the comedian Tom Arnold—the former husband of the Trump supporter Roseanne Barr—also weighed in, writing on Twitter, "Some R voting 4 him because he really is like that & worse. A man who casually uses the 'N' word, mic-ed up on camera. Ask *Apprentice* crew." (Arnold became so obsessed with finding the tapes that in 2018 he made a TV series for the channel Viceland, *The Hunt for the Trump Tapes*, but came up empty-handed.)

Manigault said in interviews in 2018 that she's heard the tapes and that they are real. Burnett told me the tapes didn't exist. In this circus of self-promoters, where everyone's acting on behalf of their own financial interests, it's hard to know who's telling the truth.

"Let me tell you," Trump says. "The mics are on all the time. You have three to four hundred people working there. Every race, color, and creed are working there. Many African Americans. If I were to use that"—he pauses, seeming, protractedly, to sift through his vocabulary to find a way to describe America's most offensive slur—"*race* word, everybody hears it, because the mic goes in every room. If I had used that word, it would have been out," he says. "You wouldn't have gone two days."

Trump denies that his outtakes from *The Apprentice* are being held somewhere by Burnett, as some have speculated. "They say it's guarded," Trump says. "It's not guarded. It doesn't exist. It would have come out fifteen different ways. No. 1, it's a word that I've never used. I've never used it in my life!" But he immediately can't resist a thought experiment where he might have said the word but never while being recorded. "Would I use it when the mics are all hot? The mics were always hot. Because, a lot of times, they would see stuff during a break that was good. They'd use stuff during the breaks, which was my idea."

As Trump attempts to dismantle this story that has followed him for years, he still finds time to pat himself on the back. "Yeah, because a lot of good stuff comes out," he says, boasting about his improvisation skills. "Frankly, better stuff comes when they don't know it's on," he says about his interactions with the contestants. "Do you understand what I'm saying?" Trump seems to have forgotten that my two tape recorders are running, or that we're speaking about the breadth of his career, culminating in his presidency. He just wants me to understand how he made great TV.

The orange skin around his eyes crinkles. He's back in defense mode. "I use that, and I've got three or four hundred people listening to every word. It's so ridiculous. It never existed, and if it did exist, it would have been exposed years ago. You don't think during a presidential campaign that tape would have been released. Right? That says it better than anything, if you think about it."

Trump could rest his case now, but he's not done. "Except Hunter Biden," he says. Manigault is in the rearview mirror. Without my prompting, we've landed on the leaked private sex tape starring the son of his successor. "You know what's amazing? It's amazing that his tape will not be aired by the mainstream media."

Since 1994, Carolyn Kepcher had been working her way up in the Trump Organization. By the 2000s, she ran her boss's golf courses, helping create what would become prized properties in Bedminster, New Jersey, and Briarcliff Manor, New York. She and Trump were close: he'd call her a few times a week and drop by to talk business. Often she'd even see him on the green with his famous friends. "Hillary and Bill, they played golf with Donald," Kepcher tells me. "We had some nice conversations. I remember them coming to the golf course, and they were getting along fine and laughed."

One day, Trump stopped by Kepcher's Westchester office to ask her advice about something not related to her areas of expertise. He wanted to know what she thought of Burnett's idea to do a reality TV show that revolved around him. "I remember Donald coming in one day," Kepcher says. "I was at Trump National. And he said he was being approached by Mark Burnett." She clarifies that's not how he described him: "He said 'the *Survivor* guy.' And I don't think I knew what that meant. *Cancer survivor*? I had no idea."

Trump quickly laid out the bigger details of the proposal for her. "He told me about the idea of doing a reality show on the Trump Organization, the business," she recalls. Being a pragmatist, and someone who wasn't deeply enmeshed in popular culture, she quickly shot it down. "And the first thing I said was, 'It's silly,'" she recalls. Kepcher told him, "I don't think we should do it. I think you're going to expose the company to the cameras, looking at contracts and negotiations."

Trump liked this quality in Kepcher—her outspokenness. They didn't always see eye to eye about everything, but she wasn't afraid to strongly voice her opinions, even when they disagreed. "He said, 'Okay, good advice, I suppose,'" Kepcher says. It turns out this would be one of the few times that he wouldn't listen to her. Several weeks passed. "And he came back and said, 'Remember I told you about the show for Mark Burnett?'" Kepcher says. "I said, 'Yeah?' He said, 'Well, I'm going to do it, and you're going to be a part of it.'"

Trump didn't have to travel as far to find his second judge. George Ross, his former mentor whom he'd hired as general counsel of the Trump Organization, sat on the same floor as he did in Trump Tower. "Donald called me into his office," Ross says. "Mark Burnett was there. Donald told me he was thinking of doing this show. Would I be a judge? Why not? In other words, basically I had a very good working relationship with Donald. I was with him for a lot of years, and if he had something he wanted done and it made sense, I certainly said okay."

On *The Apprentice*, Trump was supposed to be the consummate businessman—too busy (at least as depicted on TV) to spend the day chasing around his contestants. So Burnett devised an idea to streamline the judging on the show so it wouldn't all fall on a boss whose decision making was unpredictable at best. Burnett needed two of Trump's trusted associates to follow the contestants on the ground, take notes, and sit by his side in the boardroom. This was one area where reality TV looked a bit like reality, because Trump picked Kepcher and Ross without even requiring them to do a screen test. Better still, by keeping it in-house, Burnett initially wouldn't need to pay them much.

Trump wanted Kepcher, in her mid-thirties, because producers had told him it would be good to have a woman by his side, and he liked that she stood up to him. And for the second spot, Ross, who was seventy-five at the start of the show, proved to be the perfect extension for Trump. He dressed like his boss, wearing baggy suits, but looked less like an outsized media celebrity than a calming grandpa figure. His no-nonsense assessments, delivered in plain English and with no Trumpian drama or flair, gave the show credibility. Kepcher, youthful and conveying nerdy energy and passion for business through the screen, quickly became a fan favor-

ite, much to her own surprise. Trump says that he chose Ross and Kepcher because he thought it would be good casting. "Carolyn was a younger
generation," Trump says. "George was an older generation, and we covered
the whole gamut."

On a first season in which the defining female contestant was the erratic Manigault—and with two final contenders who were both men—
Kepcher was the solid-as-a-rock female voice. And her cutting humor and
frank comebacks showed what it took for a woman less built for drama
than Manigault to make it in Trump's world. "It was funny, because I
learned through some of the producers as time went on, apparently, I do
eye rolls or I put my hands together," Kepcher says. "I never even realized."

Kepcher and Ross were a natural fit to play Trump's sidekicks, but
they didn't get much guidance from Burnett before filming began. "It
was basically, 'Carolyn, be yourself. If you weren't a businesswoman, you
wouldn't be on the show,'" Kepcher recalls.

And Trump's two sidekicks didn't get a wardrobe budget. "I just basically wore my regular clothes," Ross says. "I wore a suit. I had to adopt the
persona of a judge—mild-mannered, fair, and not controversial, because I
never knew when I was going to get called upon. It was very impromptu,
and that's what I liked about it."

As the show came together, Burnett hired a group of junior producers—
many of them rejected *Apprentice* contestants—whom he referred to in-
ternally as "the Dream Team." These junior workers would run around
Manhattan, doing mock trials of the tasks to make sure they worked in
real time and ironing out hiccups before the actual contestants took them
on. Trump, Ross, and Kepcher did their own run-through of the first task
right before cameras rolled, still not understanding the full scope of Burnett's vision for the show. "We did a pass, so George and I knew what it
was about," Kepcher recalls. "And then the next day, we all started filming. It all happened in a few hours for me."

As Kepcher witnessed *The Apprentice* unfold, as played for keeps by
sixteen contestants who wanted a job like the one she had, she realized
that it was a much different show from the one she'd imagined. "The very

first task was the lemonade," she says of the challenge where each team tried to make money by wooing New Yorkers during their lunch breaks to a lemonade stand. "Not really knowing too much, I kind of was like, 'Are we really selling lemonade?' I was worried about people looking at contracts for the Trump Organization, and here we are!"

But as she observed the men's team strategize and duke it out, with Sam Solovey failing in his attempts to beg strangers to give him $1,000 for a glass of lemonade, she realized that there was a genius to the show's simplicity. "It was about working together as a team," Kepcher says. "It was about how you form a team. It's not about setting up a stand and pouring lemonade like you were a kid."

Still, it wasn't enviable or easy work. "After the first gig, I was exhausted running around South Street Seaport," Kepcher says. "I remember sitting on a curb, talking to a producer: *Oh my God. Is it going to be like this every day?*"

The boardroom scenes are the pinnacle of every episode of *The Apprentice*. It's the tense moment where Trump decides whom to get rid of at the end of each task, and it plays out like a protracted tribal council from *Survivor*, with one man casting all the votes. Burnett's team had built a set on the fourteenth floor of Trump Tower, with a long table and three chairs on a platform—Trump in the center flanked by Ross and Kepcher. The contestants faced them. This room was lined with one-way mirrors, because more than a dozen cameras were positioned on the other side. While for Trump and his protégés the room seemed intimate, they were being secretly scrutinized by a group of Hollywood producers and crew whose size might have shocked even the mouthiest contestant into silence.

In the boardroom, Trump would assess what exactly happened on the task (with notes from Burnett, since he didn't observe the contestants in the field). Then the project manager, or team captain, of the losing team would choose the two weakest players to stay behind and they'd dodge rapid-fire questions from Trump in a frenzied fight for survival. Although

Trump loved to say he chose whom he fired, Burnett and NBC helped make the decision for him. But sometimes, he'd go rogue, getting rid of a particularly annoying contestant on the spot.

Of course, Trump credits himself with creating the most memorable line on *The Apprentice*, and the four-fingered cobra gesture with his right hand that accompanied it while filming the first episode. "It's a funny thing," Trump tells me. "When I taped it, I used the words 'You're fired!' You remember the first one I fired?" As he poses the question, a handler in the back of the room frantically types on his laptop, trying to find the right answer—which turns out to be the thirty-one-year-old venture capitalist David Gould—but comes up empty. After a pause, Trump moves on. "I just remember the net effect," Trump says. "Those words were never thought of until that happened. It was going to be, 'You won't be back next week.' You know, less dramatic."

Ross was surprised when he watched *The Apprentice* for the first time. "The finished product was a lot different than the raw material that went into it," he says, crediting Burnett's editors with inventing story lines and even splicing reaction shots to fit a narrative. "There was a lot of rewriting done. There were a lot of revisions. They put in a smile. They put in a frown. They could tailor whatever emotion they wanted."

While Trump had initially told Ross and Kepcher that *The Apprentice* would take about three hours out of their weekly schedules, it soon swallowed up their entire lives. Trump doesn't adhere to boundaries when it comes to any enterprise associated with his name—which is why he had a habit of roaming the halls of the Miss USA pageant before the show and greeting each contestant personally in her dressing room. (The women on the other side of the door, often a bit startled, were as young as eighteen.) For this newly minted reality TV star, the players on *The Apprentice* weren't just potential Trump Organization employees or fodder for entertainment; they were extensions of his own brand. Trump's frustration was real when one of his acolytes couldn't read his mind. These were stars in a drama the onetime aspiring producer was creating. And it made sense to keep them close—at times closer than some of his children.

Trump has never been shy about giving preferential treatment. So for those on the ground of *The Apprentice*, it soon became clear which contestants were the early favorites. Amy Henry, a spunky thirty-year-old account manager from Austin, Texas, was unstoppable, winning the first ten tasks. The contestants continually switched teams, using the schoolyard-pick method; Amy was always in demand. On the men's side, the strongest players were Bill Rancic, a thirty-two-year-old cigar business owner from Chicago; Kwame Jackson, a twenty-nine-year-old Wall Street investment manager from Charlotte, North Carolina (and the only other Black contestant besides Manigault); and Nick Warnock, a twenty-seven-year-old copier salesman from Los Angeles with red hair, who provided a juicy romantic subplot by flirting with Henry, as the show's editors worked overtime to make viewers wonder if he'd stab her in the back.

Manigault was constantly in the middle of fights with her teammates, injecting conflict and tension into the competition. "During the show, she made statements and accusations that were out of control," says Heidi Bressler, who argued with Manigault when she tried to stop for a leisurely lunch on a task where they were supposed to sell an artist's work at a gallery. "She truly made a name for herself, and I gave her kudos for that."

Solovey lasted for three episodes as the show's court jester. But he'd taken the assignment seriously when the cameras weren't on. Before Solovey boarded his flight for New York, he read every book he could find on Trump. "I'm sharing this because it gets into the whole mythmaking thing," Solovey says. "I read about his father, his grandparents. My aim was to become a student of Donald Trump. And then when I got there, I watched him."

When the contestants faced Trump for the first time in an introductory meeting set in the boardroom, Solovey was surprised to witness the man at the other end of the table. "He almost presented himself as a Broadway character," Solovey says. "When you go to a Broadway show, there's a certain manner in which an actor is supposed to stand onstage, because they don't use their hands," Solovey says. "Certain aspects of posture, cadence—he adopted all of that. And it wasn't natural. I don't think people really analyze it, but it clearly was intentional. All of these sorts of affectations fed into this idea that he was like this false idol in the room, kind of sucking all of the oxygen out."

This was Trump's public image, even when the cameras weren't rolling. "I believe the way that he presents himself is a larger sort of performance art," Solovey says. "Just watching him, everything from the hands, the way he puts his fingers together and claps, the pointing fingers, the length of his ties, always wearing suits. It's all part of a persona. And I don't think it's natural—especially the speech pattern and the way he stands. It doesn't hurt that he's a tall guy and physically big. It's all part of a product."

That product mesmerized most of the cast of *The Apprentice*. They'd been told—if they somehow hadn't already been aware—about Trump's vast wealth, and he reiterated his success to them in the short monologues he delivered before he sent them on their tasks. "I observed all these young women taken by him," Solovey says. "I remember asking one of the contestants, 'Would you sleep with Donald Trump?' And she said, 'Absolutely.' And I said, 'Really? You're twenty-eight years old. He's almost sixty.'"

Trump was an *idea* to all of them, not an actual person. The group's interactions with him were limited to his appearances at the beginning of each episode, where Trump laid out the task, and at the end as the executioner. But they also got glimpses into other sides of his personality. One early interaction involved Trump reading promos with the contestants. After reciting a line from a teleprompter (never one of Trump's strengths), he turned to them, asking for reassurance that he'd delivered the words convincingly. They were taken aback by his insecurity.

Trump didn't yell in front of them, but he could lose his patience with the mundane details of filming a TV show. He hated it when a glam squad materialized in the boardroom to tousle his bouffant. It shattered the mirage, the idea that he was larger than life. "When they would stop for a tape change, all of a sudden hair and makeup would come in to fix Trump," says the contestant Bowie Hogg. "He didn't like us seeing him get done multiple times."

New York City, two years after the deadliest terrorist attacks on American soil, was still finding its feet during production in September 2003, and *The Apprentice* painted the town as the place to be—aspirational and exciting. For three months, the contestants got to live communally in digs that felt like a *Real World* spin on a Trump property. A floor of Trump Tower had been outfitted as the world's coolest dorm room, with bunk beds for the roommates to share, a basketball court for them to shoot hoops on, and, of course, more cameras than *The Truman Show*. They were told they had to be wearing microphones at all times, and nothing was off limits. In the first episode, a phone call summoned them to the trading floor of the New York Stock Exchange, with a crew capturing footage of them grumpily rising from their beds.

"I remember Mark Burnett talking to us," Hogg says. "At the start, he said, 'I have cameras everywhere in this place. The one place I don't have them is in the bathroom. The first time someone violates any rule, and two contestants go in the toilet together, I will immediately put cameras in the bathroom.'"

But Burnett couldn't help himself, and he eventually brought the cameras into the bathroom to collect footage of the contestants getting ready. "I remember one morning, I did an interview while I was in the shower, washing my hair," Hogg says. He didn't expose himself to all of America, because "it was one of those shower doors that came up to about the middle of my chest."

There was no time for modesty. "Living in Trump Tower was crazy," says Kristi Frank, the thirty-year-old restaurateur from Bel-Air. "But it becomes part of your life. And I remember one time getting dressed. There were no doors. And there was another contestant right in front of me, like a boy. Oh, well, there wasn't a whole lot of privacy."

Each contestant had packed a few weeks of clothes into their rolling luggage, with directions that they'd be responsible for dressing themselves—no frills, or stylists, allowed. "It's almost like living in a cubicle," Bressler says. And once she learned just how much she'd be on camera, she realized how badly she'd failed the fashion part of this assignment.

"I would have brought my nice bags," says Bressler, who was seen throughout the season carrying a dated Prada purse. "I would have gotten keratin. I would have made sure my hair was easy to do. I would have gotten, like, fake eyelashes. We didn't know any of that. They tell you to bring a professional nice dress."

Many of Burnett's producers and crew had come straight from *Survivor*. They had to go from choreographing challenges in the middle of desolate tropical islands to shooting in the streets of New York City. And while the living conditions looked much better than a hut in the rain, the *Apprentice* castmates would nag that their fridge wasn't fully stocked with vegan-friendly snacks. The complaining paid off. "We started getting every food," Hogg says. "Burnett's team was not used to having to feed people. This was not a show about us having to go hungry."

Although they were in their twenties and thirties, being on a reality show produced by Burnett meant that they had to surrender most of their rights. It wasn't unlike being in a luxury prison—their cell phones, IDs, and wallets were stripped from them and were held by producers. Hogg, who'd come from Texas, even forked over $5,000 in cash he'd packed in case of an emergency. This was done to limit their contact with the world outside the show and to ensure that they were all completely dependent on Burnett. And as they lived in Trump Tower and went about their tasks, they were warned that Trump was always monitoring them by watching the camera feeds.

"They messed with us," Frank says. "They said, 'Donald Trump will be watching you guys throughout the whole thing.' And they'd say, 'Oh, he's watching you. He's keeping tabs.' No, he wasn't watching us! He had no idea what we were doing."

Every few days, Kepcher and Ross would confer with Trump about who they thought should be fired. Producers would weigh in, giving him feedback, and then he'd make the decision—although he liked to keep everyone guessing. The axed contestant would leave on the spot and be sent down in the elevator to the street, where a taxi would be waiting. "They had purchased a New York City cab and blackened it on its sides,"

Hogg says. "There's a producer driving. There's a cameraman sitting in the front seat, holding a camera through a little hole. And there's a sound guy lying on the floorboard, holding the boom mic up so they can catch you. They'll drive you for as long as you want. They could drive around for, like, two hours filming." And then, after preferably shedding some curse words and tears—"There's little correlation between IQ and success in lemonade sales," pleaded the first fired contestant—the rejected castoffs met with a therapist off-camera to make sure they were emotionally stable.

But they weren't done yet. So that there'd be no spoilers, Burnett didn't want anyone returning home; *Survivor* also employed this tactic. So the axed contestants moved into rooms at the Drake Hotel. That's when they got to know the real Donald Trump, who violated the golden rule of reality TV: never get too close to the contestants. Although the genre was new, the standard Hollywood caste system still applied. The civilians on a set shouldn't delude themselves into thinking they're on the same level as the talent, and the only actual famous person on the *Apprentice* set that first season was Donald Trump.

But his grip on the contestants went beyond the show. While he wasn't obligated to ever see them again, Trump had a strong curiosity about these young people who had put their lives on hold to compete for his affection. They still didn't have access to their wallets or money; production assistants would take them out for sightseeing or to bars (or even, in one instance, to buy costumes for a toga party they decided to throw in their rooms). During the day, Trump would regularly invite them over to his office, simply to hang out. They all had the ability to reach him. All they had to do was call his assistant Rhona.

Trump was on the cutting edge of television's new era. But he still preferred a fax as a form of communication to email. "He didn't have a computer at the time, which I always remember," Hogg says. He also exhibited some hoarding tendencies: "There was so much paperwork stacked up everywhere—all kinds of development contracts and blueprints. He had this entire wall of all his magazines that he'd been in, and things like that."

Trump would sometimes suggest field trips for the ousted contestants, sending them to his golf courses and his casino in Atlantic City and getting them face time with his top executives. These activities are what kept him busy while Kepcher and Ross were chronicling the adventures of the remaining cast. Trump got so close to the contestants he'd fired that he offered the men some personal advice. "Always make sure you got a prenup," Hogg remembers him telling them. "He goes, 'Men will hire a lawyer to look at everything, but then they put half their wealth at risk, and they won't hire an attorney to protect their wealth in a marriage.'" (Never mind that most of these players didn't have any wealth to protect.) Trump had been burned by his 1990 divorce from Ivana, and while Kepcher and Ross were advising the surviving contestants on business, he took it upon himself to tell the young men he'd already fired about the tougher casualties of falling in love.

Trump even had them over to his apartment. But this is when things got *really* weird. "I remember looking at Central Park from his big floor-to-ceiling windows," says Solovey, who recalls standing next to Kristi Frank. "I sort of have this little crush on Kristi," Solovey says. "I'm dazzled by her. And he comes up behind her, right up against her with his mouth, like right in the crook of her neck. And he puts his hands on her shoulders, like, 'Do you like that view?' And I was like, 'Whoa, dude! You're fifty-seven!'"

Frank doesn't remember that encounter, but she's aware that Trump objectified her looks when she wasn't in the room. During the 2016 election, the Associated Press published an investigation where they interviewed the *Apprentice* producer Katherine Walker, who said that on the episode where Frank was fired, Trump pulled her aside. He quizzed Walker about whom he should eliminate as he "raised his hands and cupped them to his chest to ask whether it was a contestant with large breasts," meaning Frank. He didn't even know her name.

When this incident came out in the press, Frank says people wanted to know how she felt about it. But she still doesn't have anything negative to say about Trump. She recalls that even after she left the show, he'd always take her calls, would offer her career advice, and even wrote her a letter of recommendation. "Behind the scenes, he can talk about my body," Frank says. "But to my face, he was a perfect gentleman."

According to Frank, Trump told her that she would have won a different kind of contest with him. "He brought me to his office with my fiancé at the time," Frank says. "And Trump was very complimentary. He said, 'Out of all the contestants, Kristi was my favorite. If I was going to marry anyone, it would be Kristi.'" She wasn't offended by that either. "It was charming, and tongue in cheek," she says. "It wasn't lascivious."

But for Trump, there was no line he wouldn't cross. As is true of Manigault, the contestant whom he fired shortly after Frank and Hogg, he lived for the attention. *The Apprentice* had expanded his world, and he loved these doting contestants who worshipped him. He was suddenly so intoxicatingly in charge he felt like he could get away with anything.

CHAPTER 5

Ratings, Ratings, Ratings!

During our first afternoon together, Donald Trump rises from his chair to give me a tour of his favorite part of his office. Perhaps unsurprisingly, given his need to keep his most precious things close (and his reputed dislike of exercise), he doesn't need to walk far. About three steps beyond his desk, in the entryway of his den, there's the Trump wall of fame. Crammed in a jumble that would be an interior designer's nightmare, in gold frames inches from each other, his favorite magazine covers are cluttered together, including a 1984 *GQ* cover story written by Graydon Carter (whom Trump would come to hate as the editor of *Spy* and *Vanity Fair*) and a *Playboy* cover, which in 1990 captured him as Manhattan's most envied ladies' man.

Trump stands next to me as he inspects one particular artifact. This sheet of paper carries tremendous meaning for him. As Trump remembers it, his voice sounds tender and his face lights up, in the same way that someone might respond to a snapshot of a soulmate. Trump is looking at a page from the Nielsen ratings published in a 2004 issue of *Variety*— then a daily Hollywood trade newspaper, now a weekly entertainment magazine that I run—from the week after the airing of *The Apprentice*'s first-season finale. It's framed and bolted to the wall; he points to it as if he were addressing a living person, but he doesn't dare touch this valuable document, something that seems to carry as much value to him as the U.S. Constitution, if not more.

As ever, Trump knows how to pitch his audience, or maybe he's just glad to be in the company of someone professionally obligated to understand TV ratings. "Head of *Variety*—I can't bullshit you!" Trump says as he gloats about the size of the crowds he reached as the star of *The Apprentice*. "Look at those ratings!" He seems to hope I'll look at them and decipher them for him, as if he can't make any sense of the chart. What it shows is that the two-hour first-season-ending TV event drew a 34 share in the Nielsen ratings—meaning that 34 percent of adults between the ages of eighteen and forty-nine with their TVs turned on were glued to Trump's final boardroom. That equates to a total of forty million viewers. By any measurement, that's a stratospheric number that doesn't need to be spun or inflated. But Trump, who's no stranger to wresting defeat from the jaws of victory, still manages to bungle it.

Repeating the words "Look at those ratings!" he then waves his finger at the page. "Thirty-four million people!" He decides—perhaps through a braggart's muscle memory for self-promotion—that the number could be bigger (and he is indeed correct). But to admit that he doesn't remember how to read a Nielsen chart requires a humility he can't muster. He covers up his error by inventing a new statistic, pretending that there were more successful seasons of *The Apprentice* that aired. (In fact, it peaked in its first season and continued to shed viewers as the years dragged on.) "And this wasn't even the biggest show," Trump insists. What ought to have been a victory lap for Trump—there's no denying that his show was big— has grown hazy in a web of half-truths and empty boasts. "The biggest show had forty-two million people. Forty-two! What's the date of this? Do you have it?"

It was April 15, 2004. Burnett had packed two hours of melodrama into the *Apprentice* conclusion, an episode titled "Down to the Wire."

Trump had whittled down his job interview search from 215,000 applicants to 16 on-camera competitors to the final 2 candidates: Bill Rancic and Kwame Jackson. Perhaps it was no surprise that in the end Trump had eliminated every member of the original all-female team; now, on this show, there was room for only two women, the trustworthy Carolyn Kepcher and the even more trustworthy Rhona Graff.

"Everybody assumed that I was going to be picking a really beautiful woman like Amy," Trump said on TV in the boardroom as he introduced the last task. "And, hey, I'm stuck with two guys. The fact is, that you guys were the best. And when it comes to business, I don't play games." (His final business lesson of the season was about getting rid of toxic people in the workplace. "You never know what makes a loyal person," Trump said. "And guess what? If they're not loyal to you one time, don't give them a second chance—because they won't be loyal to you the next time.")

All these years later, when Trump looks back on that episode, what resonates with him isn't the words he used or the quality of the show that Burnett produced. He's singularly focused on his ranking as No. 1 show on the chart. After a pause, only a few seconds later, he adds another 500,000 people to the ratings count. "The finale had 42.5 million people," Trump says, padding his numbers more as a pathological tic than a strategic move. He's celebrating his pre-MAGA popularity—calling his ratings "higher than at the time the Academy Awards." (This isn't true. At the 2004 Oscars, two months prior, 44 million people tuned in to see *The Lord of the Rings: The Return of the King* sweep. And three weeks later, on May 6, also on NBC, the series finale of *Friends* would draw 52.5 million viewers.)

"It was always the Super Bowl, the Academy Awards, the *Apprentice* finale," Trump says, dropping another lie to keep the momentum going. "Even here you have 34 million people." He's still reading the chart incorrectly. "Look at your second." The next biggest shows of that week—*CSI*, *American Idol*, and *Survivor*—all had a smaller audience share than *The Apprentice*'s cliff-hanger hiring. That's true and impressive: those shows were forces to be reckoned with. But Trump still needs more.

Later, of course, Trump's obsession with size was woven into the fabric of his presidency, a fixation that even Freud might have thought to be too on the nose. It started as a defense mechanism: what he lacked in traditional experience, he made up for in sheer tonnage of support. The packed arenas where he held his rallies made the case that what the people truly wanted wasn't a traditional politician like Jeb Bush or Marco Rubio (or, later, Hillary Clinton). Having spent so much time questioning Barack Obama's legitimacy and birthplace, Trump, for all his braggadocio, was the one who suffered from impostor syndrome. On inauguration weekend, instead of celebrating, he spent his first days as president sulking about his crowd size being smaller than Obama's 2008 celebration. His first press secretary, Sean Spicer, lit into journalists with a fevered, Trumpian intensity on day 1, credibility be damned, as he declared Trump had "the largest audience to ever witness an inauguration, period," an untruth that Trump's surrogate Kellyanne Conway, the latter-day Carolyn Kepcher of a bizarre moment in history, referred to as "alternative facts."

Perhaps an earlier fixation on ratings explains the degree to which the inauguration crowd size nagged at his ego. Ratings could also be made to tell the story you wanted them to, and what Trump wanted was an objective-seeming measure of his success. He had been taught well by Jeff Zucker and NBC executives that the ratings determined everything—crucially, how much they could charge advertisers, proving Trump's worth to the network. After *The Apprentice* debuted on January 8, 2004, following *Friends* on "Must See TV" Thursday, Trump was sucked into the numbers game by his new Hollywood friends. His phone wouldn't stop ringing the next day, as Zucker, Burnett, and other NBC suits kept calling him to offer their personal congratulations. *The Apprentice*'s first episode was the biggest new hit of the season, with 18.49 million viewers overall. (*Friends*, in its much-ballyhooed final season, drew 25.49 million viewers that night.)

"We called Donald right after and told him what a success it was," recalls Jeff Gaspin. "What we see in his personality today, we saw back then. When you reward him, he is your biggest proponent." Trump was so invested in the ratings he started finding them on his own because he didn't have the patience to wait for NBC to send the numbers to him. "He then started calling us," Gaspin says, estimating Trump spent two hours on the phone after each episode simply talking about the ratings. "He would know what the ratings were before we did, because he was on the East Coast and we were on the West Coast. I got faxes where he'd circle a headline or rating, and wrote a handwritten comment."

The memory of those numbers still gives Trump a jolt of adrenaline. "We beat them all," he says, his face flushed with excitement. "Isn't it amazing?" Trump turns to his spokesperson Jason Miller, who is sitting in the back of his office. "He's *Variety*," Trump explains about me, forgetting that Miller set up our interview and had already vetted me.

On the night before I first met with Trump for the book, Miller called me to give me some pointers. Some journalists, he noted, mistakenly try to make small talk with Trump to break the ice. This often sends him into a verbal tailspin, eating up valuable time and causing the interview to be mostly over before it begins. Miller recommended that I just start asking questions as soon as I sit down. But now we're standing in front of his wall of egotism, with endless framed prompts for Trumpian nostalgia and boasting. I'm not sure how to end this show-and-tell and, if I don't take action, how long it might last before he tires himself out.

Trump shows no signs of stopping as he continues to study the ratings report from twenty years ago. Under glass, as if frozen in amber, this sheet of paper comes from an America where *The Apprentice* was, if for only a single week, the No. 1 show and Trump the nation's biggest star. And he seems to be traveling further back in time—he's suddenly the college boy who tried to escape his father's shadow with a career as a producer, before returning to the fold. "This is my whole life," Trump says.

His face is still, and he's no longer the angry politician who, in his mind, never got the respect and adoration that he deserved. While intended as yet another bit of self-congratulation, Trump's declaration hangs in the air, feeling sad. It's the closest he's ever come to acknowledging that his true passion in life is for showmanship, not statesmanship.

No wonder his presidency led America down a made-for-TV rabbit hole. Performing is all he has.

As the editor of a weekly print magazine, I try to be optimistic about the future of journalism, but it's hard to deny that this room full of old media is starting to feel, well, old. Like Miss Havisham from Charles Dickens's *Great Expectations*, perpetually wearing a moldering wedding gown to mourn her lost potential, Trump keeps the world of turn-of-the-century print journalism around to remind him of . . . something. If there's something about himself that keeps him from good press these days, that's too hard to contemplate, so Trump spins the idea around: it's the magazines that got small. "It used to be a real honor to be on *Newsweek*," Trump says as he surveys how reporters covered him with puff pieces. "It used to be a real honor to be on the cover of *The New York Times*. Now you read it, there's nothing to read. It's like you hand it out at a grocery store for a bargain." Coincidentally enough, the media he pillories as having lost its status and glamour is the same industry that chronicled all his missteps in the White House. There's no danger of today's coverage getting added to this wall someday.

"The show was a big hit," Trump says, moving toward a conclusion. "We had 42.5 million people for the finale." Wearied by repetition of this false number, I'm starting to understand how Spicer and Conway felt after the inauguration flop. "And," Trump says, seeming to relish that he parachuted into Zucker's and Aniston's Thursday night paradise as an outsider before blowing it up, "they didn't have a contract with me."

Although he received the episodes in advance, Trump loved to watch (or re-watch) each new episode of *The Apprentice* in real time as it aired on the East Coast. It gave him a thrill to see himself in action on TV, and it made him feel connected to the millions of Americans who were enthralled by his every word in the boardroom. But he also believed every single viewer counted; by watching *The Apprentice*, his thinking went, he was doing his duty to help keep the numbers up. For all his fixation on ratings, Trump admits that he doesn't actually know how they're tabulated. "Where do the ratings come from?" Trump asks me. "Is it still Nielsen? Can they check by the televisions themselves? Or do they have to go poll like they used to?"

Whatever the method, Trump explains that he has a policy of trying to support TV shows that are good to him. "You know what I'll do?" he tells me. "When I like a show, and I like a TV host, I'll TiVo it." Trump, never known for his tech savvy, now sounds like a Best Buy employee during the dot-com boom, pitching me on the hottest discovery of 1999. "One of the world's great inventions, by the way," he says. "I like TiVoing. I think without TiVo, I wouldn't watch television, because you wouldn't know what's going on." I ask him if he really uses TiVo, or if he's just talking about a DVR. "TiVo or its equivalent," he says. "Let's use the word TiVo—or TiVo equivalent."

Trump says that if you looked at his TV—in constant use during his presidency, when he mainlined cable news from morning to night—it's recording the same shows, even when they are on repeat. "If somebody treats me well, like, as an example: Sean Hannity is on three times," he says about the Fox News host. "So I will TiVo it three times. I'm not watching it at four in the morning, but I'll TiVo that." For Trump, that's the definition of loyalty. "I think it's representative of the way I do things," he says.

As good as Sean Hannity would later be to Trump, nothing was better to him—and more deserving of his support—than his own show. As he watched and re-watched and TiVoed *The Apprentice*'s re-airings, Trump realized he wasn't completely sold on Burnett's narrative techniques. Specifically, he had a big note for Burnett: Trump didn't understand why he was offscreen for so long, with these anonymous contestants hogging up valuable time with the cameras. Trump advocated for more Trump. Today, he says that this resulted in his "biggest argument" with his producing partner. But as soon as he makes this declaration criticizing Burnett, he hears his own words in his head and knows how this might come off. He quickly adds an addendum of contradictory gibberish: "It wasn't in the form of an argument." Although there's no reason to still be deferential to Burnett, Trump doesn't want to discredit the man who made him a star.

For Trump, the part of the show that carried substance, and the ostensible reason for *The Apprentice* to exist—the tasks for contestants and the differences in style between competitors that they exposed—was all extra. He wanted to max out the conflict. "The people didn't really like all of that stuff, all of the plans for whatever company we were doing it for," Trump says. "They really liked the boardroom. That's what they liked. And they liked the opening, when I was talking in front of them." It's perhaps not surprising that Trump's favorite part of *The Apprentice* was his own camera time, but his analysis of the show suggests that, despite his credit as executive producer, he doesn't have the strongest handle on storytelling. Without all that comes before the boardroom, who would even understand what the fighting was about?

Making any set of real experiences into a TV-friendly narrative is hard enough in the best of times. But with an agent of chaos—one agitating for an endlessly bigger role—at the center, Burnett had a near-impossible task. His special touch as a producer was to lighten the dark edges around Trump, to make his hit-or-miss track record in business seem relevant and important, orderly and coherent. Those around Trump had a sense of trepidation about watching their workplace—and their own work—launched into the national spotlight. On Thanksgiving morning in 2003, Carolyn Kepcher was in her kitchen preparing dinner for her family as she watched the parade on NBC. At the commercial break, she was suddenly stopped cold when she saw a promo for *The Apprentice*. "Oh my God," Kepcher says. "That was my first intro to what it was." That's when it really hit her: she was going to be on a TV show.

By Burnett's hand, Kepcher emerged as a breakout superstar—direct and firm, quick to correct not only the mistakes of the contestants but the excesses of her boss. (Eventually, she'd be replaced by Ivanka Trump, who was far more likely to rubber-stamp her father's thinking.) Women not only responded to Kepcher's business-executive persona but started to recognize her on the street. They rooted for her passionately and saw themselves in her. (A *New York Times* profile from 2004 called Kepcher "the ice queen of Thursday night" but approvingly noted her "reputation for being a great manager" and said that she looked "younger and more approachable" in real life than on TV.)

"I didn't go in there thinking that was going to happen," Kepcher says. "But it did. I got a lot of emails and letters, mostly from young women in business. I was the voice, the female voice. It was exciting for me. I embraced it, learning from it. There was a good amount of responsibility that went with it."

Trump, for his part, wasn't staying up late at night pondering his responsibilities as a role model. He just loved the fame. In New York, he'd get swarmed in the street by a new generation of fans as they'd shout his catchphrase "You're fired!" back at him. From the moment *The Apprentice* was ratified as a hit, Trump spent every waking moment promoting the show—and his brand. There wasn't an interview that Trump wouldn't do, which delighted NBC.

"He loved talking about himself, and he loved talking about the success of the show," says Gaspin. "He's a publicist's dream. You don't need to ask or schedule him. His answer is yes. 'Where do you want me? Point.'" Remarkably, to those at NBC, it started to feel as if *The Apprentice* were Trump's full-time job—with his real estate business a side hustle. "I don't think he was actually doing much, to be honest," Gaspin says. "I think he had people around him doing the work, and he was the figurehead. He was essentially the queen. He showed up where you needed him to show up. People wanted to see him and touch him and speak to him, and he loved it. He was great at it."

Trump could dominate an entire news cycle with his overblown score settling. Shortly after *The Apprentice* premiered, at his first Television Critics Association presentation, Trump lit into CBS's CEO, Leslie Moonves, calling him "the most highly overrated person in television." Burnett, who'd been CBS's boy wonder with *Survivor* before *The Apprentice*, had to bite his tongue as Trump continued. "If Leslie Moonves was a contestant on our show, he would have been fired by the third episode, and unlike most people I like Les Moonves." Trump's trashing of Moonves was merely payback for his canceling the Miss Universe pageants, which now aired on NBC. Zucker—who viewed Moonves as a frenemy who'd ridden *Survivor* and *CSI* to better ratings—smirked at Trump so publicly dragging the competition. There was no way for Moonves to win this fight, and so he didn't try. ("The Donald is always good for a chuckle," his spokesperson responded. "But we're not going to engage in such banter.") As Trump kept taking digs at Moonves while promoting *The Apprentice*, the CBS boss finally called Trump, asking *him* for a truce.

"Wouldn't you say he was the most powerful guy in Hollywood?" Trump asks me. "No, I'm not talking about now." (Moonves resigned from CBS in 2018 after multiple women claimed he'd assaulted or harassed them.) "Now he sits alone at the Bel-Air Club, and nobody cares," Trump says, somehow knowing his whereabouts. "Back then, during the *Apprentice* time, I would probably say he's the most powerful man in Hollywood. But in the end, he called and he really apologized."

Trump's commitment to NBC was around the clock. "It was amazing, because I would say I could get him anywhere in the world at any time," says Kevin Reilly, who served as the network's president of prime-time development. "There were times I'd call his assistant Rhona, and she'd say, 'One moment, please.' All of a sudden he'd pick up in Scotland. There was never a time when I did not get him on the phone, regardless of whatever part of the world he was in, which was pretty extraordinary."

The Apprentice started off on Thursday nights, but that was just to give the show a jump start. Traditionally, that night was reserved for NBC's block of scripted hit comedies, from *Mad About You* to *Seinfeld* to *Friends*. These shows allowed the network to charge high advertising premiums on the most important programming night of the week, before viewers went out to spend money over the weekend. "Thursday night made more money in ad sales than the rest of the week combined, putting aside the NFL," Reilly says. "It had been an incredible cash cow in the heyday of Must See TV." At NBC, unscripted programming—including *Fear Factor*—was still regarded as second-tier programming and not worthy of sharing the night with *Friends*.

After two weeks of airing on Thursdays, *The Apprentice* was moved to

Wednesday for its third episode. That turned out to be a huge mistake. The show got clobbered by the launch of *American Idol*'s third season, where the charismatic singer Fantasia Barrino would eventually win the top prize and help the show continue steamrolling the competition. In a head to head with *Idol*, *The Apprentice* went from having 20 million viewers (for its second episode) to 12.3 million viewers, and the nosedive in ratings profoundly upset Trump. Sam Solovey was axed during that episode, and he recalls meeting with Trump after he'd gone on *Today*, in a standard cross-promotional appearance for fired contestants. Ever the good soldier, Solovey had decided to extend his popularity and build buzz for the show. He used his moment on *Today* to propose to his girlfriend on live TV, while Katie Couric (enough of a Trump pal to attend his third wedding) watched.

At Trump Tower, the newly engaged couple didn't receive the warm greeting they were expecting. "I remember going to his office and seeing this miserable, very small man sitting behind his desk," Solovey says. Trump couldn't hide his pain about the disappointing ratings. "And I introduced him to my now wife of twenty years," he says. "We were engaged that day. I remember he said to me, 'Sam, did you get a prenup?'—in front of her! It was the strangest conversation. He's not a happy guy, and that was a very real, raw moment when I walked in, where I got to see him without the performance."

Jeff Zucker quickly corrected for this error. *The Apprentice* was big, but *Idol*, with its own cynically deployed mentor figure in the caustic judge Simon Cowell, was huge. The following week, *The Apprentice* was moved back to Thursday nights, out of *Idol*'s way, and its ratings rebounded. And Trump, who'd wanted to remain the sole focus of the cameras, made his own concession to get more airtime; he'd realized that surrounding himself with the contestants was a surefire way to keep *The Apprentice* in the press. So he invited them everywhere—from the Playboy Mansion to awards shows to his birthday party at the Trump Taj Mahal in Atlantic City, hosted by Regis Philbin. Trump had never been more in demand. *Saturday Night Live*, which airs on NBC, asked him to host for the first time in April 2004, before the finale. (In one sketch, he danced in a bright-yellow suit while cast members dressed as chickens frolicked around him; the sketch was called "Donald Trump's House of Wings," and the joke was that he'd slap his name on anything.)

Solovey says he had lengthy discussions with Trump about joining the Trump Organization as an employee, but Trump said he couldn't hire him before the finale. Trump told Solovey that Burnett wouldn't allow it, because they were worried about optics. If one of the fired contestants still got a job from Trump, they didn't want the game to look, to use a Trump word that would crop up again, "rigged." In the short term, Solovey became a Trump mascot, continually appearing in public with him in the hopes that it would lead to something later.

"I met with him privately in his office," Solovey says. "He had his lawyer there taking notes. And then we did all these things together. We were on QVC, and we shot television commercials. I mean, the stuff I subjected myself to. He did a promo for the Miss Universe pageant, and I put on a dress. I was just, like, doing this. I remember Trump saying, 'Sam, I hope they're paying you.'" But Solovey collected only a nominal fee, and he eventually got tired of playing Cousin Greg in the *Succession* episode that was Trump's life. Solovey says he stopped engaging with Trump about a job and went back to his real life as a real estate agent.

Others couldn't escape Trump's orbit as easily. In fact, Trump enlisted the fired contestants as his helpers long before the first episode of *The Apprentice* aired, back when they were still being held without their wallets in New York City hotel rooms during production. One day, he called them into his office to show off his next great invention: he told them in confidence that he was about to roll out Trump Ice, a new bottled water brand with his face on the label, against a red-and-blue patriotic background. He polled them for feedback, but the room was mixed. They suggested he try different colors on the label—something more inviting that would actually make you want to drink water.

Trump listened to the feedback, but he was sticking with the design.

He had another task for them—one that wasn't for the cameras. He asked them to go to Brooklyn to meet with bottle manufacturers. He wanted a good deal, and he figured these young hustlers could act as unpaid interns to help him negotiate. "We spent a couple days meeting with bottlers and helping them get everything lined up," Bowie Hogg says. The product hadn't been announced, so they couldn't use Trump's name. Since *The Apprentice* hadn't aired yet, they were perfect as incognito workers. "But yeah," says Hogg, "we did the legwork." The contestants never complained, because they actually thought Trump was trying to teach them how to succeed in business.

As far as entertainment value goes, the first season of *The Apprentice* still holds up, even after the Trump brand has changed so much. Part of it is the sheer absurdity of the tasks: Bill Rancic and Kwame Jackson were competing to be the next great American mogul, but their final challenge cast them as party planners. They both had to oversee star-studded events under the guise of charity fundraising at different Trump properties, and the show brought back some former contestants to help them (including Omarosa Manigault, because Burnett wanted to squeeze out every ratings opportunity he could).

Rancic's task was to hold a celebrity golf tournament at Trump National, where a missing sign from a sponsor threatened to derail his success. But the real heat of the episode comes from watching Jackson's team set up a charity concert at the Taj Mahal Hotel and Casino in Atlantic City, headlined by Jessica Simpson. It's fair to say that Jackson lost his chance at being the Apprentice the second he selected Manigault for his team. Given the job of handling Simpson, who arrived with her father, Joe, and her then husband, Nick Lachey, Manigault kept losing the pop star. The cameras tracked long shots of Trump trekking through the casino to say hello to Simpson with no success. He was accompanied by Melania, who on *The Apprentice*, like later in the White House, came across as an enigma. The future first lady didn't have much of a story line, but she confessed to being a huge fan of *Newlyweds: Nick and Jessica*, Simpson and Lachey's MTV reality show about their married life as celebrities.

The final boardroom was taped live, as the *Survivor* tribal councils used to be, to stoke the feeling of it being an event for NBC. Trump inverted his favorite line, telling Bill Rancic, "You're hired!" to a cacophony of applause. Rancic accepted the $250,000 job offer and chose to work on the new Trump International Hotel and Tower in Chicago, where he lived. It's not surprising that Trump selected a safe, good-looking white man, who didn't rock the boat, to represent him.

"I thought Bill Rancic was very good," says George Ross, before offering a more lukewarm assessment of the first winner of the show. "I didn't find him overly aggressive. He was okay. I can't say anything plus or minus. He handled it very well. I didn't find him overly impressive as far as I was concerned. As far as his personality, I didn't find him overly dynamic or dramatic."

Trump was now contractually done starring on *The Apprentice*. But as he well knew, NBC couldn't afford to lose him. The ad sales team crunched the numbers and came back with staggering results. A single season of *The Apprentice* starring Donald Trump was worth $200 million in profits to NBC, according to one insider. With numbers like these, Zucker thought the network's strategy needed to evolve on reality TV. And the data showed that the audience of *The Apprentice* was affluent, because the show positioned itself as smarter than run-of-the-mill unscripted programming.

Burnett had batted around names like Virgin Group's CEO, Richard Branson, as a successor to Trump for future seasons. But for NBC, losing Trump wasn't an option. As far as Zucker was concerned, Trump was the show, and NBC had to keep him happy, no matter what it cost. So Zucker offered to help with the negotiations, even though Burnett was technically the one who'd employed Trump through his production company.

And that's when things got ugly for the first time between Donald Trump and Jeff Zucker.

CHAPTER 6

Trump v. Zucker

When it came time to negotiate with Jeff Zucker for the second season of *The Apprentice*, Donald Trump was determined to get a real payday from NBC. And as an outsider to Hollywood, he saw no need to comply with the standard showbiz rituals. Having proven his agent wrong by making *The Apprentice* into a massive hit, he decided to steer the deal making on his own.

Just the memory of it makes him come alive in conversation. He sparks with vim and energy in our conversation at his office at Trump Tower as he narrates the art of his deal with NBC. Reflecting on his rise from mere Manhattan tycoon to that wondrous thing—a television star—Trump can't help waxing rhapsodic about his own unique power. "When you're successful, you negotiate your own contract," Trump says. He sits back in his chair, flashing a mischievous grin. He's about to weave a tale that will show me—years after NBC fired him—just how irreplaceable he was to the network.

These are blissful memories for him. In our days together, Trump is happiest when he talks about *The Apprentice* and crankiest when he relives his years as the commander in chief. The stark difference in his temperament, as Trump shuffles through his recollections of his two major public jobs—hosting a reality show, running the country—reveals a man who believes he was only really in charge in one of these scenarios.

But it makes sense. For Trump, image is all that matters. *Playing* an authoritative person was so much more fulfilling than the burdensome weight of executing his responsibilities as the nation's most powerful official. And besides, getting rehired as chief in the boardroom turned out to be substantially easier than getting swing voters in the Rust Belt to approve him for four more years. NBC "offered me a lot," Trump says. "They offered me five years. They don't do that!" (In fact, they do; it's common practice for a TV network to lock down talent for as long as possible.)

"So anyway," Trump says, practically salivating as he gets the chance to talk about something that interests him, "here's the story."

The $25,000 an episode that Trump earned for the first season of *The Apprentice* was humiliating. It wasn't that he needed the TV money to live off, and the free advertising the Trump Organization got from the series was likely better than any pay package. But it was a status thing: bigger, according to Trump math, was always better. Trump felt that NBC had no choice but to multiply that number by a number so huge it would make him one of the wealthiest men in entertainment.

His negotiations for a second season took place as NBC's biggest hit, *Friends*, was ending after ten seasons. Trump says that he knew the network was desperate to keep him. "They were really in the basement, and we brought them back—big league!" While *Friends* still outperformed *The Apprentice* overall that season, Trump gleefully noted that some weeks his show did better. This wasn't a fair comparison: the final season of *Friends* was only eighteen episodes—six episodes fewer than the previous few seasons had been. As a result, NBC aired *Friends* reruns for seven weeks in the spring of 2004 in the lead-up to the show's grand finale, while *The Apprentice* was new each week. In other words, new episodes of

The Apprentice outperformed reruns of *Friends*. But for Trump, a win is a win, no matter what the circumstances.

And these wins were potentially very valuable. It was widely known that Jennifer Aniston and her quintet of TV besties were raking in a staggering $1 million each per episode from NBC for that last season.

So what was the logical thing to do? Getting paid $1 million an episode was, to anyone reasonably versed in how the business worked, out of the question. It had taken years of massive ratings, as well as a collective-bargaining push by all six stars, to negotiate the *Friends* paycheck, and besides, reality TV salaries were much smaller. It wasn't clear yet whether the genre had real staying power, and the network was still toying with the idea of swapping out *The Apprentice*'s star every season, a maneuver it couldn't easily have pulled with Lisa Kudrow or Matt LeBlanc.

But NBC was in a hurry. In the early spring of 2004, with season 1 still airing, the network had begun scouting contestants for a second season of their newest TV phenomenon so they could quickly bring *The Apprentice* back in the fall. And Trump sought to take advantage, with a proposal that was the equivalent of holding Zucker at gunpoint.

"*Friends* had six people," Trump explains to me. "They're getting $1 million an episode each. That's $6 million. So if they're getting $6 million, and I have higher ratings than they do—because this is the end of *Friends*, and they were fading out—I said, 'You should pay me $6 million an episode.'" The recollection of this big ask seems to make Trump physically swell; he stretches out his shoulders and arms, as if trying to reach around the pile of money he feels he'd earned from the series.

It was not to be, Trump says. "They went fucking crazy." Zucker, specifically, became vocally angry that Trump would even consider asking for such an unfeasible payday. (Some non-Trump math, which is to say a type of arithmetic rooted in business realities: The second season of *The Apprentice* had fifteen episodes. If the network had met Trump's demands, he would have made $90 million for three months of playing himself in the boardroom.)

"And they said, 'We're not going to do it. It's over.'" Then Trump counteroffered his own offer. After he kicked off the conversation with a stratospheric number, his strategy was to leave the door open to see what NBC would bring back to the negotiating table. "I said, 'Here's what we're going to do. Give me something less than six. If you're paying *Friends* six, and I have higher ratings than *Friends*, you should pay me six! But give me something less than that. I'm reasonable!'"

Reasonable or not, Trump's erratic maneuvering didn't sit well with Zucker, an executive who could seem cool on the surface but had an explosive temper when he didn't get his way. "And they went nuts," Trump says. "They said, 'We're going to get someone else.'" Trump knew that he could be a perennial annoyance. But he also knew that he'd truly alienated Zucker when the NBC boss—flexing his own deal-making chops—had called him personally to tell him to get lost. "We're not doing it," Zucker hissed to him on the phone. "We already have someone else lined up."

Pretending a star can be easily replaced in order to scare him into reducing his demand is a classic Hollywood negotiating ploy. Still, Trump started to wonder whether he'd overplayed his hand. "I thought the deal was dead," he says. "I thought I just killed myself." At the time, *The Apprentice* was just new and fun; he didn't view it as a career-changing enterprise yet. "They walked out—they were so angry. I said, 'That's all right! Get somebody else.'"

Not surprisingly, in Trump's retelling of these negotiations, he emerges victorious: he claims that Zucker caved. Trump says he got what he wanted—not $6 million an episode, but at least Zucker's admission that he needed Trump to give NBC a continued ratings boost. "The end result is Jeff called back like a day later, and said, 'We got to make a deal.' I said, 'Why? You couldn't get somebody else?' He said, 'No. We've got to make a deal.' And I agreed to a fortune. You know, they paid a lot of money. A lot! It was a great experience."

Trump's final salary on *The Apprentice* involved more complicated math than he's inclined to initially share. To ensure Trump's participation on the show, Burnett, who was talking to both sides in these negotiations (as a reality TV expert, he'd long ago mastered the craft of playing on everyone's team), had already agreed to a costly concession. As the show's creator and mastermind, Burnett told Trump they'd finally be cashing in on their product placement deal.

"It was part of Mark's shrewd producing, which is sort of like, 'I'm going to do these little deals, and don't worry about that,'" Kevin Reilly says. "Some of these deals had been struck on lesser unscripted shows." In the early days of reality TV, networks didn't always own the revenue from product integration; that money could go to the production company, which would negotiate with brands directly for on-camera product placement. "As the network was hemorrhaging money, I don't think they even knew the extent to do the math," Reilly says. "Certainly, a few years later, they were aware it was really significant."

On *Survivor*, and especially *The Apprentice*, Burnett had realized that these deals could be profoundly lucrative. Signing away half of the dollars his company would earn from product placement was a way for Burnett to appease Trump, keep him in the fold, and even make him feel a bit like Jennifer Aniston. Given that Trump and Burnett were running dual businesses—they were making a TV show and essentially overseeing an advertising agency—it's no surprise that *The Apprentice* pushed product placement further than any reality TV show had at the time. Each episode involved a new task, usually in the realm of marketing or promoting an existing product. So there was always a natural entry point for companies to appear on the series, and their executives' appearances didn't necessarily feel like blatant advertising, even as Trump promoted Mattel toys, Crest toothpaste, Levi's jeans, Pepsi, and M&M's.

All of those brands participated in the second season, after the show had been proven a ratings machine. But in the first season, because no brands had seen the show yet, Burnett's producers had mostly designed the task around Trump companies, giving him all the free publicity. The business leaders who appeared on season 1—such as George Steinbrenner, the principal owner of the New York Yankees—participated as a personal favor to Trump.

"We had a great sponsor, a very high-end sponsor," Trump recalls of shooting the first season. (While not usually one to worry about burning a bridge, Trump keeps this mystery advertiser a secret, as if *The Apprentice* were still on the air and he might need this company one day—or as if I might judge it as slightly less than high end.) "They canceled right before the show. They said, 'We don't want to have a problem with a failed show.' I said, 'That's a bitch.' So I got Steinbrenner. We went over to Yankee Stadium. It was going to be for fifteen minutes, and he went on for two hours about winning, and it was incredible television. I'm telling you!" Trump takes a moment to eulogize his friend, who died in 2010, but not without acknowledging, in his characteristic way with a vague euphemism, that Steinbrenner had been a convicted felon. "George was great. For me, he was. For other people, not so good."

But in season 2, Trump didn't need to call in favors from pals anymore. In its sophomore season, *The Apprentice* was massive, averaging more than sixteen million viewers an episode. Burnett demanded that brands fork over millions of dollars to be part of one of the most innovative and talked-about shows on TV. Just a few months before Christmas, the second season's premier episode, "Toying with Disaster," had the two teams duking it out to invent a toy for Mattel; the winners created a short-lived line of race cars, which sold in stores under the name Morph Machines. And they got rewarded with a dinner with Trump and Melania Knauss, who would soon be photographed for the cover of *Vogue* in her wedding gown.

On TV, this new class of pupils were done selling lemonade on the cheap. Instead, they put their culinary skills to the test by inventing a flavor of Ciao Bella Gelato, developing an ad campaign for Crest, launching a restaurant that was judged by the *Zagat Survey*, selling cleaning products and kitchen appliances on QVC, and even collaborating on a Levi's mailing catalog, featuring the season's must-have jeans. As Whitney Pastorek, a senior writer for *Entertainment Weekly*, said in her episode recap at the time, "The project was a giant Levi's commercial: Hey! We're Levi's! We still make jeans! *And* they make your ass look good, sorta! Whooo!"

In the brand-integration scenes, major CEOs would appear briefly to explain the identity of their company and how the contestants' work would need to cohere with their objective. They'd usually also judge the final product, although they never made it into the final boardroom; Trump was still the only one with the power to fire contestants. It wasn't too far off from how *American Idol*, for example, would later invite Lady Gaga and Miley Cyrus on as guest mentors and to plug their music. (One key difference: *Idol* didn't make its creators richer by asking Gaga and Miley to pay for the privilege of airtime.) For Trump, this scenario proved to be all upside—with only more upside. On *The Apprentice*, seeing Trump rub shoulders with business leaders only added to his clout, reinforcing his image as a globally connected boss. "It was such an experience," says Carolyn Kepcher. "Because you were able to meet executives and learn how they work—Mattel and these other big companies. We got a lot of background."

Unlike Kepcher, Trump was so set in his ways that he'd never take a lesson from a peer. But in performing curiosity about how other companies functioned, he, along with Burnett, laughed all the way to the bank. "We had a unique thing on *The Apprentice*," Trump says. "Mark and I, we were equals. I got a star fee. But then we were allowed to keep the advertising dollars. General Motors would come along and pay us $5 million to do an advertising campaign for their new car, and so on and so on."

Suddenly we feel far from both the Oval Office and the soundproof soundstage of the TV boardroom; a construction crew outside Trump's New York office makes themselves known with the racket of jackhammers. For today, the former president is just like any other New Yorker, straining to be heard over the relentless hum of the city. But the ease with which he trudges along, without even noticing the loud drilling outside his window, confirms that this man is a creature of Manhattan at heart, finally free from the constraints of Washington, D.C.

Pitching his voice up slightly, he goes on. "So we would have eighteen—or whatever the number was—people doing advertising campaigns for the new car of General Motors. And they would pay us a lot of money. The network got none of it. We kept 100 percent of the money. There's never been a show that's probably made more money."

Just how much money did Trump make from NBC on his fourteen seasons of *The Apprentice*? "It's got to be over $500 million," Trump insists. (In 2015, in a filing with the Federal Election Commission, Trump self-disclosed his total income from the show to be $213,606,575, which included the royalties he'd earned from licensing the show to different hosts around the world.) Trump's memories of *The Apprentice* tend to come down less to what was learned than what was earned. It's not about the contestants or the show's influence in the culture. It's about the profits he made. Consider a special cable news debate that's cemented in his brain—one that he loves to tell so much he repeated it to me on two separate occasions.

Shortly after that filing, in 2015, the MSNBC anchor and host of *The Last Word*, Lawrence O'Donnell, was a guest on *Morning Joe*, where he sneered at Joe Scarborough for believing that Trump had made a fortune from hosting a reality TV show. "It's a lie, Joe," O'Donnell said at the time. "It's a complete, total lie." The two cable news pundits then engaged in a prolonged online feud about it. These were the days when a Donald Trump presidency seemed like alternative-reality fiction—a complete impossibility—so joking about the particulars of what it could mean was a fun parlor game.

Not to Trump. "Lawrence O'Donnell was always an enemy, because he's a sick human being," Trump says. "He was on Joe Scarborough saying I made no money on *The Apprentice*! Joe said, 'That can't be possible, because the show is so successful.' This was when Joe Scarborough would do anything for me." In Trump's retelling, he adds new details that never happened. "And O'Donnell got on his show, and NBC made him apologize and he was crying," Trump claims. "He actually broke down, and he was crying. It was one of the great moments, because he was such a prick!" (While Trump's summary of the argument between the hosts is accurate, O'Donnell never backed down, nor did he cry on air.)

As we keep talking, Trump returns to how Zucker didn't want to pay him his asking price of $6 million an episode, and he leans forward in his chair, blinking rapidly to convey his rage. "That was Jeff," he says grumpily. He suddenly comes across as less of a real estate developer or a politician than an actor who can't forgive bad blood with a studio head.

He looks past me to the suited, unobtrusive adviser seated behind me. "Can you believe I got that son of a bitch a job, Jason?"

Jason Miller, true to form as the silent partner in this interview, simply nods.

After his early salary negotiations, Trump vented to other NBC executives that he didn't trust Zucker. Even so, they managed to play nice for years. Trump was savvy enough to know that he needed to stay on Zucker's good side to succeed at NBC. "They teased each other, and they had respect for each other," says Ben Silverman, who in 2007 became co-chair of NBC Entertainment, replacing Kevin Reilly. "Jeff was cocky and Donald was cocky. It was almost, like, fratty, in how they communicated with each other."

In all of our meetings, just the mention of Zucker's name would invariably lead to Trump's telling a convoluted story about how he helped secure Zucker his job as the president of CNN in the winter of 2012. Small details would shift in the story: Trump was at a lunch or dinner when he met Phil Kent, the CEO of Turner Broadcasting, overseeing networks like TNT, TBS, and CNN. And at that meal, according to Trump, he effusively praised Zucker and persuaded Kent to hire him to run CNN. After telling this story, Trump would fume about his onetime close confidant in the entertainment business.

"No good deed goes unpunished," Miller echoes back that day in Trump Tower. Perhaps the best way to stay in Trump's good graces—as Miller had, in the early days of the post-presidency—is to never verge beyond the kind of soothing affirmation one would expect from a Magic 8 Ball.

"I always said there's no way he's doing bad about me, and he did. Because a lot of people are scum." Trump pauses, as if he were about to conduct a firing. But the only power he has away from the Oval Office is the familiar intensity of his venomous contempt, now directed at Jeff Zucker. "He's human scum."

Maybe you can't rise to the top without a few past co-workers thinking you're human scum, and few media-industry rises have been more dizzyingly rapid than Zucker's. After graduating from Harvard in 1986, Jeff Zucker went to work at NBC, starting as a researcher in the network's sports division. He ended up as a producer at *Today*, earning a reputation as a wunderkind; at twenty-six, when most people in TV are still working their way up from the entry level, Zucker was managing what would become the most profitable morning show on TV as executive producer. *Today* was emerging from a period of instability, after the controversial firing of the popular anchor Jane Pauley in favor of the young and less experienced Deborah Norville. Zucker's watch began in 1992 with Katie Couric, a political correspondent who had taken over as morning TV's new queen bee the previous year, sitting next to the mainstay Bryant Gumbel. With this team in place, *Today* dominated in the ratings, trouncing *Good Morning America*.

Zucker had the benefit of good timing; Couric in particular was a master of the high-low mix, as comfortable speaking to presidents as she was doing lighthearted cooking segments. But he was an innovative thinker, expanding the remit of a morning-news show into all-out pop-culture spectacle. He began programming concerts, coaxing pop stars to rise at the crack of dawn and perform live outside at Rockefeller Plaza. It was a winning proposition for both sides, because celebrities drew eyeballs away from *GMA* (which had to launch its own concert series to compete), and musicians got a prime promotional opportunity. Under Zucker's tenure, *Today* opened up Studio 1A to the Plaza so that everyone's favorite weatherman, Al Roker, could break free from being stuck indoors and meet his fans. And when Gumbel stepped down in 1997 as the show's longest-sitting co-host at the time, Zucker didn't miss a beat. His succession plan involved promoting the show's newsreader Matt Lauer into the anchor chair and sending him on a globe-trotting adventure during sweeps under the catchy premise "Where in the World Is Matt Lauer?" By 1998, *Today* was beating *GMA* by such a wide margin—6.1 million viewers to 3.5 million—there was no risk it could fall to second place.

When it came to news judgment, too, Zucker's tastes as a producer were well matched for the morning-show audience. He gravitated toward scandalous and tragic stories, often illustrated with sensationalistic sit-downs. The 1990s, with tabloid-culture feeding frenzies like the unsolved murder of JonBenét Ramsey, the trial of O. J. Simpson, and Bill Clinton's affair with Monica Lewinsky, provided plenty for his hosts to chew on. Zucker was driven—like his protégé Trump—by an obsession with numbers. After eight years of running *Today*, the rising-star executive was promoted to be NBC Entertainment's president in 2000, overseeing the network's prime-time lineup during the heyday of *ER*, *Will & Grace*, and *Friends*. This last show was briefly endangered by *Survivor*, which CBS aggressively programmed against *Friends* on Thursday nights at the peak of castaway fever. Zucker helped preserve his biggest hit by extending episodes to a "supersized" forty minutes, generating buzz and a sense that what was going on at Central Perk was truly unmissable.

But that was an established show, one for which viewers had a long-running affection. It seemed as though every new success story on TV matched the Myspace generation's interest in what some might call authenticity—others might call it oversharing. Zucker green-lighted *Fear Factor*, a program that took the *Survivor* segment in which contestants ate grilled rats and made it into a franchise. The host, Joe Rogan, egged on unfortunate competitors as they scaled heights, hung from helicopters, and devoured insects.

Outside *Today*, Zucker had battled colon cancer twice in his thirties, with the support of his wife, Caryn, whom he'd married in 1996. (Zucker's life was so centered on NBC he'd met her in the building; she'd worked as a supervisor on *Saturday Night Live*.) His ability to power through, taking brief leaves and returning to work while undergoing chemotherapy, cemented his legacy as an unstoppable executive at

30 Rockefeller Plaza. "I don't think people would describe me as laid-back, OK?" Zucker told *The Washington Post*'s Lloyd Grove in a 1998 profile. "I still want to win, but I don't want to kill somebody or kill myself getting there."

Like Trump, Zucker loved the thrill of spectacle—especially if he was at the center of it. The two men's fortunes intersected once again in the summer of 2016, when Trump's unlikely and tumultuous campaign for the presidency was an undeniable ratings booster for CNN, which Zucker was overseeing. When Zucker sat down to talk to me for a *Variety* cover story about his strategy for running a news network during an intensely fractured time in American history, it wasn't lost on him that he'd had a major hand in bolstering the candidate who was already a destabilizing force in U.S. politics. But what Zucker took away from that was that CNN had an opportunity to keep on winning—even if democracy lost. "We've got our largest share of the prime-time audience in fifteen years," Zucker told me, sounding not unlike the man he'd taught to become fixated on ratings. "We have 34 percent of the prime-time audience. We're within two share points of Fox. They're at 36. And we've got our largest advantage over MSNBC in prime demos in seventeen years."

Zucker believed that Trump had a path to winning the presidency, even as many pundits and members of the media elite thought his candidacy was a joke. According to employees who worked with Zucker at the time, he'd say that Hillary Clinton, despite her years in the public eye as a U.S. senator and first lady, was still a mysterious figure to millions of Americans. The Republicans were successful in piling on Clinton, he thought, because she hadn't fully defined herself. On the other hand, Zucker was all too aware that Trump, despite his many shortcomings as a politician, had the ability to connect to blue-collar workers, especially in Middle America. Zucker had seen it firsthand; after all, he'd helped to build the image. And he knew that deep down many Americans saw something familiar and exciting in a man who'd spent years playing a likable, benevolent billionaire on television. They saw Trump as the leader he'd been in the boardroom—the ultimate straight shooter.

In the early days of his campaign, the reality TV star candidate would often ring up his old boss for gossip and guidance. This was before anyone took Trump seriously as a politician. Throughout 2015, Trump's polling lead was treated as a mirage, one that would collapse as soon as voters actually had to make their choice. Trump losing the 2016 Iowa caucuses to Ted Cruz, then claiming voter fraud, was treated as proof that he was ultimately a made-for-TV candidate, not a future president.

The rest is well-known history, with Trump's constant rallies being broadcast live on cable news, their backdrop becoming a sort of American wallpaper as he cruised to the nomination and then to a shock victory over Clinton in November 2016. Along the way, Trump's and Zucker's intertwined professional lives came to imitate the art they'd made together. Once inseparable in their shared quest for ratings, the two men—still in search of the highest possible number, be it viewers or electoral votes—found themselves squabbling like reality TV contestants once Trump began sweeping primaries. For any observer schooled in the tropes of the genre, this wasn't a surprise. Zucker and Trump's alliance worked for them when they both stood to profit. Using Trump as a free publicity machine and indulging his tendency to say whatever popped into his mind benefited Zucker and NBC. Yet in this new phase of Zucker's career, as the head of a cable news network guided by the responsibility to report on what was actually happening on the campaign trail, Zucker could no longer protect Trump.

That's not to say that Zucker didn't initially help candidate Trump. In 2015, Zucker gave Trump's campaign legitimacy by making the pivotal decision to air his rallies unedited on CNN, which Zucker saw as an easy layup for ratings. He persuaded Trump to talk to Jake Tapper for a series of interviews, making accommodations when Trump wanted to be patched in by phone so his voice dominated the airwaves. "We can be politically correct if you want," Trump said in September 2015 when asked by Tapper about offensive comments about Muslims made by a voter at a campaign stop. "Are you trying to say we don't have a problem? I have friends that are Muslims—they are great people, amazing people . . . but we certainly do have a problem."

The coverage would inevitably get tougher as Trump closed in on the Republican nomination. And as CNN started fact-checking his lies in real time, Trump felt that Zucker had betrayed him. "Trump talked very positively of Jeff right up until the point Jeff talked negatively of him," says Piers Morgan, who won the first season of *The Celebrity Apprentice* in 2008 and took over for Larry King on CNN in 2011. "There's no doubt that Zucker made Trump the TV superstar that he is, and it's Trump's stardom that won him the election because people were voting for a celebrity. I think Jeff knows he played a very big part. Once he realized that might happen, and he might get blamed for it, Jeff tried to perform a screeching U-turn. But by then, as Dr. Frankenstein had discovered, the monster had left the building."

Things came to a boiling point in October 2016, when Trump raged that a CNN roundtable unfairly criticized his performance in the second debate, after he'd shrugged off the leaked *Access Hollywood* tape. "You are the most disloyal person," Trump wrote to Zucker in an email quoted by *The New York Times Magazine* in April 2017.

Yet only a few months before that, when I spoke with Zucker for my *Variety* article, he seemed to think that his relationship with Trump wasn't beyond repair. Trump had already started publicly bashing Zucker, but Zucker was modulating his network's coverage to be, if not overtly Trump-friendly, then at least his own version of "fair and balanced." (Of special note was his hiring Corey Lewandowski, Trump's former campaign manager, as a political commentator in June 2016, even though he'd been fired after several ugly controversies, including forcibly grabbing a female *Breitbart News* reporter by the arm after a press conference.)

When we met, the Republican National Convention was weeks away. Zucker's modest office, with a wall dominated by eleven mounted TVs playing the competition, featured a framed tweet Trump had posted in happier times. In it, the fledgling candidate Trump, who'd used Twitter to feed cable news in getting his message out, had offered generic praise to CNN for its coverage. Perhaps it was little wonder Zucker figured Trump's opponent, Clinton, was unknowable; she wouldn't compete with Trump for Zucker's attention. Meanwhile, there were few media figures Zucker understood better than the candidate who hung tokens of his own success on the walls of Trump Tower. Certainly no Hillary memorabilia hung on the wall at Zucker's CNN office.

"We made an early bet that this political season would be a big story before anybody realized it would be a big story, and that has paid off well," Zucker told me. "That's what's been responsible for the success." This answer seemed dubious; presidential elections—even the 2012 one, a relatively low-stakes snooze-fest in which Barack Obama cruised to an easy reelection over Mitt Romney—were always huge stories. What Zucker's critics, of whom there were many, would say was that the CNN boss had found the O. J. Simpson or JonBenét story within the election—converting the race for the White House into the ultimate empty-calorie entertainment, aided by Trump's uniquely ostentatious campaign.

I asked Zucker what it was, in particular, that CNN had been missing before his arrival. He took a brief pause before answering. "It felt like the spare tire in your trunk that you only took out when you needed it," Zucker said. "I think the challenge was to make it somewhere people wanted to go when there wasn't a crisis. The air had to be more interesting and more exciting and more engaging *and* more compelling. I think that prime time had to be more vibrant and alive."

It's no wonder Zucker had formed such a close attachment to Trump. But Zucker, in contrast to the star he helped make, seemed the ultimate man behind the curtain. When I arrived at CNN five minutes before the interview that summer day, as I waited for my bag to pass through a metal detector (CNN has far stricter security than Trump Tower), his publicist called me. She had a tone of panic in her voice as she told me Zucker didn't tolerate tardiness. I wasn't yet late, simply on time, but perhaps that wasn't good enough. Or maybe Zucker was haunted by his past dealings with the man of the hour that political season. Donald Trump treated time as a theoretical mechanism; his calendar flowed fluidly depending on how engaged he was with whoever sat before him in that moment.

When I got upstairs, Zucker greeted me tersely; he didn't relax until he got into the back-and-forth, tennis-style rhythm of our interview. (Zucker had been a tennis phenom in his suburban Miami high school, and, probably more pertinently, he was someone who could easily get bored in conversation if he didn't feel challenged.)

As we spoke, there were two other spectators in the room. One was Barbara Levin, CNN's vice president of communications who handled Zucker's press; she would later tell me that Zucker's attention had been sufficiently piqued by my questions. But there was someone else who didn't need to be there: Allison Gollust, CNN's head of marketing, who'd previously worked with Zucker at NBC. She frequently interrupted her boss as if we were simply guests at the same dinner party.

Like many others in New York's media bubble, I'd heard the rumors that Zucker and Gollust were having an affair. They were so close that she'd moved her husband and family to the same building in the Upper East Side that Zucker shared with his wife and kids. But Zucker wasn't careless. He'd required months of back-and-forth just to agree to do an interview, and I knew that he'd vetted me before he agreed, calling on a colleague to see if he could trust me. Allowing his supposed mistress to sit in on an interview seemed like an unforced error. Or maybe Zucker, like Trump, thought he was so invincible that no one would call him out on his inappropriate behavior. When you're a star, as we would later hear Trump say that campaign season, they let you do it.

That afternoon, the only time that Zucker looked visibly put off was when I suggested that CNN's marketing had taken a page from *The Apprentice*, with splashy promos that announced the network's latest town hall with a voice-over that felt more suited for a Mark Burnett reality TV show. Zucker didn't like the comparison to anything *Apprentice* related. "Look, I can't take credit for that anyway," he said flatly. He then changed the subject: "Allison"—the guest in the room—"oversees our marketing. I think the promotion and marketing is better on CNN. I think that's a tribute to Allison. I do believe in strong, aggressive marketing."

Gollust piped up. "I would say that's a big difference from the previous administration," she said. Her stray voice was eating up my valuable time with her boss and, as would later be confirmed, boyfriend. "He has a keen understanding of what marketing and promotion means, probably more so than most other executives."

And that understanding, as affirmed by someone who knows him intimately, has been the secret to Zucker's success. It's also why his detractors have blasted him for pursuing style over substance. What bound Zucker to Trump and to Burnett was a thirst for closing a sale. Indeed, for most of their time together, Zucker was the one finally calling the shots—the ultimate deal maker among a crew of self-styled business geniuses.

Trump is not the only "problematic" man Zucker enabled. Bryant Gumbel's replacement as the male half of the *Today* anchor team, Matt Lauer, brought into the job in 1997 under Zucker's regime, was fired in 2017 following explosive allegations of workplace sexual misconduct. Zucker wasn't at NBC then, but he'd always protected Lauer. "That is not something I was ever aware of, or had even heard of, or had ever been suggested, or anything like that," Zucker said at a media conference the day after Lauer's firing. "It's just incredibly heartbreaking."

Zucker kept his distance from Lauer in public, but he'd been one of Lauer's core supporters at NBC, and his fondness never faded. According to insiders, if you're among the guests at one of Zucker's Hamptons parties, a Lauer sighting is inevitable.

Another of Zucker's news protégés was Don Lemon. "I think moving Don Lemon to prime time has been one of the most underappreciated moves," Zucker told me in 2016. The anchor was fired in 2023 after accusations of misogyny, including referring to Nikki Haley as "past her prime" on live TV, and of abusive behavior. But Zucker—who'd resigned from CNN in February 2022 for failing to disclose a consensual relationship with Gollust—still went on a group Italian getaway with him. And Gollust became Lemon's new publicist.

Back in 2007, Zucker was promoted again to president and CEO of NBC Universal, where he made a costly blunder that almost ended his career as an executive. Zucker had two problems: NBC's cupboard of hits was increasingly bare, and it was time to refresh *The Tonight Show*, even as the incumbent host, Jay Leno, wasn't ready to leave. The executive tried to solve both at once, converting the 10:00 p.m. time slot, usually reserved for adult dramas, into a nightly Leno talk show while installing Conan O'Brien at *Tonight*. It was cheap to produce *The Jay Leno Show*, but a nightly dose of his comedy when viewers expected *Law & Order: Special Victims Unit* flopped, and hurt O'Brien when viewers turned their sets away from NBC before the late-night hour. It also alienated Zucker from top Hollywood agents who were furious that he was trying to block their actors from receiving scripted paychecks.

In 2010, as Comcast acquired a majority stake in NBC, Zucker left with a huge payout—a reported $30 to $40 million—in disgrace. But he had an idea for redemption, to recapture the magic of *Today*'s 1990s by pairing Couric and Lauer as daytime talk show hosts. Lauer, still in his heyday at *Today*, didn't bite. Couric, who'd been cut off from her genuine gift for connection to her audience as CBS's evening news anchor, was floundering in the ratings and decided to take Zucker's offer. So she hopped back to daytime with ABC's *Katie*, debuting in the fall of 2012.

If this was something of a comedown for Couric, whose takeover as the first solo female anchor on a network evening news broadcast had given way to grinding disappointment when she couldn't merge her personality with the culture of CBS News, it was a far more precipitous decline for Zucker. He'd gone from running a network to producing a syndicated daytime show. But at least he had a close friend's support: one of the first guests Zucker booked for *Katie* was Donald Trump.

"Jeff Zucker said to me, 'Could you do me a favor for Katie Couric's opening show?'" Trump recalls. "'Could you sit down with her right in New York City on top of a bus?' So I rode in New York City on the top of the bus with Katie Couric. Remember the show she had? It wasn't successful. Not great. But that was Jeff's show, you know?"

Katie proved to be an expensive ratings misfire, because Couric once again failed to find the balance of hard news and soft lifestyle content that had defined her time with Zucker on *Today*. At CBS, she'd been perceived, if unfairly, as not serious enough to take on the stories of the day. Beaming into stay-at-home parents' orbit every afternoon, she wasn't quite credible doling out celebrity dish and makeover tips. The talk show's dismal failure (canceled after two years) led to a falling-out between Couric and her longtime boss Zucker, who left before the show wrapped up. And as Zucker jumped ship (or was fired, according to Couric's 2021 memoir, *Going There*), he aggressively lobbied to take the reins at CNN, which was looking for a new network president.

That's when Trump claims he came to the rescue. In the email obtained by *The New York Times*, Trump told Zucker, "The dumbest thing I ever did was get you the job at CNN." At the time, CNN denied Trump had anything to do with his hiring, but Trump still believes he played a central role in Zucker's ascension. Trump is so convinced of this fact that he tells the same story to me on three different occasions.

"I'm sitting there at the Plaza hotel for two and a half hours," Trump says. "The head of CNN Turkey, who is a friend of mine, is being honored. I was sitting next to one of the heads of Time Warner. I said, 'What do you do?' He said, 'I'm going to hire the new head of CNN over the next week.' I said, 'Anyone I know?' He gave me four names, and the last one was Jeff Zucker. He had no chance. I said, 'What about Jeff Zucker?' He said, 'No, he didn't do a good job at NBC.' I said, 'No—he did! He did *The Today Show*. He did *The Apprentice*.'"

The three times that Trump tells me this story, the details are always crisp and mostly the same. And for once, Trump admits to making a mistake. "And after an hour and a half, I convinced him to hire Jeff Zucker. How stupid of a move was that?" Sensing that we've gone way off subject, he clarifies that this story is still on the record. "You can use it if you want. I could care less." After that meal at the Plaza, Trump says he called Zucker to fill him in. "I said, 'Jeff, congratulations. You're going to be the new president of CNN.' He said, 'No way.' He told me the same names I'd been told by the gentleman on the left, who was a nice guy."

Whatever happened that day, Trump credits himself. "So I gave Jeff a sell like few people can sell," Trump says. "And by the end, I think the guy was going to put his hand over his ears and say, 'Leave me alone!' I convinced him that Jeff was the guy for the job. Jeff was told the next day he was the chosen one." He can barely let this hang in the air for a moment before returning to dumping on Zucker. "This guy didn't like him. He thought he was an impossible guy to get along with. And I got him the job."

Trump concludes by spinning out the story of Zucker's ultimate betrayal. "And by the way, when I was running, I said, 'CNN is going to treat me great.' It's called loyalty. I got the guy the job. And as I was campaigning, people would come and say, 'Sir, CNN is hitting you a little hard!' I would say, 'That's not possible. Go back and check.' And I'd call Jeff." Trump imitates Zucker's voice, adding a parodic layer of prissiness: "I'll look into that. I'll look into that." Trump says he finally lost patience and stopped talking to Zucker, because he realized Zucker was secretly driving the tough reporting about his campaign.

One possible reason for the eventual toughness of CNN's coverage—with real-time fact-checking and brutal commentary from anchors such as Lemon—was that Trump became a serious political force and the network took seriously his chances of winning. In the summer of 2016, at the Democratic National Convention in Philadelphia, where Hillary Clinton was named the first female presidential nominee of a major political party, Zucker's deputies were quietly whispering what their boss already believed: Trump could win.

The election signaled multiple turning points in Zucker's life. He split from Caryn, his wife of twenty-one years, in 2018. But even then, he kept his relationship with Gollust a secret. Not disclosing this romance eventually cost Zucker his job running CNN, and Gollust was forced to resign shortly thereafter following an internal probe about her own journalistic lapses. She'd blurred the lines with an ex-boss, the former New York governor Andrew Cuomo, by helping prepare him for an interview on CNN.

Gollust was among the staff who made the trip to Philly in 2016. In talking about Zucker, she always hinted at an implied intimacy. Her CNN colleagues would discuss how she'd make insinuations that suggested she knew *they knew* she was dating Jeff Zucker, beginning sentences with "Jeff and I . . ." When Gollust would deliver her hints about Zucker, they were always coded in some level of ambiguity; Zucker and Trump's shared bluntness couldn't be Gollust's way.

I witnessed her odd manner for myself at Zucker's *Variety* cover shoot in 2016. Zucker was stiff on this hot day, and he wasn't particularly comfortable with having his picture taken. So to loosen him up, our female photographer complimented him on the plain collared shirt he was wearing, telling him he looked good. I was standing next to Gollust, observing the exchange, when she leaned over and whispered something in my ear. "I think your photographer has a crush on Jeff," she said to me.

No, she really didn't. And it was the kind of declaration that seemed to encapsulate everything strange about Gollust's public intimacy with her superior. Zucker might have known how to gin up ratings, but he had cast himself in a warped reality TV show, complete with a forbidden workplace love affair constantly being teased to a captive audience. Their workplace behavior was so out of control that if they'd been contestants on *The Apprentice*, even Trump would have fired Jeff Zucker and Allison Gollust.

"I didn't know her," Trump tells me, although he too had been tipped off about Zucker's affair. "I heard about it. Everybody heard about it."

The second season of *The Apprentice*, which debuted on September 9, 2004, kept Trump's winning streak alive. For one thing, the potential contestant pool was vast: tens of thousands of Americans looked at this unusual job opportunity as a means to get rich and famous fast. Rob Flanagan, then a thirty-two-year-old corporate branding salesman from Frisco, Texas, recalls getting an email with a link to the application from his second-grade best friend. "And I forwarded it to my wife," Flanagan recalls. "And I just said, 'Should I?' And she hit me back with 72-point text in all capital letters: 'ABSOLUTELY!' And so I filled it out."

For Mark Burnett, the increased visibility of the show didn't deter him from his tradition of hazing the contestants, often viciously. Flanagan recalls sitting through rounds of interviews he endured while staying at a DoubleTree hotel in Los Angeles. "There were some attacks, not from Mark, but his team," Flanagan says. Having done an extensive background check on Flanagan, the show's producers made up quotes from the widow of one of his friends who'd recently died. "They said, 'Cece says that you can be lower than petrified cat shit at the bottom of a swimming pool.' My neck started getting red." Flanagan says he had to resist the urge to "jump across the table and choke" the questioner who made this outlandish accusation.

Then Burnett chimed in. "He asked me, 'Has anybody mentioned anything to you that you look like anybody?' And I said, 'Yeah.' I told him that I looked like George W. Bush. And the other person is Kurt Russell." Flanagan didn't realize that he had the perfect chance to stroke Burnett's ego and he missed it. "What he was getting at, and I didn't realize, people had mentioned that I looked like him," the former contestant recalls. "So he was fishing for that, and I didn't fucking catch it. Otherwise, I would have ran with that." It didn't matter; Burnett couldn't reject his doppelgänger.

In another grilling, Burnett told Chris Russo, a thirty-year-old stockbroker from Long Island, that he was cutting him from the vetting process because his wife was pregnant. "I don't need the hassle," Burnett told him. "What's going to happen if something happens? You're going to want to leave." Russo promised him that he wouldn't, that his word was his bond. Burnett then made Russo repeat his loyalty to *The Apprentice* over his unborn child until the producer was satisfactorily convinced. "You're in," Burnett finally told him.

"I think they wanted me from the beginning," Russo says. "But they were testing me to see how fucking crazy I was. And how much I wanted it."

The teams for the second season of *The Apprentice* were divided up again, with Flanagan serving as one of the project managers. But he flubbed the first task, which required them to invent the toy for Mattel. In the boardroom, he didn't think he'd be the one who was fired—particularly when another member of his team crassly insulted the looks of the small children who were part of the focus group that judged the toys. But after a boardroom meeting that lasted an astonishing four hours as Trump kept dragging the process out, Flanagan got fired.

"I mean, the first thing that went through my mind—other than 'I can't believe this shit'—was I felt bad for my wife," Flanagan says. "Our son was six months old, and we had a three-year-old daughter. And here I am stuck. I can't do anything. I can't get home. And then I felt bad for all the shopping that she did. Because she went out and bought, I don't know, fifteen different neckties for all these boardrooms I was going to be on. It totally sucked."

The contestants weren't the same blind novices from season 1, who had shown up at Trump Tower without any armor (or TV-ready wardrobes). They'd come more polished, aware that they had to perform for the cameras. Regis Philbin showed up as the emcee of the finale from Manhattan's Alice Tully Hall, where Trump crowned another central-casting white man—Kelly Perdew, the thirty-seven-year-old president of a software company from Carlsbad, California—as the winner of the season, defeating the other finalist, Jennifer Massey, a thirty-year-old attorney from San Francisco. Perdew's project within the Trump Organization was helping develop a new Trump property in Manhattan—close to the mother ship. The three-hour season 2 finale attracted seventeen million viewers, more than a 40 percent drop from the first-season finale, but still a big enough audience to keep *The Apprentice* as one of the top shows on TV.

As the series continued to be successful, Kepcher recalls that she had to find a way to squeeze the filming into her packed schedule. "Sometimes I was running from an event or running from work on the golf course," says Kepcher, who still didn't have a driver. "I remember getting off the train, running on Fifth Avenue, trying to make the boardroom. I even had my hair up—I went in and there was no time." She simply performed her role on TV as Trump's associate coming straight off the street. "If you ask what the years were like, I was constantly running around."

The pace wasn't about to slow down. Trump's mainstream star power was ratified by his wedding to his third wife—the future first lady of the United States Melania Knauss Trump—on January 22, 2005. The ceremony landed a glowing story in *The New York Times*, which plugged Mar-a-Lago's "newly refurbished $42 million ballroom featuring 24-karat-gold moldings and 11,000 square feet of marble flooring." Trump was now a national celebrity, with wall-to-wall tabloid coverage of his big day in *People* magazine and on *Extra!* and *Access Hollywood*.

He could now pack a room with some of the biggest stars in the world. The newlywed Trump was still available for press, but his time was limited. My phone calls from *Newsweek* to his office would still go through, yet they were getting shorter. He'd answer one or two questions and then promptly hang up. Still, I managed to get him on the phone on the weekend of his wedding, where he fed me superlatives about Melania in a two-minute call from his golf course in Florida.

A few months later, in the spring of 2005, I worked on a story for *Newsweek* where I trailed Perdew and Bill Rancic to chronicle their professional lives in the Trump Organization. Although Trump had offered to make the winner of the show a president within his organization, he held back, bringing both of them on with the unglamorous title of "owner's representative."

"It's a little bit too much to ask someone to be the president of a $800 million building when they haven't had that kind of experience," Trump had explained to me at the time, referencing Rancic's project in Chicago.

When he wasn't in the Windy City, Rancic spent his time in New York, promoting Trump. Perdew's office in Trump Tower was in a small space without any windows, next to Melania's, and he admitted to me that he didn't even have his own assistant. But he, too, was dispatched to spend much of his day to sell the Trump brand, including Trump's pet project, Trump Ice, the bottled water line he'd deployed the fired contestants from season 1 to research.

Both men were vanilla characters, as if they'd been chosen for their ability to blend into the background behind Trump. "I'm not going to be a twenty-year employee," Rancic told me. "I'm an entrepreneur; my goal is to go on and do a deal of my own."

As we drove back from Trump's golf course in Briarcliff Manor, New York, in a shared town car, the only thing that stands out from my day with Rancic is him talking about how he'd recently worked out at Equinox Columbus Circle, which he described as a much nicer sports club than anything he'd seen in Chicago. On another day, *Newsweek* photographed Rancic and Perdew standing next to Trump in a boardroom at Trump Tower; it was the only time I saw Trump interact with his *Apprentice* winners (for publicity's sake, naturally). It was a moment that passed quickly: Trump hated the wide camera lens our photographer was using, thinking it wouldn't flatter him, and stormed off the set, cutting our session short.

The show's first two winners seemed neglected at best. On TV, Rancic and Perdew loomed almost as large as Trump, dreaming that they could one day follow in his path. But while Trump lived up to the image he'd built for himself—never deviating from how one might expect him to behave—these two men, decorated as winners on TV, seemed smaller in real life. It was as if when they'd finally tried to collect the pot of gold at the end of the rainbow, they learned their prize was too heavy to lug back home. They'd won a contest where the reward was becoming spokespeople for a boss whose shadow they couldn't escape.

Trump denounced the *Newsweek* article as soon as it came out. He didn't exactly use the as-yet-uncoined phrase "fake news," but he told his mouthpiece *Access Hollywood* that *Newsweek* had gotten it wrong. I knew we hadn't. And the headline that accompanied my story, about how first place on *The Apprentice* wasn't much of an honor, said it all: "What's Second Prize?"

CHAPTER 7

Will & Grace Under Fire

Donald Trump may remember his first Emmy nomination more clearly than his first nomination for the presidency. The summer after season 1 of *The Apprentice* aired, he received good news from his producing partner. "I got a call from Mark Burnett," Trump says. "He said, 'Congratulations—you were nominated for an Emmy!' He said, 'You should win.' I had the hottest show in many years." His voice is steady as he says this, but his head bounces like one of the Trump bobblehead dolls that became a ubiquitous accessory during his presidency. Watching this in person is mesmerizing: Trump jolting his head around is the Donald equivalent of a parrot puffing up its feathers in a display of dominance.

Trump was nominated as an executive producer of *The Apprentice* in the newly added category of outstanding reality-competition series—an acknowledgment of the genre's success that the Emmys had added for the first time only the year before. In 2003, the trophy had gone to *The Amazing Race*, the CBS series that sent contestants on a globe-trotting adventure with an army of quick-moving producers and camera operators. The series was relatively low rated, but it had a patina of genuine quality, with its reliance on skill over manipulation, invoking awestruck wonder for viewers at the grandeur of different places and cultures. In 2004, *The Amazing Race* was a heavy favorite once again, and indeed it eventually beat *The Apprentice* (as well as *American Idol*, *Last Comic Standing*, and *Survivor*), continuing what would eventually be, to Trump's great displeasure, a seven-year winning streak for the CBS show.

"I thought I'd win too," Trump says, still looking disappointed all these years later. He gives himself a pep talk. "But I killed *The Amazing Race* in ratings," Trump says. "I'd never even heard of the show. I knew it was done by all of Hollywood royalty. They had many producers. I think even Harvey Weinstein was there. They had all the biggest people in Hollywood." Trump's gift for mudslinging is not rooted in accuracy, even when reliving the years he remembers most fondly. Weinstein produced another popular reality TV series, *Project Runway*, but the disgraced mogul had nothing to do with *The Amazing Race*. (Although the *Top Gun* producer Jerry Bruckheimer did have an executive producer credit.)

Trump assumed that his name would be called when the envelope was cracked open. "I really deserved it," he says. "I had the highest ratings. It was the talk of the whole country—beyond, even." Trump had already taken the stage earlier that evening with another reality TV royal, Simon Cowell from *American Idol*, to present the award for best supporting actress in a comedy series. "Okay, and the Emmy goes to . . . ," Trump said as he tilted the envelope, taking up the spotlight from a grinning Cowell, "Cynthia Nixon, *Sex and the City*." It was the final season of the beloved HBO series, and Miranda's win over the fan favorite, Samantha (played by Kim Cattrall), was something of a shock. ("Do I wish I had gotten my Emmy from somebody else?" Nixon would say in 2017. "Yes, I do. Absolutely I do. But it's not like he picked me. He just passed off the trophy.")

But the surprise that some viewers felt in that moment was no match for Trump's bewilderment at going home empty-handed. During his category, Trump had already proclaimed himself the winner in his head. "And I stood up to start walking down the aisle," Trump recalls. "They said, 'The winner is . . . *The Amazing Race*.' I said, 'Oh shit!' And I sat down." He remembers that one of his seatmates, Howard Stringer—who'd soon be named the CEO of Sony Corporation—turned to him and said, "Donald, you got screwed!"

"And *Amazing Race* kept winning it, winning it," Trump says with disdain. "*American Idol* was so powerful at the time. It was not fair that every year it was *The Amazing Race*. It was nothing special!" He's suddenly handicapping decades-old Emmy ceremonies like political races, sounding off with the passion of a cable news host waiting for the vote count in the Rust Belt to come in. "I said, 'I can't believe it! *Amazing Race* won again?' Honestly, it was a joke. They shouldn't have won over me."

In dissecting the awards show results, Trump borrows a term he's frequently heard about himself on Fox News. "But it was pure establishment," Trump says of the relatively scrappy *Amazing Race*, in which contestants slept on airport floors to get ahead in the game. "And I was antiestablishment. And Mark was antiestablishment too." He pauses and realizes that this assessment isn't quite right. "Mark is pretty establishment," he concedes, "but Mark Burnett was not establishment at the time."

This analysis doesn't make much sense, and it doesn't need to. Trump's messaging—that he was somehow burned by corrupt forces out of his control—is a familiar page from his conspiracy theory handbook. After *The Apprentice* premiered, in his new life as an entertainer, Trump breathed in the exclusive air of A-list fame. The new attention he received as a businessman and as a celebrity padded his ego beyond its already inflated size. As a young man, Trump couldn't summon the courage to pursue his dream career as a producer, and so went into the family business. But Trump had, at age fifty-eight, found his voice—and his true calling—in stardom.

"It's a very rare thing that a show is successful," Trump tells me one afternoon, circling back to one of his favorite subjects: his own on-camera charisma. "I used to have the stats on that." Rather than pump himself up, on this particular day in the fall of 2023, shortly before he'd decide to take the stand in a New York City court for his civil fraud trial, Trump is uncharacteristically reserved about putting his TV chops front and center.

Instead, he rattles off some statistics without citing any particular source: "I think 10 percent of the shows make it, 5 percent are successful, 1 percent are very successful. That sounds like Broadway odds, right?"

That's Trump's way of telling me he's in the 1 percent. *The Apprentice* maximized Trump's footprint all over America, and the country hung on his every word—including his attempt to carry a tune in front of millions of people. When Trump was nominated for another Emmy the following year, in 2005—which would turn out to be the final nomination for the show in the outstanding reality-competition category—the Emmys producers asked him if he'd participate in a contest called "Emmy Idol." Playing off *American Idol*, a juggernaut much bigger than *The Apprentice*, the Emmys recruited several TV stars to compete by belting out popular theme songs, with the viewers asked to vote on the best act.

Trump was up for anything, as long as a stage was involved. So he agreed to dress up as the character on *Green Acres* played by Eddie Albert, a farmer in denim overalls, and carry a rake during his turn—crooning the show's theme song. Trump's duet partner was Megan Mullally, the comedian best known for playing the shrieking millionaire Karen Walker on *Will & Grace*, who channeled the Hungarian princess Lisa Douglas (played by Eva Gabor) in a green suit with a fur collar. Ellen DeGeneres, the Emmys host that year, could barely contain her smirk as she introduced the duo. Trump and Mullally charmingly belted out their tribute to the popular 1960s sitcom—the *Schitt's Creek* of its time—about a couple that leaves their Manhattan luxuries behind for rough farm living. Mullally laughed through Trump's opening verse, which he kept largely on key, though without much of a sense of rhythm.

"I didn't know her," Trump says of Mullally, "but she was the star of the show." And to Trump, that's all that mattered. Mullally scored brownie points for switching one of the song's lyrics—where her penthouse-living wife lists the indispensable perks of city life—from "Times Square" to "Trump Tower," which had become just as important a landmark to those watching at home.

"They said, 'Would you participate in a skit?' They came in with stuff. I said, 'All right, I'll do it. So I did it.' William Shatner did it. Other people did it, very well known. Who are they?" Trump stumbles, admitting he can't remember. "You'll figure it out." (The other contestants included Kristen Bell, who sang the song to *Fame*; Macy Gray and Gary Dourdan, with "Movin' On Up" from *The Jeffersons*; and Shatner, who warbled the title sequence of *Star Trek* with the opera singer Frederica von Stade.)

Trump might have lost the Emmy again to *The Amazing Race* that night, but he still takes pride in his consolation prize—that the viewers voted for his performance as the night's best, beating out the other three acts. He asks to go off the record, as if he were about to reveal national security secrets, to brag about the percentage of the vote that he allegedly received.

"But at the end of the evening, I won with a massive—it was something like . . . ," he says, giving me a number, not for publication. "I got almost all the votes. I sang 'Green Acres,' and I was dressed in overalls and a straw hat." He clarifies that he didn't need to take singing lessons to prepare. "No, no, no," he says. "But I have an aptitude for music."

Trump's love of Broadway musicals—especially *Evita*—stems from what he believes is a natural gift. Trump doesn't usually volunteer detailed stories about his childhood, but here he makes an exception. "You know, when I was young, my parents took me to a place, and they said, 'What's up with this guy? We think he's really smart!'" He's referring to himself. "They gave me all these tests. And I'll never forget, they told my father, 'Your son has an unbelievable aptitude in music.' Like they play a note . . ." To make this story come to life, Trump offers his own sound effects. ". . . Ding, ding!"

He continues: "And then they play it again. And then twenty minutes later, they asked, 'Which is the note we first played?'" The sound effects return from Trump's own lips: "Ding. Ding. Ding." It was, in Trump's telling, an early marker of his genius. "They said, 'He has an aptitude in music.' Anyway, so I did 'Green Acres.' I'm telling you, we brought the house down. You have the clips of it?"

Trump's face lights up as he presses me for a favorable review of his singing skills. "Do you agree?" he asks me. "It brought the house down." He then starts to wonder about his partner. "How has Megan Mullally treated me over the years? Do you have any idea?" He twitches suspiciously, eager to add another name to his lengthy Hollywood enemies list. "I know she loved her time up on the stage," Trump says about Mullally. "She loved doing it. We rehearsed the day before, and she said the same thing: 'You have a great feel for the music, the song.' Anyway, I did the song, brought the whole house down, and they voted." And this time, Trump won the popular vote.

Trump is jubilant that he managed to outperform the star of *Veronica Mars* in a TV singing contest. He even revisits how fun it was to resurface his brief turn as a singer on social media from the White House. On December 20, 2018, Trump tweeted out the Emmys clip, saying, "Farm bill signing in 15 minutes! #Emmys." (Mullally, an outspoken Democrat, tweeted back "omg" and then: "if you guys need me, i'll be in a hole in the ground" with a dead face, skull, and goodbye emoji.)

What inspired Trump, as the president of the United States, to reclaim past glories, to remind the American public of this kitschy moment? "Somebody gave me the idea," Trump says, vaguely. "What a great idea! We passed legislation." Trump doesn't dwell on the specifics of the bill, which offered $867 billion in aid to farmers and legalized the production of hemp. "And that was a sensation."

Trump says when he tweeted out the clip, "that thing had hundreds of thousands of hits. And the farmers liked me, and I won the farmers both times by a lot." From Trump's vantage point, all of his enemies—from the deal makers in Congress to the producers of *The Amazing Race*—are no match for his gift-from-the-heavens voice. He's on such a high, he can't resist telling me his favorite lie. "I won both elections, by the way," Trump says. "By a lot!"

Even now, after all his years in the spotlight, Trump struggles to contend with one of the downsides of fame—his haters. And one particular facet of Trump's unique sort of stardom is that many of his critics are among those he most wants to court: other celebrities. Many of the Hollywood pals first cultivated during his *Apprentice* years would later turn on him as president, which of course remains one of his biggest fixations. Here, in his Trump Tower aerie far above New York City, his enemies from the entertainment industry still occupy his thoughts around the clock. It's as if he were being jabbed by a pebble in his loafers all day long.

Take his obsession with Debra Messing, another actress from *Will & Grace* who figured prominently in his past. Trump still remembers the day he met Messing—who played the self-centered New York interior designer Grace Adler on NBC—around the time of *The Apprentice*'s second season. "So I'm in line," Trump recalls. "The show had gone to No. 1, and we're ready to do the upfronts, which I'd never heard of." As a new TV star, he was quickly catching up with Hollywood jargon: upfronts are an annual presentation that networks give in May, trotting out their stars to charm advertisers ahead of the upcoming TV season. "And Debra Messing came up to me. She had a show at a similar time."

He doesn't seem able to say the title *Will & Grace*—but then again does he need to? Messing's sitcom remains widely remembered and even beloved years after its first incarnation left the air. (It returned, first with a 2016 viral clip of the characters endorsing Hillary Clinton for president and then with a #Resistance-ready reboot in 2017. The first episode featured Messing's character repulsed that she's been hired to redesign Trump's Oval Office. She ends up leaving a "Make America Gay Again" cap on his desk.) In its heyday, the series was part of the Must See TV block of programming on NBC that led into *The Apprentice* on Thursday nights. More notably, it was an Emmy-winning, groundbreaking smash hit. Joe Biden, announcing his support for gay marriage in 2012, cited the show as priming America to accept same-sex couples, although its true emotional heart lay in its depiction of a platonic, loving relationship between a single gay man (Eric McCormack) and his best friend (Messing).

"She came up to me with her beautiful red hair," Trump says about Messing, pausing on this detail a beat too long. "And she said, 'Sir—I love you! Thank God for you! You're saving the network, and you're saving my show.' Because in that world, which I know a lot about now, when you have a hit, a lead-in, it's a massive difference." I point out to Trump that *Will & Grace* came on before *The Apprentice*, which would mean that it wouldn't have received a ratings bump from viewers tuning in to *The Apprentice*. "A lead-in—or a lead out," he clarifies.

"She was so thankful," Trump says. "She said, 'I can't thank you enough.' Do you believe this? I've been watching her. And I'm saying, 'She'd do anything for me.'" As he makes this claim, Trump's words are lathered with a suggestive grease, similar in tone to his boasting about women finding him irresistible in the leaked *Access Hollywood* tape. ("I'm automatically attracted to beautiful—I just start kissing them. It's like a magnet. Just kiss.")

"She was so effusive," Trump concludes. "And when I see the hatred coming out of her mouth today, it's incredible."

On Twitter, throughout his campaign and first term as president, Messing had been one of the most vocal actors bashing Trump. She once called him "a weak, scared, stupid, inept, negligent, vindictive, narcissistic criminal." When Trump was set to attend a Beverly Hills fundraiser in late August 2019, Messing tweeted, "Please print a list of all attendees please. The public has a right to know." With a possible category 3 hurricane making its way to Florida, Trump's attention instead lay with his onetime network-mate. He shot back at Messing on September 5, 2019, venting on Twitter, "Bad 'actress' Debra the Mess Messing is in hot water. She wants to create a 'Blacklist' of Trump supporters, & is being accused of McCarthyism." Trump then suggested Messing was racist, without providing any details. "If Roseanne Barr said what she did," Trump claimed on Twitter, "even being on a much higher rated show, she would have been thrown off television." (Barr, a Trump supporter, had already been fired from her eponymous sitcom on ABC in May 2018 for making a racist remark about the former Obama White House adviser Valerie Jarrett.)

Here in New York, during his early months outside the White House, Trump hasn't moved on. Messing is on his traitors list, and he can't shake the hypocrisy—in his mind—that she once supported him as a reality TV star. "She probably wouldn't even admit it," Trump says about Messing's supposed flattery from more than fifteen years ago. "She came up to me in front of a group of people. I've never seen it. She was begging for acceptance!" He takes on a higher-pitched voice that's supposed to be Messing: "Thank you so much for what you've done for me, my show, and for NBC. It will never be forgotten."

Trump pauses dramatically. "Well," he proclaims, "it was forgotten. She was just a nasty person. Her and many others. So many people have come up to me over the years and said, 'Thank you!' Once I ran for office, that stopped."

The next time we talk, Trump brings up Messing again, and he confirms something that he'd only dropped hints about in our last meeting. During the early years of *The Apprentice*, Trump even had a crush on *Will & Grace*'s leading lady. Maybe that's why he can't quite shake the bitterness that now exists between them. A former president who can't win over a star almost sounds like the premise of a corny romantic comedy, but for Trump, Messing's rejection is still a sharp dagger to his heart. "This Debra Messing, who I always thought was quite attractive—not that it matters, of course . . ." Their squabbles on social media continue to live rent-free in his mind. "Debra Messing was so thankful," he says. "And then I watch her today, and it's like she's a raving mess."

Then he starts to quiz me about whether or not Megan Mullally ever betrayed him. As he comes up empty on that front—clearing her of any backstabbing behavior for now—he finally says, "You should tell that Debra Messing story. To me, it's disgusting."

By the time the third season of *The Apprentice* had started airing in January 2005, Trump was forced to do something that didn't come naturally to him. He needed to learn how to share. Mark Burnett had started partnering with other celebrities who were trying to copy Trump's success. The Svengali producer was busy behind the scenes hatching *The Contender*, a search for the next great professional boxer. Given the notoriety and ratings Trump had brought to *The Apprentice*, and the failure of *The Restaurant*, Burnett was on the hunt for other stars who could drum up drama. On *The Contender*, which he produced with the DreamWorks co-founder Jeffrey Katzenberg, Burnett recruited the *Rocky* legend Sylvester Stallone and the professional boxer Sugar Ray Leonard to mentor sixteen wannabe fighters who squared off in the ring until one winner was crowned with a championship belt and $1 million. Though the prize was four times what the winner of *The Apprentice* received and Stallone had a blue-collar-friendly persona and level of fame that surpassed Trump's, the show didn't connect. Still, Trump kept a close eye on the competition, because the prospect of being displaced by Stallone in Burnett's orbit ruffled his feathers.

But Burnett was savvy about handling Trump. To soothe his ego, Burnett trash-talked Stallone and Leonard's hosting abilities, telling Trump they were no match for his natural talents. It's a confidence-boosting tale that Trump clings to all these years later, bringing it up repeatedly in our different conversations. "I have a great memory, and I can do things right," Trump tells me one day in 2023 while we're sitting down together at Mar-a-Lago. In the past, Trump had said that *The Apprentice* was completely unscripted. It turns out, he now admits, there'd be written lines he'd need to deliver at the top of each episode. "I'd read a script in the morning. They'd sometimes give me four or five pages," Trump says, improvising in this moment some made-up dialogues involving an address, a task, a sponsor, and the family lineage of the sponsor to show me just how complicated it could all be. "And I don't think I ever missed a take. And I had tremendous facts!"

Now, as Trump revisits all the intricacies of filming a reality show, his inner thespian comes to the surface, and he reconsiders the quality of the dialogue he was forced to deliver. "Some of these things were just factual bullshit," Trump says, about plugging the sponsors on TV. "And you have to be able to say it, ideally, in one take, or it's not great. I don't think I ever missed a take."

According to Trump, Burnett told him that his new stars just didn't have the delivery skills to measure up. "Mark said Sly and Sugar Ray Leonard would take days on simple little presentations," Trump says, recalling Burnett telling him, "You do it in fifteen, twenty minutes. These guys take two days to do basically the introduction of the show, because Sly's memory is not the greatest, and Sugar Ray Leonard had no memory whatsoever!"

As he says this, Trump realizes that it might sound harsh—coming down so hard on a beloved, elderly Black athlete who has never taken a shot at him—so he eases up on Leonard. "He had a great left jab, and a fucking great right. He may not have had a good memory, but he could fight, that guy—I'll tell you." Trump quickly redirects the storytelling back to the real champion in the reality TV ring: himself. "Mark said I made the job a lot easier, saved a lot of money, too, because those cameras, when they roll, it's expensive," Trump says. "I had a lot of fun doing it."

Ultimately, there was no reason for Trump to be threatened by *The Contender*. The series, which Burnett had sold to NBC in a heated bidding war for more than $2 million an episode, premiered to only eight million viewers in its Monday night time slot—a sizable audience in the fractured media environment now, but back then it meant losing to *CSI: Miami*. Ultimately, it was canceled by NBC after one season. Burnett found a new home for it on ESPN for two additional seasons with Leonard (but no Stallone); a fourth season hosted by Tony Danza on Versus, a short-lived sports network owned by NBC; and a fifth season fronted by the boxer Andre Ward on Epix. Needless to say, *The Contender* was no match for Trump.

Yet at NBC and among Burnett's top producers as season 3 of *The Apprentice* premiered in January 2005, there were concerns that this reality

TV heavyweight could be on the decline. Because *Joey*, Matt LeBlanc's spin-off to *Friends*, didn't live up to the ratings its predecessor earned on Thursday nights, NBC's future looked bleak. Under Zucker's watch, the network aired two seasons of *The Apprentice* a year, with occasional two-hour supersized episodes, so the risk of viewer burnout was real. On *Survivor*, which CBS also began airing twice a year, the different locations around the world provided new texture and tension to make each competition stand out. But since Burnett was tied to the same *Apprentice* host and to Trump's hometown, the only way to differentiate the show was through the various contestants and the challenges. It seemed as though that might not be enough.

"Philosophically, had it been my call, I would have never put it on Thursday nights," says Kevin Reilly. "I knew we were smoking crack. I knew it was going to be the beginning of other problems for NBC as we needed to rebuild. But as it was waning, I called Trump, every conversation was the same: 'We're No. 1!'" Reilly would have to tell Trump otherwise. "He just keeps repeating the thing on a loop, like he does now, and eventually people start going, 'It's No. 1.' I found it kind of amusing, where someone can just keep pressing on that agenda no matter what the facts said."

For season 3, Burnett decided to divide the contestants into two teams based on their education—those who'd gone to college ("Book Smarts") and those who hadn't ("Street Smarts"). This had been his original plan for *The Apprentice*. But because the producers weren't happy with the non-college talent pool, Burnett changed the premise of the show, making it a battle of the sexes. It turns out, there's a reason he had to make that adjustment.

On the first day of filming season 3, Burnett surprised the contestants with this twist after they'd already been cast on the show. "Everyone I was in business with assumed I'd finished school," says John Gafford, then a thirty-two-year-old technology firm owner from Tampa, Florida. "I'll never forget—I was sitting in that boardroom when they announced that, and I was like, 'Holy shit! This is going to fucking *ruin* me.'" Later, he discovered that nothing changed for him professionally. "The funny thing was nobody cared," Gafford says. "But it would have been nice to know that, prior to it being sprung on us."

Even while multitasking to further expand his dominance on TV, Burnett remained a central force on the set of *The Apprentice*. One day, as the crew was struggling to set up a shot, one of the contestants tried to make a joke at Burnett's expense. "You're treading water today, aren't you, Mark?" she said. This didn't sit well with the most powerful man in reality TV. "I never tread water," Burnett sniffed. "I swim."

And Burnett didn't let up on the mind games either. Gafford recalls meeting with Burnett in the final round of his audition in a sequestered conference room at the Embassy Suites in Santa Monica. "I said, 'How are you doing, Mr. Burnett?' I stuck out my hand to shake his hand. He was sitting there eating M&M's, and he didn't shake my hand. He put an M&M in my hand. In the next fifteen minutes, he says, 'Oh, I heard your buddy says your girlfriend is going to break up with you any day.'"

Gafford realized why he couldn't find a foothold in the conversation. "It had nothing to do with my wonderful attributes for business," he says. "It was just a fuck-with-me meeting. And it did not go well."

A few hours later, one of the assistants summoned Gafford back to the conference room for another gathering with Burnett and NBC brass. "I opened the minibar real quick, hit that, and then walked upstairs to the double doors. And right when I got to the front of them, I smashed them open as hard as I could. Everyone inside jumps." Gafford was ready to deliver the drama he knew the room was craving. "I looked at Burnett and said, 'Before you open your mouth and tell me one more fucking thing about myself, let me tell you something: When you make an investment in me, you make back a hundred times what you invest.' And I pulled out a bag of M&M's from my pocket that I'd taken out of the minibar and I threw it in his face and I walked out of the room." He holds for a second on that detail. "And," Gafford continues, "that's how I got on the show."

Burnett and NBC had huddled with Trump before production began on the new episodes, advising him that for the third season he should probably select a female winner—to change things up from the previous two white men who'd triumphed in his boardroom. Trump, who still cherished having final say over whom he could fire, was amenable to this note, but he couldn't keep it private. He blurted out the network's game plan at his first meeting with the contestants.

"I will tell you exactly what he said, and it shocked me," says Alex Thomason, then a twenty-nine-year-old attorney from Brewster, Washington, who played on the "Book Smarts" team. "The very first words that came out of his mouth, he looked us over and said, 'I'm sick and tired of hiring educated white guys to work for me. This season should be different!'" Thomason, still a fan of Trump's, uses this interaction as evidence that the former president isn't a hateful person. "When people say that he's racist, I take umbrage against that, because I know that's false. He says crazy things, but he does it to get someone's goat."

Gafford remembers something else from that day. In the contestants' first meeting with Trump in season 3, all of the players were lined up as a group to take publicity photographs. "It's the first time we ever saw Trump," Gafford says. "Someone tells Trump to take his spot, and he stands next to me." The photographer on set climbed up the ladder and took only two pictures before he was rudely interrupted. "Trump walks out of the photograph and says in front of everyone—like, not even under his breath—he just says it out loud. He goes, 'You have to move this guy! He's taller than I am!'"

Of course, since Trump was the boss on the set of *The Apprentice*, he got what he wanted. "Sure enough, they move me to the front," Gafford says. "I sit down, and they proceed to take a thousand photographs. And I was like, if this guy won't take one picture with me, there's zero chance I'm going to win this."

But in the event that he somehow pulled out a win even after Trump felt threatened by his height, Gafford—who'd clinched his spot on the show by delivering chaos—had one last twist in mind. If Trump were to hire him, he planned on turning down his job offer on national TV to pursue other opportunities. "Dude," he says, laughing, "it would have been incredible."

Gafford's stunt might well have reinvigorated a show that, while still huge, was beginning to lose steam. The third season averaged fourteen million viewers an episode, down from an average of almost twenty-one million in the show's first season. And the idea of pitting people with college degrees against those who didn't graduate from a fancy university failed to show the contestants to their best advantage or connect with viewers. "At the time, the real estate market was booming," Gafford says. "A lot of the people on the Street Smarts team were in the real estate industry and not good, savvy businesspeople."

There was also something else about this crop of contestants. They were nice and actually got along with each other. Even before Burnett was engaged to his girlfriend, Roma Downey, on Thanksgiving in 2006 and experienced a spiritual awakening, he'd recruited a crew of contestants who seemed to be distinguished by one common characteristic: many of them were well-behaved practicing Christians. "I don't know what the dynamics were on the other seasons of the show," says Kendra Todd, who joined the show as a twenty-five-year-old real estate broker from Boynton Beach, Florida. "But a lot of us had some deeply enriching personal relationships on our season. A bunch of us even prayed together during the show. It bonded us."

While the silent thoughts inside these prayer circles were often recorded by the cameras, it didn't translate to compelling TV. "We had some really eclectic personalities, but there was no villain," Todd says proudly. "There wasn't an Omarosa. Were there some people who at times were catty? Yes, but it wasn't a prevailing theme." Unfortunately, it had been that prevailing theme that had made the show work. Something had to change.

In 2005, Donald Trump, famous as he'd ever been, seemed to have less time to hang out with the contestants as he'd done in previous seasons. His potential hires would get glimpses of the man they wanted to work for as he'd crash their living quarters, not to say hello, but to give his own business partners, or those he wanted to woo, an exclusive visit to the set. "He had learned the value of the show," says Tara Dowdell, a then twenty-eight-year-old senior government manager from New York. "Going behind the scenes was a hot ticket. He would bring in executives or investors—people that he had some sort of business dealing with—and give them these private tours."

What the executives didn't see was that the set was becoming an increasingly tense place. In the absence of contestants who hated each other, Burnett pushed the envelope by making the challenges more demanding. While he and Trump continued to collect tens of millions of dollars from sponsors, Todd recalls getting only three hours of sleep a night. She and her teammates would stay up late trying to crack tasks, including selling a new hamburger for Burger King, creating a thirty-second commercial for Dove, renovating a motel on the Jersey Shore, and building their own miniature golf course at Chelsea Piers. "Here's what you have to understand," Todd says. "The experience on that show was so stressful, and we were so sleep deprived, I literally have black spots in my memory. There are details that I do not remember from that time—just because of the extreme stress. It felt like I was given ten bucks, a pack of gum, and a toothpick and told to build a skyscraper. That's how every task felt, like, 'Go achieve the impossible!' And, gosh darn it, we did."

When Trump wasn't invading their personal space, most of his time with the cast would come in the form of the boardroom. The production team had by now learned that they needed to clear an entire afternoon or evening to film Trump's off-the-cuff remarks and final verdict. There was no other reason, beyond the demands of one person, that the climax of each episode needed to take so long to shoot. Indeed, despite Trump's gloating at being fast at delivering his lines, the boardroom had become his vanity project. If he couldn't get NBC to air these scenes uninterrupted, at least he'd get a high from holding court. It was a telling detail of set design that Trump's seat was on a platform so he sat higher than the contestants cowering before him. It was as though the production designers anticipated that he would feel the need to go through each shoot as king for a day.

"One of them went five hours," George Ross recalls. "The vitriol was unbelievable. These women really went at it. They used language—I was in the Army—I'd never heard. I thought it ought to be cut short maybe after two hours. Donald said, 'No, let them go!' When it finally got edited down, it was maybe eight minutes." Ross explains why Trump was so entertained: "Donald was always up for an argument. As long as it was a good argument, he kept it going."

For the contestants, the hours of shooting boardroom sequences came across as proof of Trump's devotion to the show—rather than his obsession with himself. Paradoxically, the less of him the contestants saw, the more enamored they were. Trump was able to win them over by offering even more lavish prizes to the team that won each challenge, such as a day on the golf course with him or a dinner on a yacht with the publishing titan Steve Forbes.

In an off-camera moment of candor during that maritime meal, Trump reprimanded Forbes for running for president in 1996 and 2000 on what Trump saw as a losing platform. "You went overboard on this pro-life nonsense," Trump told Forbes, according to Thomason, who witnessed the exchange. The former contestant is certain Trump didn't believe in banning abortion then—or even now. "I know his heart didn't change," Thomason says, supporting Trump's decision to use himself as a vessel for the Republican Party. "I view it as incredible integrity to the people who elected him." If that sounds like something Kellyanne Conway would say, many of the contestants from that season speak about Trump in language that a campaign surrogate might use.

"I was not anticipating how involved and engaged he would be with the process," Kendra Todd says. "It was incredible. Some of those boardrooms took three to four hours. I'm not exaggerating. I only know this because I was waiting for people to come back from them." (Todd never experienced this herself because she became the first contestant to make it to the finale without ever getting sent to the boardroom.) "He could have used the show as, 'I'm Donald Trump. My name is enough.' That was not his attitude at all. He was super involved with making the right decision on who was fired. I found that fascinating."

While this extra face time with Trump could be valuable, it could also be draining—and occasionally disturbing. After a task with the Home Depot—during which the contestants were supposed to create a customized experience for shoppers—the *Apprentice* house was abuzz about what Trump had supposedly said to Erin Elmore, a twenty-six-year-old attorney from Philadelphia, in the boardroom. On the episode, she's seen flirting with Trump, even winking at him before she gets the boot. But at some point, Trump allegedly boasted to her, "I'll show you my nine-inch power tool," as she pleaded ignorance about her knowledge of home repair. (No one knows for certain whether Trump was wearing a microphone when he made that lewd joke or if a recording exists.)

Trump didn't get in trouble for it. Indeed, since the moment didn't make it to air, it might as well never have happened. "There's no truth to it," says Elmore, a Republican strategist who worked as a surrogate for Trump's 2016 presidential campaign. "It's kind of hearsay."

Trump's Teflon-like skills at avoiding blame for his relentlessly crass behavior might not have begun on *The Apprentice*, but the show certainly cemented his image as a harmless figure of fun. It's this era of *The Apprentice* that brought out some of his most vocal supporters—including Elmore—when Trump ran for president. Stephanie Myers, then a twenty-nine-year-old consultant from San Diego, later served on his National Diversity Coalition and campaigned for him in 2016 and 2020. Not only does she defend his policies; she also weighs in on the age-old question of what's happening on the top of Trump's head. "I'm one of the rare people that has seen the roots of his hair," she says, describing the day she won a glamorous photo shoot with Trump after one of the tasks. "So I got to get my hair done next to Mr. Trump. And we did an amazing shoot. I have the photo in my house."

Myers, who was fired after a task that required the teams to deliver Domino's pizzas, says that Trump asked her to stay after her final boardroom. He blamed NBC for the firing and praised her work ethic and integrity—she lost because she wasted time traveling to Brooklyn to drop off pizzas, keeping her word to customers who lived there. "He told Mark Burnett to stop filming so he could talk to me and tell me what a great person I was, and how much I accomplished and how great I did," Myers says.

Thomason also speaks highly of Trump. "I'll tell you the moment that changed my viewpoint," says Thomason, who references a boardroom moment that stuck with him—the firing of Chris Shelton, a twenty-one-year-old real estate investor from Las Vegas. "Chris burst into tears, was sobbing, and walked away," Thomason recalls. "Mr. Trump changed and softened. He became who he was. From that moment, I realized that's the true Donald Trump, and the exterior he projects is all for advertising." Thomason believes that the real Trump is "that caring, gentle father who covers up with an incredibly gruff exterior. Do I think he's a good man? You're damn right I do."

Despite the goodwill and loyalty of the cast, Trump found himself struggling to fulfill the commitment he'd made to the network. While he had vowed to find a winner who wasn't a white man, both the Black women contestants on the season saw their screen time cut short. Verna Felton, a thirty-one-year-old business manager from Seattle, quit the show under a cloud of stress during an all-nighter when the teams attempted to renovate a Jersey Shore motel. She actually tried to flee by foot, but didn't get far without her wallet. "Luckily, Carolyn came by and gave me a ride back to the motel," Felton told *TV Guide* after her exit.

Dowdell, who made it on the show for a few more episodes, found herself holding back out of fear that she'd be portrayed badly. "My biggest trepidation was that they would try to paint me as a stereotype of a Black woman," Dowdell says. "And certainly I think they wanted me to be this stereotype of a Black woman."

Dowdell says she didn't trust the *Apprentice* producers, especially when they asked her questions in her confessional interviews alone to camera. "I just remember them saying, 'Didn't it make you upset when . . . ? Didn't you think they meant X, Y, and Z?' They were clearly trying to goad me in those moments. I just didn't take the bait." She got fired in the sixth task, and was never portrayed as a prominent character on the show. "I was so concerned I actively worked not to give them anything they could use," she says. "That resulted in me not being featured as much on the show."

When it came time for Trump to choose the third-season winner, the contest came down to two white women: Tana Goertz, a thirty-seven-year-old sales executive from Des Moines, and Todd, whose victory proved anticlimactic given that she was the front-runner. Not surprisingly, "Book Smarts" triumphed over "Street Smarts." "It didn't matter to me if I won or lost," Todd says. "For me, it was a life-transforming experience, and there were blessings that came from that."

For her job within the Trump Organization, she chose to refurnish Maison de L'Amitie, a mansion that Trump owned in Palm Beach, just a stone's throw away from Mar-a-Lago. She thought it was kismet that she could return to her home state, working in her chosen profession. But because the renovation wasn't ready for her yet, she spent the first three months shadowing Carolyn Kepcher at Trump National Golf Club in Briarcliff Manor, New York, and doing interviews to promote *The Apprentice* and Trump. She saw it all as a learning opportunity. She says that her time with Kepcher at the golf club allowed her to see a different side of Trump, too—when he didn't need to perform for the cameras. "Can you envision Trump driving a car and pulling up? I got to see him do that," Todd says. "I got to see him having normal human interactions. He would drive up to the golf club—'How are you ladies doing?' It was a place where he could kind of unwind. He didn't have to be the New York Donald Trump. He could be the golf aficionado. He was more laid-back."

Todd recalls hanging out with Trump during these check-in visits. "He cared about what I was doing and if I was happy." When he couldn't make an in-person visit, she'd get phone calls from Trump on her cell phone. "He didn't really have an agenda," Todd says. "He wanted to make sure I had everything I needed, and that things were going well with me and Carolyn." Based on their time together, Todd believes that Trump was, at his core, a good boss. "One on one, he's very engaging and a thoughtful person. My business interactions with him were always serious. I had a positive experience. The whole thing was positive for me."

After her stint in New York, Todd returned to Florida to oversee the mansion renovation. "We did a retrofit of the interior," she says. "We added more bedrooms, and did a bunch of exterior renovations. I supported the real estate brokers that we hired, and I managed all of the press. *The Wall Street Journal* wanted to fly down to make it a front-page story. We had various magazine shows that wanted to take tours through the house."

Her contributions to the property later helped find it a buyer—the Russian billionaire and oligarch Dmitry Rybolovlev, who forked over $95 million in a record-breaking sale. (Years later, Debra Messing's fictional renovation of Trump's Oval Office on the *Will & Grace* reboot would see her extracting a Russian-English dictionary from under the Resolute desk.) When reporters were trying to get dirt on Trump as the Republican nominee for president, they kept contacting Todd to see whether she could confirm any of his previous business dealings with Russia. "I can't tell you how many people called me during Russiagate, trying to fish for information," Todd says. "It was the most pathetic, lazy journalism I've ever seen. I'm like, 'Guys, it was *The Apprentice*! It was 2005. He wasn't even thinking about running for office! And he didn't know the Russian oligarch.'"

Granted, Trump had floated running for president many times before *The Apprentice* began, including, most notably, with a Reform Party run in 2000. But in the early years of *The Apprentice*, he was solely focused on TV stardom. "I'm like, 'Come on,'" Todd says. "There are so many people on the 'Let's get Trump' train. I'm not going to play the game."

Todd moved on from the Trump Organization after she completed a year on the job. She later hosted *My House Is Worth What?*, a successful real estate show on HGTV. Todd had learned some lessons from her boss about using her time in the spotlight to advance her own career, but she says she wouldn't describe herself as a die-hard *Apprentice* fan. "I think the show inherently changed after the third season," she says. "It wasn't quite the same."

And Trump suddenly found himself newly against the ropes. Forget about Rocky Balboa. For the next season of *The Apprentice*, Trump had to defend his turf from a new foe—one so tough she'd just been sprung from jail.

CHAPTER 8

Mad About Martha

Trump's politics—and the animosity toward him in today's Hollywood—have shrunk his Rolodex. Once upon a time, not only did Jeff Zucker practically make Trump a regular *Today* co-host to promote *The Apprentice*, but Bette Midler came over for dinner. "I had her in my apartment," Trump says. "And then she says the nastiest things." While Couric and Midler are the media and the industry elite, Trump has been especially stung by the loss of the support of a fellow entrepreneur and personal-branding genius who, like him, had used reality TV to emerge from catastrophic failure. Martha Stewart stumped for Hillary Clinton in 2016. "Martha Stewart and I were on great terms, to put it mildly, until I ran for politics. But then, you know, she became hostile."

If these celebrities Trump spent time with while he was on top no longer call, a rising generation of new stars see him, simply, as a villain, never having experienced his glad-handing side. During one of our conversations, in the winter of 2023, I ask Trump what he thinks of the biggest celebrity of our times: Taylor Swift, who was at the time selling out stadiums globally on her Eras Tour. (She opened her tour with her 2019 song "Miss Americana and the Heartbreak Prince," widely perceived as being about the division sown by Trump.) Trump, usually one to punch back at critics, is smart enough to know Swift's fame is on another level. "She's got a great star quality," Trump says. "She really does." Trump is effusive as he uses one of his favorite adjectives to describe women—"beautiful"— several times in a row. "I think she's beautiful—very beautiful! I find her very beautiful. I think she's liberal. She probably doesn't like Trump. I hear she's very talented. I think she's very beautiful, actually—unusually beautiful!" It's her fame, not her songcraft, that fascinates Trump. When asked about Swift's music, played so frequently on the radio that it's inescapable in daily life, he says, "Don't know it well."

Beyond Swift's looks, what intrigues Trump the most is the idea— frequently bandied about online before she endorsed the Democratic Senate candidate in Tennessee in 2018—that she could secretly be supporting him. "But she is liberal, or is that just an act?" he asks me. "She's legitimately liberal? It's not an act? It surprises me that a country star can be successful being liberal." I tell Trump that Swift is no longer a country star; she's been making pop music for years. He doesn't seem aware of this, but he reaches for a different name. "Garth Brooks is liberal. Explain that! How does it happen? But he's liberal." Trump trails off. "It's one of those things . . ."

If Trump were more familiar with Swift's songs, he could probably relate to her scorched-earth lyrics. Trump and Swift share little politically, but Swift's skill as an insult comic—and her ability to strike back hard against those who've wounded her—coexist alongside a sort of hopeful belief in reconciliation. And even if Trump never cues up "All Too Well," he's leaving open the possibility that some of his biggest detractors secretly love him. He's constantly floating this theory to reassure himself that he is, in fact, winning at the game of life. "I actually got along great with Martha Stewart until I ran for office," he tells me. "I guess she's obviously a different persuasion, or pretends to be," Trump says. "A lot of people that are saying they are a different persuasion voted for me. I can guarantee you that! I guarantee you that a big percentage of Beverly Hills voted for me. A big percentage of Bel-Air voted for me."

Trump's gaze moves beyond Taylor Swift's Tribeca or Martha Stewart's Westchester to the zip code that's home to some of the biggest mansions on the West Coast. Trump, who locked up the swing states in 2016, then lost them in 2020 (just don't tell him that), seems concerned with making the case that he overperformed in the all-important Hollywood vote. He's suggesting that the town that never awarded him an Emmy covertly supports him as a president and that many celebrities are lying about being Democrats. "I think *most* of them, if you want to know the truth," he says about these invisible voters. "But then they walk out and say, 'I voted for Crooked Joe Biden,' okay? I think in your world, they won't say it."

He doesn't offer any evidence to support these claims. But then he never explained exactly how it was that he really won the 2020 election either. Maybe it all makes sense when you look at it through the eyes of a reality star: he who gets the most attention wins. For Trump, celebrity is the ultimate currency, and that's why he needs to pretend that famous people secretly like him. To be truly rejected by Hollywood, and the world's biggest movie stars, is not something that gels with his definition of success. His time on *The Apprentice* made Trump into a president who looks less like a statesman and more like an old-school studio mogul. "This book, if it's good, will be a big hit," Trump tells me, after he's done speculating about all of his hidden voters in the entertainment industry. "It's going to be a very big smash. I've never had a book that wasn't."

It wasn't true that Trump "got along great" with Martha Stewart. He wasn't on "great terms" with the self-made billionaire whom the country trusted for advice on how to maintain a happy home. The two New Yorkers became embroiled in a tabloid feud long before she endorsed his 2016 opponent. It all started, naturally, because of *The Apprentice*.

With the show's ratings dipping in seasons 2 and 3, Mark Burnett was looking for a stunt to keep America glued to the premise of a megalomaniacal boss teaching mentees how to succeed in business. And even though Burnett's partnership with Trump was supposed to be ironclad, Burnett was the kind of overachiever who was always looking over the shoulder of his dance partner, in case someone better walked into the room. Later, with NBC's *The Voice*, Burnett kept ratings momentum going long after *American Idol* had fallen off by swapping out the original celebrity mentors Blake Shelton, Adam Levine, Christina Aguilera, and CeeLo Green in favor of a revolving door of pop stars that's included Shakira, Usher, Gwen Stefani, and the original Idol, Kelly Clarkson. Burnett, sensing that doing business with Trump had an expiration date, hadn't given up on the idea of rotating in new business moguls. Maybe what the boardroom needed was a refresh not of the contestants but of the person doing the firing.

Enter Martha Stewart. Like Trump, she was a beloved and feared celebrity figure with a knack for understanding the value of self-generated publicity. Unlike Trump, who had the benefit of family wealth, she'd managed to build her own vast enterprise, Martha Stewart Living Omnimedia. On the morning of the company's initial public offering, Stewart served brioche and fresh-squeezed orange juice at the New York Stock Exchange. She leveraged her lifestyle lessons into a billion-dollar company in the late 1990s, informing baby boomer women about cooking, cleaning, gardening, decluttering, and hosting the perfect dinner party. She even served as the editor in chief of her own magazine, *Martha Stewart Living*, launched by Time Inc. (She later bought it back for her company on an $85 million loan.) But what intrigued Burnett the most about Stewart was her sudden, humiliating public downfall.

Stewart had been accused of insider trading involving a 2001 stock sale of ImClone Systems, a biopharmaceutical company, in the amount of $229,513. It was a drop in the bucket for her, but in July 2004 a judge sentenced her to five months in prison, in a wall-to-wall media circus that dominated the airwaves. Later, Bravo's *Real Housewives* franchise would feature numerous white-collar crime trials, but years earlier, Stewart was the realest housewife of all. On late-night TV, Jay Leno and David Letterman couldn't tell enough jokes about this snobby perfectionist in an ill-fitting orange jumpsuit.

"Perhaps all of you out there can continue to show your support by subscribing to our magazine, by buying our products, by encouraging our advertisers to come back in full force to our magazines," Stewart said on July 16, 2004, outside the courthouse in downtown Manhattan shortly after she'd been sentenced. Stewart, then sixty-two, still demonstrated Trumpian zeal for the cameras, pivoting all the attention on her to her businesses. "Our magazines are great. They deserve your support, and whatever happened to me personally shouldn't have any effect whatsoever on the great company Martha Stewart Omnimedia."

Burnett, never shy about seizing the moment, decided he could extend his own power in entertainment by helping rehabilitate Stewart. Before she surrendered herself to Alderson Federal Prison Camp in West Virginia in October 2004, he managed to arrange a series of meetings and sign her as his latest star. Burnett agreed to pay Stewart $8 million annually for *Martha*, a syndicated daytime lifestyle show on NBC, on which Stewart would teach secret cooking recipes and dispense entertaining tips to stay-at-home moms. She'd previously hosted *Martha Stewart Living*, a morning talk show based on her magazine's self-help principles, for eleven seasons on CBS, but it had been canceled due to her jail sentence. Betting that Stewart would emerge from prison more popular than ever was a major risk, but Burnett had a vision. And the talk show was secondary: what Burnett really wanted was Stewart as the next host of *The Apprentice*, bringing new vitality to one of the biggest TV shows in prime time.

Like Roxie Hart in *Chicago*, who saw her prospects for free media attention dim when the vaudeville singer Velma Kelly joined her in prison for murdering her husband, Trump couldn't compete with Stewart's homemaker-in-distress image. In media circles, there was round-the-clock speculation about whether Stewart's career could survive once she was released from prison. What many saw as professional death, Burnett—like Roxie's Svengali, Billy Flynn—saw as a golden opportunity.

"She was hot as a pistol, because she was coming out of prison," Trump recalls. "It was my idea: 'Why don't we try Martha Stewart?'" That's not accurate: Burnett had approached Stewart without Trump's knowledge.

"Yes," Burnett texts me, before Christmas 2023, confirming that Stewart was his—and only his—brainchild. I ask if we can talk on the phone, and he writes, "Can it wait til after the new year. Family all arrived and we've committed to no work stuff." And in the new year, he ghosts me again.

When I push back on the origins of Stewart's *Apprentice* to Trump, he mutters, "Both of us"— meaning he and Burnett created Stewart's version together. "It was just an idea I had."

The terms of Burnett and Stewart's arrangement were a little sketchy. Burnett told reporters in February 2005, near the end of Stewart's jail sentence, that he'd been visiting her behind bars every week. "Her mood is fantastic," he said at the time. "She's a really brave woman. Very few people could have withstood what she has."

Burnett claimed that he couldn't talk about business with Stewart on his visits to prison. Once she was out, she would serve another five months of house arrest at her 153-acre, $16 million estate in Bedford, New York, but she'd get forty-eight hours a week to run errands, buy groceries, and work. That's when she'd be able to film *The Apprentice*. She called the schedule "hideously challenging" in an interview with *Entertainment Weekly*, because she had to race to Manhattan to quickly debrief and dismiss contestants before returning to her compound. The downside of the production challenges of Stewart's legal drama wasn't balanced out by the potential ratings bump of her actually discussing her situation on TV. Stewart shut down any conversation about the glaring imperfection strapped around her ankle. She kept her court-ordered ankle bracelet hidden under her pants instead of using it as an opportunity to milk ratings. It was an early sign that she might not be the future of the franchise: part of the show's success, though not as much as Trump might have liked to believe, could be traced to its star's willingness to say anything.

As the cameras started to roll that spring, Stewart was already in a prickly mood about the circumstances under which she'd entered her new TV endeavor. When Burnett persuaded Stewart to accept *The Apprentice*, she thought she'd be the lone host of the show. But as soon as Trump caught wind of that plan, he was outraged, refusing to step aside graciously. Burnett could have made the decision to keep Trump off *The Apprentice* for a single season so Stewart could give the series a legitimate run, but nobody wanted to piss off Trump and lose his loyalty. After Trump's intense objections, Burnett and Zucker decided that they'd simultaneously air Stewart's edition with Trump's version in the same cycle. That meant Stewart would have Wednesday nights for her spin-off, *The Apprentice: Martha Stewart*, while Trump took Thursdays. It was an awkward custody arrangement that seriously risked oversaturating an already at-risk franchise.

"I mean no, I didn't think more of that was the answer, but I was getting the shit kicked out of me," says Kevin Reilly. "Every week, someone thought I was going to get fired. I'm championing things like *Friday Night Lights* and *The Office*." Neither of those series was a hit out of the gate for NBC. "Half the town was like, 'This guy doesn't get it. He's hanging his hat on these losers.'"

All these years later, Trump still holds firm on his decision not to surrender his seat in the boardroom. "Martha said she was under the impression that I was going to end the show. I said, 'Use your head! Why would we end the show? No, we are putting on a second version by a female. It should be great.'" He feigns a tepid endorsement, before admitting that he never thought Stewart could surpass him. "I said, 'Wait a minute. We have one of the top shows. Why would you stop it?'" Trump was credited as an executive producer on both shows. "I didn't even know I was the executive producer," he says. "They probably put my name on it."

Trump started to distance himself from *The Apprentice: Martha Stewart* before production even began. "It's going to be a very different show," he told the New York *Daily News* in February 2005. "Different in every sense."

At 6:00 a.m. on February 4, 2005, a dreary, cold morning in New York, I found myself on Wall Street, wearing a loose-fitting suit and a red necktie with a cut on my face from shaving while half-asleep. NBC was holding in-person auditions for *The Apprentice*, and my editors at *Newsweek* thought it might be a fun idea for me to go undercover and see how far I could get. This wasn't just a stunt piece: it was also a chance to try to learn a little about how Martha Stewart was approaching her return to the public eye. Since the network had just unveiled the Stewart version, Burnett decided to host dual casting calls side by side—a preview of a showdown that would pit not just contestant against contestant but host against host.

More than a hundred people were already huddling in the cold at the crack of dawn. "I want to be No. 1," Sean Grant, then a thirty-one-year-old options trader, told me as he stood at the very front of the line. He'd arrived at 4:00 p.m. the day before to secure the first spot. "Waiting seventeen hours for the chance of a lifetime isn't such a bad thing," he said, then added, "I lost complete feeling in my feet."

I was struck by one thing as I made my way through the line, interviewing these would-be competitors: Stewart didn't seem to have nearly as many die-hard supporters as Trump did. Most of the people in the crowd said they would prefer to be on the Trump show. These fans were surprisingly discerning in their search for their fifteen minutes of fame, and Stewart didn't offer anything they wanted. What difference did it make if they could baste a turkey or deep clean an oven? Trump was willing to get down and dirty with contestants, while Stewart's persona—even after prison time—remained aloof.

As my own feet started to feel numb, a man with a clipboard asked us to give our preference for which version of *The Apprentice* we wanted to apply for—Trump's or Stewart's. The line barely moved; almost everyone stayed where they were for the original *Apprentice*. Yes, a few stragglers, perhaps sensing a competitive advantage, shuffled to a different door for the spin-off opportunity, but it wasn't necessarily inspired by their devotion to Stewart. It was anyone's guess what skills made someone a successful candidate on *The Apprentice: Martha Stewart*. The few people I met who were genuine fans of Stewart's were mild-mannered and polite, not the typical brash reality TV characters who could go toe-to-toe with Trump. "I make draperies, ottomans, paintings on glass," Darlene Mays, a forty-five-year-old stay-at-home mom, told me. "I can fold napkins like origami."

Four hours later, I reached the front of the line and entered a ballroom space at 40 Wall Street, the seventy-two-story building for office rentals with Trump's name on it. The crowd was mostly dressed in business attire—plain suits and skirts—but this group didn't come across like the smartest or most successful people in Manhattan. They were more like reality TV superfans attending a convention (years before BravoCon). In fact, if you didn't take home the top prize of making it on TV, you could still buy Trump memorabilia. There were tables set up selling Trump mugs, buttons, and the talking doll that said, "You're fired!" And to the delight of the crowd, you could also hear the real thing. In a reality TV plot twist no one in line had seen coming, Trump had decided to crash the auditions. "Look at all the beautiful people!" he said as he waved to his fans. They responded with shrieks and cheers as dozens of news camera crews followed his every handshake.

This was unlike any job interview I'd ever attended. Trump's working the room into a fervor, I'd only later realize, looked a lot like his 2016 political rallies, posing for photos with his loyal viewers. "Back in the day, I tried out for *Teen Jeopardy!* and Alex Trebek was nowhere to be found," I would write in my *Newsweek* story. It was a line that I'd recall when I saw Trump running for president on TV years later, reflecting on just how much he loved to be loved.

From the very beginning of their respective seasons, Trump was determined to outshine Stewart, an easy layup since Stewart was still behind bars and couldn't fight back. She didn't even have any merchandise on display, not a cookbook in sight. Trump would later tell *The New York Times* that he flew to Los Angeles to personally select seventeen of the final eighteen candidates for *The Apprentice*'s upcoming season 4. He said he felt that Burnett had failed him in selecting a dud cast for season 3, after Trump said he'd spotted better personalities at another early casting call. "I was very nice," Trump explained to the *Times* in August 2005. "I said, 'You see that guy in dreadlocks? I would like him in the show if possible.' There was a girl I wanted. I said, 'I'd like to see if you could have her in the show.' It wasn't typical Trump." In other words, he approached things politely.

Trump somehow thought he was so attuned to stardom that he could determine if ratings would follow just by looking at a person. When he finally met the contestants for season 3, he claimed that none of his top picks from the auditions were among the group. "I went through the roof," Trump said in 2005. "Then I became the real Trump—because I didn't like the cast."

So how would I get Trump to like me if he didn't know I was a journalist writing about him? Sensing that my time would be limited, and with no actual desire of joining *The Apprentice*, I decided my strategy for my audition was to be as annoying as possible. I was going to write a humorous column about how the other contestants responded to my stupidity, similar to something Joel Stein would publish in that era's iteration of *Time* magazine. At around noon, six hours into this adventure, I finally got my shot.

Once inside, all the applicants were separated into small groups and seated at mock boardrooms next to each other, positioned like tables in a high school cafeteria. A casting director assigned to our table would then throw out a prompt, and we were encouraged to respond with as much flair as possible. The other people at my table ranged from an elderly doctor to a twenty-two-year-old surfer type wearing an Armani headband to a woman who developed film at a pharmacy. Interestingly enough, it didn't seem as if any of these applicants had actual jobs that required them to work during the day in an office. Nevertheless, I relished my chance to create a fictional reality TV villain.

The first question was a softball: Why do you want to work for Donald Trump?

"I want to work for Donald Trump because he is the greatest leader in the world," I said theatrically as Trump strolled by our table, within earshot.

"He's good!" Trump said, pointing to me. The casting director looked annoyed.

The second question was a hypothetical one about whether a woman should disclose her desire for having children when applying for a job. Everyone at my table said she didn't need to, but taking the contrarian viewpoint, I told them that it should be illegal for her to hide such information. "Women are biologically different than men," I replied in my most chauvinistic voice, mocking the group and stoking outrage. The film developer looked heartbroken that she'd trusted me with her life stories while we were in line.

The interview ended with everyone going around the table, picking one person to fire—and I won. Or, technically, I lost because everyone voted for me. But having their attention on me counted as a win in *Apprentice*-land.

The casting director asked me to stay behind for a few seconds. "If you want to get on this show," he said, "this wasn't the way to do it." He folded our stack of applications and tossed them in the reject pile. I was twenty-two, and I felt as if I'd been handed a slip to report to detention. I was embarrassed for attempting to play the role of a chaos agent and not being a good enough actor to pull it off. For the fourth season of *The Apprentice*, the show didn't want players who were so desperately clamoring for attention. It turns out, there was an art to succeeding in reality TV: being entertaining and obnoxious, but not so obnoxious as to come across as artificial. But part of me felt that if Trump had seen the entirety of my performance, he still would have put me through to the next round.

Jim Bozzini, a thirty-six-year-old advertising executive from Gilbertsville, Pennsylvania, excelled where I didn't in playing a reality TV bad guy on his *Apprentice* audition that year. "I actually applied to be on Trump's, not Martha's," Bozzini says. "I didn't even realize Martha was doing one. I just sent a really goofy video. It was very irreverent, showing off my bartending moves." Bozzini made it so far that NBC flew him to Los Angeles to meet Trump, but the show's lead producer that season—Jay Bienstock, taking on a bigger role as Mark Burnett focused on Stewart's launch—thought he could too easily see the strings behind Bozzini's shtick.

"They called me and said I wasn't going to be on the Trump one, so I was pretty crestfallen and upset about that," Bozzini says. "But then they called me back, like half a week later, and they said, 'We think you might be right for the Martha Stewart show.' I said, 'I didn't apply for that one.'" It still meant a chance to get exposure on national TV, so Bozzini accepted the offer. (Bozzini thinks he missed out on the Trump version because they were looking to cast a mean villain, not a humorous one: "And then later, much later, I saw the guy they had put in my place and he was a real weasel.")

But even if he didn't get a chance to play Trump's jester, Bozzini ended up stealing the spotlight away from Stewart. Within a few weeks, in a story planted by NBC, the *New York Post* would dub him the male Omarosa. "He's loud, rude, combative and obnoxious," the tabloid declared. But unlike the real Omarosa, Stewart couldn't afford to lose Bozzini. Her show immediately collapsed in its time slot against the second season of *Lost*, ABC's water-cooler drama set on a desert island—stealing back the idea from *Survivor* and repurposing it for a scripted series. Bozzini needed to survive in order for Stewart to attract any viewers at all.

He hadn't originally planned on being so awful on TV. Bozzini says that when he arrived in New York to start filming, he was suddenly gripped with fear that producers would misrepresent him. "I had a panic attack. I was like, 'Oh my gosh, everyone in the country is going to see me on television. I don't know if I'm ready to reveal who I am.' So I created a character right then and there, and the character was Jim. He was a villain, and he was ruthless and nasty and backbiting and all the things

I gleaned that got me accepted in the first place. So that's who I became. I was the troublemaker."

Bozzini's continued presence on *The Apprentice: Martha Stewart* was a sign that something was off. The spin-off series premiered on September 21, 2005, only a day before Trump's season 4 premiere, to a lackluster 7.1 million viewers and continued to tumble from there. The show felt familiar—with contestants racing through Manhattan to write the best children's fairy-tale book for Random House as their first challenge, and living together in a loft downtown—but different, as Trump predicted. It didn't have any of the fun or high-wire spark of the Trump version.

In the first episode, as Stewart floats through the halls of Martha Stewart Omnimedia, dressed in a pantsuit, she maintains an icy smile, struggling to wave naturally and make small talk with her office minions. "I love that, don't you?" she says to a young woman, without even pausing long enough to see what she's working on. On TV, in this artificial setting, Stewart came across as erudite, stiff, awkward, and uncomfortable—all words that would also be used to describe Hillary Clinton years later.

"Well, let's get down to business," Stewart says a few minutes into the episode, greeting the contestants. "Money can't buy what you're going to learn here. In the Renaissance, a young person would buy an apprenticeship, would pay a certain amount of money to an artisan or a craftsman or a famous weaver and learn that craft." Stewart, in her diction and posture, seemed more like an uptight professor at a liberal arts college. Trump's off-the-cuff improv existed in the sweet spot of reality TV, while Stewart was asking viewers to travel back to the sixteenth century.

She was allowed to deliver her lectures. But in its pacing and tasks, the series never fully embraced Stewart's world. Where Trump could pretend to be interested in everything and everyone, Stewart had more narrow tastes. "I think I was expecting it to be much more like the magazine, inclined toward the creative," says the contestant Marcela Valladolid, then twenty-seven, a cooking instructor from Tijuana, Mexico. "We had that one cooking challenge. And of course I was leading that challenge.

We won, and that was awesome." Burnett had decided that viewers could watch only so many shots of ovens, wedding cakes, and food. The show even recycled a task—getting celebrities to participate in an auction for charity—from Trump's season 1.

Stewart had her own sidekicks to help judge the contestants, but they didn't measure up to George or Carolyn. She'd rely on the advice of Charles Koppelman, a music executive who was serving as the chairman of Martha Stewart Living Omnimedia (his odd tic of dangling an unlit cigar between his lips was like a visual reminder of the show's missing spark), and Stewart's soft-spoken daughter, Alexis. "I thought their relationship was a little, like, dry and cold," says Sarah Brennan, a twenty-five-year-old event planner from Washington, D.C., while Howie Greenspan, a thirty-three-year-old fashion company owner from Closter, New Jersey, adds, "I didn't get the vibe her and her mom were that close." (Alexis Stewart later appeared on a niche cable show, *Whatever, Martha!*, a kind of *Mystery Science Theater 3000* series in which she mocked her mom's old segments, with the co-host, Jenny Koppelman Hutt, daughter of Charles Koppelman. It ran for four seasons.)

"The daughter thing, that was not good," Trump says about Alexis. If Stewart couldn't even seem to connect with her own daughter, what hope did she have to appeal to viewers?

"We knew immediately, as soon as we saw the episodes, she wasn't the dynamic reality star he was," says Jeff Gaspin. "She was very low-key. She wasn't in your face the way he was."

Stewart's emergence from prison, grinning while wearing a poncho a fellow inmate had knit her, gave a false sense of her confidence on camera. In fact, Stewart receded into her shell, concerned that she'd alienate her devoted fan base. "She was very self-conscious about not trying to come across as too mean," Gaspin says. "She was trying to resurrect her image. She didn't want to show that negative, tough personality. She was trying to be more constructive. And, frankly, that didn't make for good TV."

The other problem stemmed from Stewart's genuine lack of interest in the contestants. She was visibly flustered and exhausted by her schedule, confined to her home for so much of the week. "I took it upon myself to read every biography I could get my hands on, authorized or not, on her," says Brennan. "And I was sort of feeling like, 'She can't be that difficult.' But I found her to be challenging for sure." Brennan elaborates: "Many people would say she can be kind of sharp. And I don't mean intelligent."

While Trump would regularly draw a smattering of applause from the crew when he appeared on the set of *The Apprentice*, Stewart didn't love the way the reality TV cameras followed her every move. "They're always filming, so there wasn't a time when the cameras weren't on," Brennan says. "And I saw she was burning waffles or something, and she got really irritated with the cameraman who was filming it." Stewart hissed at him, "You're not supposed to be filming this part!" The outburst startled Brennan. "She got kind of nasty with the cameraman in front of me. And I was like, 'Oh, okay, some of the unauthorized biographies might be accurate.'"

Other than Bozzini, the rest of the Stewart contestants didn't make much of a dent in pop culture, save for a thirty-four-year-old natural foods chef from New York named Bethenny. Yes, Bethenny—as in Bethenny Frankel—scored her reality TV debut on *The Apprentice: Martha Stewart*, introducing America to her caustic one-liners and eye rolls years before she became one of Bravo's most popular and successful Real Housewives. Being on *The Apprentice* gave Frankel a foothold into fame, but it's not a chapter from her career she loves to revisit. ("We're definitely not friends," Frankel later said about Stewart on a podcast. "But we almost did this TV project together despite the fact that she can't stand me. And I can't really stand her either.") But there was no way that Burnett could let Frankel win. In the first episode, producers revealed that, by complete coincidence, Frankel had dated Koppelman's son years before, so the show couldn't fully embrace her as an underdog mogul, for fear of the game seeming fixed.

Stewart did her dismissals (she never called them "firings") in a conference room at her company. Unlike Trump's execution room, which was lit like a haunted dungeon, Stewart glowed under such flattering lighting that it looked as if she were conducting her show from heaven. When she let a contestant go, she'd use the milder catchphrase "You just don't fit in," often reading detailed notes on her BlackBerry before delivering her weekly edict. "I knew she didn't know anything from anything," Bozzini says. "You could tell Mark Burnett was telling her what to say, more or less."

Bozzini also thinks that the show was—to use a Trumpian term— rigged and that producers helped him win some of his tasks so he wouldn't go home. "So I'm pleading my case," he recalls about one conference room interaction. "I hear laughter coming from behind the windows," where Stewart was sitting. "So I'm like, 'Okay, they got a focus group out there, probably. Whoever gets the reaction is the person they are going to keep on the show.'"

Trump's firings were carried out like public floggings. Stewart's process was so much gentler and poorly suited to a brutal genre that Trump had helped pioneer. After she'd send a contestant home, Stewart would sit alone in her conference room and write them a handwritten letter, which she would then read in an earnest voice-over. The outcome was as bad in real life as it played on TV. "She has terrible penmanship, by the way, which is hilarious," Brennan says. "Like, abysmal. And her note to me was so nice. I shouldn't be ripping on her so bad, but I was blown away by how terrible her penmanship is."

The letter-writing exercise still draws mockery from Trump, even as he claims not to have watched: "I didn't see the Martha one." But then he manages to describe her method of getting rid of contestants in such specific detail. "She'd sit down and write, 'Dear Jim, it's wonderful getting to know you.' I said, 'You got to be kidding!'"

As for the rewards, Stewart—who was limited in how far she could travel due to her house arrest—sucked all the fun out of that too. "A lot of it was charity-related," says Howie Greenspan. "So you'd, like, do this crazy task and be up for a day straight. Finally, you win, and whereas in the Donald Trump one you'd be whisked off to a private island to get dinner, we had to go work in a nursery and plant trees for underprivileged neighborhoods, or we would go to a dog shelter. And I didn't mind doing it—but who wants to see this? I just thought it was a stupid version of the other one."

In the third episode, Burnett enlisted Trump and Melania to make a crossover appearance, getting dinner with the winning team that designed the best wedding cakes. The contestants, despite some preconceptions, were impressed by how much warmer he was than Stewart. "I went in thinking, 'This is the most tactless, classless guy ever,'" Brennan says. "And I remember telling people I was blown away by how charming and engaging he could be in small settings."

Stewart balked at notes from the network, which tried to shape her performance after they saw how stiff she looked on camera. "There were conversations about trying to get her to be a little more aggressive and to be a little more out there," Gaspin says. "But in the end, she was very controlling of who she wanted to present."

Bozzini didn't think that Stewart was invested in actually finding a future mentee. "It was all for Martha just to get her back on track, because she'd just come out of jail," he says. "She had zero allegiance to any of us. I mean, my wife gave birth while I was on that television show. This woman's a home-lifestyle guru. She didn't send anything for my baby! She's a punk in that respect."

By the time the finale aired, the contestants knew that Stewart was the one getting fired. The show came down to Frankel and Dawna Stone, a thirty-seven-year-old magazine publisher from St. Petersburg, Florida. And Burnett even bungled the landing, by giving Frankel—the future multimillionaire behind the lifestyle brand Skinnygirl—second place. Stone took the top prize, and she accepted a role in the publishing arm of Stewart's company.

How cooked was Martha? She pretended she didn't have time to continue as a reality TV host. Soon after, she returned to the relative safety of her talk show, which puttered on for years with its pleasantly calming household tasks. But she had missed the opportunity to redefine herself, and her *Apprentice* chapter was quickly forgotten.

Trump still gets the last word. "So we had Martha," he tells me. "How can you get better than Martha? And it failed miserably." He discusses her demise in the same manner that he talks about wiping out a political rival. "She bombed," Trump says. "Somebody said, 'Are you happy she bombed?' I said, 'Probably.'" Edging out media's most legendary type A figure, a striking blonde who struggled to connect with the very people whose support she needed—well, Trump wasn't tired of winning yet.

CHAPTER 9

"Beauty Is an Unfair Advantage"

The Apprentice positioned itself as the ultimate job interview for the best minds in business, but it had a better track record ginning up drama than finding potential Trump Organization executives. Still, the show sometimes managed to stumble upon candidates with quantifiable success in the real world. For season 4, airing in the fall of 2005 on the night after Martha Stewart's version, Donald Trump had originally suggested moving the show in a direction that NBC would never have allowed. He wanted to divide the teams by race—white versus Black contestants. The idea was deemed so offensive it never made its way to top executives at the network. Instead, Mark Burnett decided to amp up the show's business acumen and cast players with more impressive résumés.

And Randal Pinkett proved himself to be one of the most dynamic, accomplished contestants to compete on the series. A Black Rhodes scholar who'd earned five academic degrees, Pinkett, then a thirty-four-

year-old consulting firm owner from Somerset, New Jersey, auditioned
for the show at his wife's suggestion. He made it all the way to the end—
having joined the cast not knowing he was about to get sucked into one
of the most unhinged seasons of *The Apprentice* ever. Even as the latest
edition had been stacked with impressive professionals, they were subject
to the maelstrom caused by Trump, who finally got to call all the shots
without the supervision of Burnett, busy taking care of Martha Stewart.

To prepare for the show, Pinkett approached his audition as if he were
about to testify before Congress, not to play a game that mostly came
down to charisma and luck. In the spring of 2005, while in Los Angeles
for his final round of interviews, Pinkett purchased the season 1 DVDs
and started studying the early episodes during the hours of downtime in
his hotel room. "I watched that season three times over the course of a
week," Pinkett recalls. "I took notes, and I noticed what got people fired,
and what were the strategies that Bill and Kwame used to get to the final
two. I was extraordinarily familiar with it by the end of the week."

Pinkett remembers meeting Trump during this time. Feeling the heat
from Martha Stewart, Trump had followed through with his plan to get
even more closely involved with the contestant search, elbowing Burnett
out of having the final say and creating some awkwardness behind the
scenes about who was calling the shots. "My impression was he was this
larger-than-life persona," Pinkett says, describing Trump. "Of course,
I knew Donald. I grew up in New Jersey—I probably knew more than
most people knew about Donald. But I didn't know all there was to know
about Donald."

The dynamic of interviewing with both Trump and Burnett was a
whiplash-inducing challenge previous seasons' competitors hadn't faced.
"I walked into the room and made eye contact with Trump, and held
eye contact," says Kristi Caudell, then a twenty-four-year-old sales executive from Gainesville, Georgia. "And Mark Burnett was like, 'Oh, I love
a confident woman. Tell me about yourself.' And Trump, still staring
at me, he's like, 'I think she's intimidated.'" Caudell knew that she had
to win Trump over—and she did. She laughed, and shot back rapid-fire

comebacks in her southern drawl. "I was like, 'We're just people. We're at different stages of life.'"

According to Pinkett, Trump presented two different versions of himself to contestants that season. "One you see on the campaign trail now," Pinkett says. "He's funny. He's inviting. He's engaging." Pinkett pauses for a moment. "The other part was seeding division. I don't say that to sound colloquial. He would say in the interview, 'So why do you think you're better than him? What makes you more qualified than the guy sitting next to you?' You could already see from the initial auditioning process he was trying to pit us against each other."

Pinkett continued to observe both sides of Trump—the charming entertainer and the divisive provocateur—while filming *The Apprentice*. During their interactions in the boardroom, Pinkett had a front-row seat to how Trump regarded women. Beyond keeping the ratings up, Trump's biggest fixation that season was on Jennifer Murphy, a twenty-six-year-old ad sales manager and the 2003 winner of Miss Oregon USA, part of the Miss USA pageant system owned by Trump. "It was mostly among the men, where he'd say, 'Oh, she's hot. Oh, I'd love to sleep with her,'" Pinkett says. "Jennifer Murphy—that's who he'd talk about."

The Apprentice had returned to its gender-war roots, dividing up into teams of men and women. So in the beginning of season 4, Trump once again found himself in hours-long boardrooms with just the male players, during which he was able to speak freely. Emboldened by his stardom, Trump openly bragged about his desire to have sex with a woman seeking his employment. "I felt it was inappropriate, and not knowing Donald as well as I do now, it was in some ways shocking," Pinkett says. "This was a business show about business professionals. There's no place for those conversations in a business context. It was unacceptable."

The nation and the world would come to know Trump's approach to discussing women in the workplace. The infamous *Access Hollywood* tape, in which Trump told the TV host Billy Bush that he likes to grab women "by the pussy," was released toward the end of the 2016 campaign, but was recorded in September 2005—the month Pinkett's season of *The Appren-*

tice began airing. And on set, without Burnett as an interceptor of bad behavior, Trump wasn't holding back in season 4.

In the seventh episode, for instance, the teams had to teach a class at the Learning Annex. The losing group had picked a lesson on sex at work, parceling lessons about the intricacies of dating a co-worker. Trump was confused at how poorly the contestants did in explaining the boundaries around sex in the workplace—perhaps because for him there were none. In the boardroom later on, Trump asked one contestant, "Are you a homosexual?" before expressing his own support of gay people with a convoluted analogy. "That's why they have menus in restaurants, you know?" Trump said, to comedic effect, on TV. "I like steak; someone else likes spaghetti. It's a great world." Trump then blurted an inappropriate question at the project manager, Adam Israelov, twenty-two, asking him, "Have you ever had sex before?"

"Honestly, sir, I don't feel comfortable answering that question," replied the terrified contestant.

"How can you be afraid to talk about sex?" Trump said. "Sex is, like, not a big deal. How can you be afraid?"

Trump wasn't done humiliating Israelov. "Listen, Adam isn't good with sex. He might be in ten years, but right now you don't feel comfortable with sex. Do you agree with it? Someday, you will. It's gotten me into a lot of trouble, Adam. It's cost me a lot of money. Do you understand that?" Trump was giving America a glimpse into how he might have taught his own kids about the birds and the bees, and it wasn't how an average dad in America would approach the topic.

In a previous episode, Trump's object of affection, Jennifer Murphy, had lost a task where she was supposed to design a parade float for the upcoming Sony Pictures film *Zathura*, the sci-fi children's movie from the soon-to-be *Iron Man* director Jon Favreau. Murphy, as the project manager, brought only one other teammate—the outspoken Caudell—into the boardroom with her. Producers were angling for Murphy to get the ax, because she kept mispronouncing the name of the movie in their presentation—a rookie mistake that made for good TV. But Caudell committed the bigger error of taunting Murphy in front of Trump. "She was just a beauty pageant girl who sold Yellow Pages ads, nothing accomplished before the show," Caudell says now. "And so when I'm sitting with her, I'm just saying, 'Can you even spell "integrity"? Can you give me a definition?' I was just young and rude." In the boardroom, Trump lost his temper with Caudell's abrasiveness and asked her to beg for his mercy. When Caudell refused, he went off script and fired her instead.

There was a special visitor to the set that day. "Actually, Martha Stewart was getting ready to film, so she was behind the glass, and I didn't know it," Caudell says. "She and Mark Burnett, they watched." Burnett was trying to coach Stewart on Trump's TV-ready directness in firing people, but the lesson didn't go as planned, as chaos erupted backstage. Instead of observing how Trump got rid of contestants, Stewart saw the show scramble to try to save someone who shouldn't have been dumped.

"So I get on the elevator—get right back off," Caudell recalls. The producer Jay Bienstock, who was running *The Apprentice*, had asked her to wait. "And they hold me for four hours. Because Burnett and Bienstock are asking Trump, 'What the hell did you just do?' And Trump's like, 'Bring them back!'" Trump was evidently willing to reshoot the entire boardroom with a different firing. But Burnett decided it was too late, and it would be too scandalous if it ever came out they had tried to stage a new outcome.

For all that, Pinkett managed to have a largely positive experience. As a former athlete on the Rutgers track-and-field team, he found himself deeply invested in the competitive aspect of each episode. When he watched his season back, he saw that he and his teammates all looked sleepless and haggard, but there was a thrill in trying to outmaneuver each other—with the strategic jiu-jitsu, introduced in season 1, of each week's losing team getting to steal an opposing player. Pinkett, who was the person that each team wanted to steal during season 4, quickly became the clear front-runner—winning all three of his tasks as project manager. As Pinkett revisits his memories from the show, he recalls Bienstock telling him, "Your job is to try to win. Our job is to try to get ratings. Don't confuse the two."

Not that Pinkett needed any reminders. He'd strategized with his employees and friends before filming began, and played out different scenarios before he'd arrived at Trump Tower. He shaped his public TV persona around two guiding principles. First, he saw the show as an opportunity to present himself as an innovative businessman. "We decided, 'Brand yourself as a problem solver,'" Pinkett says. "But the second piece, which I actually think was more important: 'Treat people fairly.' Don't succumb to stabbing people in the back, finger-pointing, ratting people out in the boardroom, undermining the project manager." Pinkett also had a deep emotional arc on the show, one he never could or would have planned. He tugged at America's heartstrings when he had to leave for a few days due to his grandmother's death. (Burnett was more forgiving than he had been on *Survivor* in letting *Apprentice* contestants go home when faced with such circumstances.) Overall, Pinkett had set a high bar for himself: "Maintain the same integrity as you maintain outside of reality TV."

Remarkably, Pinkett's take-the-high-road strategy worked for a genre in which integrity (the word Caudell had suspected Murphy couldn't even spell) usually results in getting the boot. And for the viewers at home, Trump's antics—including uncontrollable boardroom histrionics that went on for three or four hours—were tidily covered up in the editing room.

The editors had to work overtime to make sense of one particular boardroom scene in which Trump, supposedly frustrated with many of the players, conducted a mass firing. In the sixth episode, the teams were supposed to stage an interactive event to help drive sales at Dick's Sporting Goods. The losing team—which had set up an indoor baseball field to play a game—saw sales drop by 34 percent overall because they'd taken up too much space, distracting customers from shopping. As a result, Trump supersized his toughness, knowing that it would play in contrast to Stewart's softness on Wednesdays that same season. In that episode, Trump fired four contestants in a single swipe. "Life continues," he said on TV, dressed in a tuxedo for a formal dinner he was attending later. (Has there ever been another prime-time host who couldn't be bothered to change for his own TV show?) It was a dramatic plot twist that NBC milked in promos, hoping to win back some of the show's erstwhile fans.

To the relief of everyone who worked on the show, the mass firing meant that Trump would finally get separated from his latest obsession. Murphy, along with three men, was among the casualties of that board-room as Trump finally caved to the producers' wishes. But not before she became among the season's most talked-about figures: *Entertainment Weekly*, then the arbiter of pop-culture taste, had nicknamed her "1987 Hair Barbie."

Donald Trump might have been beating Martha Stewart, but on Thurs-day nights *The Apprentice* was now getting its clock cleaned by *CSI*. But Trump didn't let the Nielsen ratings stop him from pretending that he was still TV's top star. The season 4 premiere of *The Apprentice* debuted to 9.9 million viewers, down 6 million viewers from season 3, and it be-came immediately clear how badly Jeff Zucker had misjudged the public's appetite for competing versions of the show. Still, between the two hosts, Trump was ahead by a margin of several million viewers. He found joy in clobbering Martha Stewart, privately blaming NBC for diluting his brand, but resolving to charge ahead. Trump juiced the finale with an-other twist that—even in the show's weakened state—became one of the most memorable moments of the TV season.

The last episode came down to two capable, likable contestants: Pin-kett and Rebecca Jarvis, a twenty-three-year-old financial journalist from Chicago. While Pinkett was still the favorite, there were warning signs that Trump could be wavering in whether to hire his first Black Appren-tice. Pinkett recalls reading an interview in *Us Weekly* where Trump of-fered adjectives to describe each finalist. "When asked about Rebecca, he said, 'She's beautiful,'" Pinkett says. "When asked about me, for the lead-ing contestant, he said I'm lazy. Based on what?"

As a writer for *Crain's Chicago Business*, Jarvis had auditioned for *The Apprentice* so she could write about the process, just as I had. But she never published her article because . . . she got on the show. Jarvis managed to find a way to shine on TV despite a painful injury. She broke her ankle three days into production, during a reward in which her team got to play hockey with the New York Islanders. Jarvis gained Trump's admiration by powering through the rest of the season on crutches, hobbling in and out of the boardroom with a determined smile on her face. In the final task, yet another charity auction, Pinkett raised $11,000 during a softball game he hosted for Autism Speaks, while Jarvis thought it was tacky to ask for in-person donations at a comedy show for the Elizabeth Glaser Pediatric AIDS Foundation. Her tally was effectively zero dollars.

Trump knew he had to choose Pinkett, the clear favorite on the show, even if he personally liked Jarvis. On the night of December 15, 2005, on live TV at Lincoln Center, Trump said, "Rarely have I seen a leader as good as you. And you lead through niceness . . . Randal, you're hired." Then Trump kept talking: He'd secretly decided, along with Burnett, that he wanted to offer a second job to Jarvis. But rather than reveal the surprise himself, he'd pose the hypothetical to Pinkett, asking whether he should hire Jarvis too. Trump thought that when Pinkett agreed, the show would engineer a feel-good moment entering the holidays and thrust the final stake in the heart of Stewart with a big celebration around his double winners.

Only that's not what happened. Pinkett had heard murmurs that Trump might be naming two winners that night, and he'd come up with his own plan. "If he had said, 'Randal, I'm hiring both of you,' I had a scripted response prepared," Pinkett says. "And it was, 'If you cannot see, Donald, that I'm the sole and only winner, then guess what? I quit. You're fired!'"

Trump spared himself that humiliation. His uncanny intuition for made-for-TV moments might have tipped him off about playing too fast and loose with someone as strategic as Pinkett. After shushing the crowd cheering for the first Black *Apprentice* winner, Trump presented his question to Pinkett about offering a second job to Jarvis. Genuinely surprised that he was asked to steer this decision, Pinkett told Trump that he shouldn't hire Jarvis. "I firmly believe that this is *The Apprentice*—that there is one and only one apprentice. And if you're going to hire someone tonight, it should be one," he said on TV. Suddenly, Pinkett had gone from being the guy America loved to someone who was getting loudly booed. Trump's feel-good finale ended suddenly on a sour note as he abruptly closed the show with one winner, leaving the country to debate what had just happened.

"I think he made himself unpopular by not doing it," Trump says now, when asked to revisit that moment. "He said no, and most people thought—especially the way I put it—he'd say yes. It was a very interesting time. I thought he was going to be, you know, a little more generous. He wasn't. That's his problem."

Pinkett counters by saying that Trump tried to dilute his win because of the color of his skin. "In retrospect, I would argue this: it was a combination of racism and sexism," Pinkett says. "I think he was enthralled with Rebecca and the story with her broken leg. And he was not wanting to see a Black man as the winner of his show."

At the cast after-party at Planet Hollywood in Times Square, a nascent TMZ, which had come into existence the month before, reported that the only thing anyone could talk about was Pinkett's decision to block the show's runner-up. "I think everyone was surprised," Jarvis told TMZ that night. "It seemed out of line with how Randal has endeared himself." The reality-TV-focused news site Reality Blurred called Pinkett's decision "selfish," and many viewers agreed. But the discussions being had that night were very different in living rooms in Black households across the country.

Trump had succeeded in sowing division. "My dad and I would talk about it years later as the first red flag," says Arisha Hatch, who served as chief of campaigns at the progressive nonprofit Color of Change, devoted to overcoming obstacles that hold Black people back. "Black people remember that moment. You know how you'd watch a reality show, rooting for someone? That was Randal to many Black families—a 'respectable Black.' Probably, at the time, he was one of the first Black reality TV winners, and Trump tried to take it away from him."

Pinkett didn't have time to reflect on what had happened before NBC sent him on a press tour where he was bombarded with questions about his decision not to share his victory with a white woman. Before Twitter, an arena where viewers would be able to push back on pop culture moments in real time, the narrative around the finale soon made it seem as if Pinkett's hiring were somehow controversial. "After I win this show, I'm on this media frenzy," Pinkett says. "I didn't have any real one-on-one time with Donald."

Pinkett finally got the chance to voice his concerns in a meeting at Trump's office in Trump Tower. "I confronted him after the finale. Top of my mind is, what in the world just happened? I'm mad. I'm angry. You insulted me, and this wasn't a tie." Pinkett had hired the show's publicist, Jim Dowd, to represent him, as some of the other contestants had, and Dowd sat in to mediate. Trump normally loved spending time alone with the winners, to congratulate them, offer them praise, and encourage them to drum up press for the Trump brand. Yet that day was full of tension.

"By that point, I had already had a chance to reflect on the finale," Pinkett says. "I had seen interviews with Donald, with his post-finale analysis, where he started out saying things along the lines of, 'Randal should have shared the title with Rebecca.' And then he'd pivot to, 'Randal's decision is more like art; the more I look back on it, the more I think he showed toughness, and it was the right decision.'" Pinkett thinks Trump started to tread carefully based on some backlash, because he didn't want to hurt his own image. "I think because he took heat for what he pulled. Although I took my own heat."

Since Dowd had told him that Trump wanted to fix things, Pinkett presented him with a list of requests. "I said, 'Donald, I think you should fund publicity for me to enact some sort of damage control—put a more positive spin on this. I think you need to say something more definitive in support of me as your apprentice.' He said, 'Randal, I can't do that.'"

Trump, never willing to shoulder even a little blame in the event that it would make him look weak, wasn't about to issue a public statement in support of his chosen winner.

"And then," Pinkett recalls, "Dowd kind of stepped in and said, 'We can figure out some other strategies together, and how we can get some puff piece.' I remember he said 'puff piece.' I didn't know what a puff piece was until then."

For his apprenticeship, Pinkett was tasked with overseeing the $110 million renovation of Trump's three failing Atlantic City casinos—the Trump Taj Mahal, Trump Plaza Hotel and Casino, and Trump Marina. (Not even *The Apprentice* could save them. All three would go bankrupt, and after bleeding $350 million in a span of a few years, the Taj Mahal shut down on October 10, 2016, just weeks before Trump was elected president.) Even after the negative circumstances surrounding his hiring, Pinkett tried to be a good, hardworking employee for Trump. "So I did not bite my tongue in terms of my opinion of the finale, but I also did seek to establish a productive working relationship with him and the other executives with Trump Entertainment Resorts," Pinkett says. "I would go to casting calls. I was invited to Trump Tower for press conferences. I was embraced into that inner circle."

As he went about his year, Pinkett noticed something. "I was the only Black person or person of color that I met in an executive position for my entire year at the Trump Organization," Pinkett says. Pinkett recalls that among executives at Trump Mortgage, GoTrump, Trump Ice, Trump Institute, Trump University, and Trump Entertainment Resorts, he'd be surrounded by a homogeneous group of leaders. "There was not only no racial diversity," Pinkett says. "I would argue there was no diversity of thought either. If you disagreed with Donald, he put you out of his inner circle. He didn't invite in differing perspectives. He invited affirming perspectives—yes-men, yes-women, 'Yes, Donald.'"

It's not surprising that Pinkett and Trump didn't remain on favorable terms. When Pinkett returned to give an update on his apprenticeship at the season 5 finale, which had become customary for the show's winner, he took a few seconds on TV to plug his own website. Trump erupted backstage, "Who does Randal think he is, promoting himself at the finale?" Pinkett didn't understand the fuss. "Donald is furious. I played the game; the game didn't play me."

Pinkett was supposed to be in Los Angeles the next week, to fill in as a guest judge on an episode of season 6—to be filmed for the first time outside New York. But Trump tried to rescind the offer. "Jay Bienstock calls me and says, 'Donald says you can't come to Los Angeles. He's pissed.' I said, 'Jay, how can he be mad at me for doing what he does? He's the king of self-promotion. I did exactly what's according to the Trump playbook.'" By appealing to his ego, Pinkett got Trump to back down. "I said, 'Tell Donald I apologize for the self-promotion.' Jay speaks to Donald, calms him down. I came out and filmed the episode."

There was a certain co-dependence between the reality TV boss and his apprentice. While Trump might have preferred to fire Pinkett, he knew it still benefited him to keep him in the fold. As for Pinkett, *The Apprentice* undeniably opened doors. In 2009, even though he didn't have any political experience, Pinkett cropped up on the then New Jersey governor Jon Corzine's short list for a lieutenant governor running mate, and Trump enthusiastically endorsed him.

Pinkett didn't get the job, but he continued to run his consulting firm, published a book, and became a motivational speaker. In April 2016, he was back on Trump's bad side when he held a press conference with five other *Apprentice* contestants—including the first-season runner-up, Kwame Jackson—to disavow Trump's campaign for president.

"When I'm announced to be a possible lieutenant governor, Donald says, 'Randal is wonderful; he'll do a fantastic job,'" Pinkett recalls. "When I come out against his candidacy, he says, 'Randal is a loser and a failure.' And he went public with that. Petulant—that's the word for Donald."

There's another word that Pinkett uses. "I think Donald's a racist," Pinkett says. "And I think he consciously and unconsciously and deliberately cast Black people in a negative light." Pinkett doesn't question for a second whether he made the right call in not accepting Trump's suggestion to share the title with Jarvis. "As an African American, there's a particular point of pride that can almost bring me to tears," Pinkett says. "I will tell you to this day the thing that people say to me most frequently when they recognize me from the show is, 'I remember the finale and how you stood up to Donald, and you didn't accept sharing the title.'"

Trump, for his part, still doesn't understand why Pinkett refused his offer. "I thought it was a cool idea," Trump tells me. "I thought it was great for everybody." Even though the finale didn't go as planned, Trump still regards it fondly, because he got *The Apprentice* back in the news. "I thought it would be good for him," Trump says of Pinkett. "I don't know what happened to him. Some of these guys did great afterward." Like the season 1 winner who never gave him pushback in public—even when he was in the White House. "Bill Rancic did great. He worked for me for a while, and he was good. A lot of these guys work for you for a while. Some of these guys are less good."

One non-winner Trump stayed in close contact with was Jennifer Murphy. For years after she was fired from *The Apprentice*, Trump continued to see her, flirt with her, and even kiss her unexpectedly outside his office. This extended a relationship that had begun even before she'd appeared on the show—a serious conflict of interest, even by the relatively lawless standards of reality television. "I was a Donald Trump fan from the age of probably eighteen or nineteen," Murphy tells me, describing how she'd read *The Art of the Deal* as a teenager, before her success in beauty pageants. "It took a few tries, but I finally did become Miss Oregon. I think I was twenty-five at the time." That's when she decided that she might be equally suited for a different competition. "My favorite show was *The Apprentice*," she says. "My goal was to become a contestant."

In April 2004, Murphy was in Los Angeles, competing as Miss Oregon USA in the Miss USA pageant. She received a tip from someone that Trump would be making a detour backstage, as he loved to do, before the start of the show. "I hear, 'Last call!' Pageant is about to start," Murphy says. "I grab my shoes. I'm barefoot, running through the hallway, and I run right into Trump. I literally fell right on top of him. He's like, 'Who are you?' I said, 'I'm sorry. I'm Miss Oregon, but I'm late for a pageant and I've got to run.' He and his security guard were standing there, chuckling."

As she took her position on TV, Murphy could see Trump in the audience, pointing and smiling at her, offering his approval. "I said, 'I think he's rooting for me,'" she recalls. "I made Top 15, Top 10, and then I didn't make it to Top 5, so I was out. The pageant ends; the winner is crowned. Trump walks up on the stage and straight over to me, and he says, 'Miss Oregon, you're my favorite! But I can't get involved with judging.' I was like, 'Thank you so much.'" She told him that she loved *The Apprentice* and would love to be considered for it. "He said, 'You'd be great. Here's my card. Make sure to call me. I'll make it happen.'"

Murphy says at the after-party, she got into a fight with her then boyfriend and somehow lost Trump's card. That night, she also met the man who would later become her husband, Bill Dorfman, a dentist to the stars featured on *Extreme Makeover*. Her exchange with Trump was just one part of an eventful evening, and Murphy decided later to make a run for *The Apprentice*, even without Trump's contact. "I decide to try out for the show the old-fashioned way," says Murphy, who booked a flight from Medford, Oregon, where she was living, to San Diego, one of the cities where the production was holding auditions for season 4. "I was wearing my same suit that I was wearing for Miss Oregon and for Miss USA for the interview," she says. "It was my magic suit."

The producers, not knowing that she'd already brokered a backstage handshake deal with Trump to join the show, put her through as a finalist to Los Angeles. In the sequestered hotel room, she remembers hearing that she should be prepared for anything on the last day. "They lined me up with four other women and walked us in—and there's Donald Trump!" Murphy says. While Trump didn't know she'd be there, he greeted her affectionately. "And I said, 'Mr. Trump!' He goes, 'Miss Oregon!' I go, 'I lost your card. I had to try out like everybody else, but here I am.' He's like, 'I'm so glad to see you here.' The other women were pissed."

Trump made no secret of his appreciation for Murphy. He even broadcast his attraction for her in the interview about the show's retooling that ran in *The New York Times* ahead of the season. Trump called Murphy "one of the most beautiful women I've ever seen" in the paper of record. He described to the *Times* how he overruled other producers—he was referring to Burnett, though he didn't name him—in choosing her. "They said she was too beautiful. I said, 'Excuse me, there is no such thing as too beautiful.' They said, 'Donald, she's so beautiful, she's not credible.' I said, 'No. 1, she happens to be smart. No. 2, she's very beautiful—congratulations, she's going on the show.'"

In a rambling answer that invoked the Declaration of Independence, Trump, playing into the conceit that the show hadn't already filmed, admitted to the *Times* that he'd have a hard time firing Murphy. "I try to be objective," he said. "But beauty is an unfair advantage for certain people. When they came up with the wonderful statement, all men are created equal, never has there been a more false statement. It sounds brilliant; it reads beautifully. But some people are geniuses. Some are beautiful."

Behind the scenes, there had been real pushback from Burnett about Murphy's inclusion, given that the mandate for the season had been to cast only business overachievers—not beauty pageant winners. But Trump, who'd granted himself ultimate say in selecting the contestants as payback for Martha Stewart making a run for his crown, ignored Burnett's objections. He thought that Murphy would make good TV, equating her looks with ratings.

During the second episode, the contestants were supposed to create an advertising campaign for Lamborghini. Murphy credits herself with coming up with some of the best marketing ideas on the women's team, and before they'd even won, Trump was her biggest supporter. "After we gave the presentation, Trump said, 'Jennifer, come over here!' He had me meet the people who were the heads of Lamborghini." Murphy recalls Trump telling them, "Jennifer is Miss Oregon. She's my favorite," just a few feet away from the other players.

As the doting continued, some of the players began to resent Murphy. "They're like, 'We've got to get rid of her, because Trump likes her so much,'" Murphy says. "It was really challenging for me to be on the show with that situation going on. But it was okay. I stood my ground, and stood up for myself." Yet even *she* admits that the extra attention would sometimes be uncomfortable. "We'd be right in the middle of a heated debate in the boardroom, and Trump would say, 'Jennifer, have you always been so beautiful?'" There's little wonder the other contestants were envious.

Trump says that he was smitten with Murphy and that's why he cast her on the show. "I thought she was really beautiful. You know what I mean?" Trump says, years later, when I bring up her name and ask whether she was his favorite contestant. "Not a question of favorite," Trump answers. "Somebody said, 'Who do you think was the most beautiful?' Okay. I don't know if she was good or bad."

Trump turns to Margo Martin, his deputy director of communications, who replaced Hope Hicks after he left the White House and brought new elegance to his inner circle. The twentysomething aide, often disguised in designer sunglasses (and once mistaken for Melania by Fox News), travels by Trump's side, preferring to chronicle "the real @realDonaldTrump the media won't show you!" with her iPhone videos. The *Daily Mail* described Martin as "VERY glamorous," the rare case, perhaps, of a newspaper giving Trump good publicity.

"You know who I'm talking about?" Trump asks Martin. "Jennifer?"

Martin's at a loss; she was only ten when that season of *The Apprentice* aired.

"I get along with everybody, to be honest," Trump says. "I kept a lot of them. Some did very well. Some didn't. It's like the *Ziegfeld Follies*." (The famed theatrical revue was also before Martin's time.)

When Trump finally fired Murphy in the surprise boardroom massacre, she was furious. "I threw my microphone off in the elevator," she says, re-membering the moment producers escorted her out of Trump Tower. "I was like, 'This show is rigged.' But then I realized I got to stay in New York for a full month on Uncle B." That's what the Thursday night contestants that season called Burnett, who was like an absentee relative because he wasn't around.

According to Murphy, Trump's attentiveness actually helped her re-gain her confidence in business. "I don't feel that beautiful all the time," she says. "I was one of twelve kids and chubby-cheeked with braces." Her conservative Catholic parents didn't watch *The Apprentice*, because they didn't think it was wholesome. "Trump standing up for me and even over-ruling Mark Burnett's decision to this day has a lasting effect," Murphy says. "It's helped me feel like I can push through boundaries and some of the self-doubt that I had to overcome."

After she was fired, Trump called her the next day to check in. "I didn't want to fire you, but the producers kind of made me. But I still want to hire you," Trump told her. To avoid the appearance of impropriety, he explained, as he had to Sam Solovey in season 1, "they don't want me to make an official offer until after the season airs, but let's talk about it."

Murphy says that Trump sent her on meetings with his top execu-tives, including Ivanka, and he'd offer her two jobs—to work in the Miss Universe organization or at Trump National Golf Club in Rancho Palos Verdes, California. She appreciated his mentorship. "I think he looked at me in a way like he does his daughter," Murphy says. "But also, I did think he had the hots for me a little bit."

As she was weighing his job offers, after a meeting with him in his office one day, Trump walked Murphy to the elevator. No one was around, and he leaned over and kissed her on the lips. "I mean, he didn't push it," Murphy says. "It was like, one, two, three—no tongue. I just let him give me the kiss. And I kind of turned red."

Murphy doesn't think it was necessarily inappropriate. "I wasn't of-fended," she says. "He didn't grab me. It was done in a way where I could have pushed back. I know the difference, and I can feel the difference when someone is being predatory versus someone just really likes beautiful women. I think, if anything, he likes beautiful women too much—if that's a flaw."

She decided to turn down both jobs, because she wanted to move to Los Angeles to pursue acting. She remembers getting a call from him one night when he was in town, asking her to come meet him in his room at the Beverly Hills Hotel, but Murphy drew the line. "I have a conscience," she says. "I have integrity. I made up a reason I was busy."

But when she was planning her walk down the aisle, she asked Trump for a favor: she wanted to get married at one of his properties. "The director of sales said, 'Don't even ask him. He never gives a discount,'" Murphy says. "I called him up: 'I am getting married. I know you don't like giving discounts, but can I have a discount at your Palos Verdes golf estate?' He said yes." How much of a discount did Trump give her? "It was 20 percent off."

Murphy also persuaded *Access Hollywood* to do a week of segments on her July 2006 wedding, narrated by Billy Bush—no stranger to Trump's approach to women—and Nancy O'Dell. Murphy called Trump again, to ask if he'd tape one of the spots with her, as good promotion for both of them. "He said, 'You know what? Sure. I'll only have fifteen minutes, but let's do it.'"

He ended up staying a lot longer. "He loves the cameras," Murphy says. "We were filming for quite a while that day. He gave me a kiss on the cheek on camera." And then he broke away from the crew to tell her that he couldn't believe she was marrying her dentist fiancé. "He put his arm around me," Murphy says. "It was off camera. I think he smacked my butt a little. I was like, 'Goodness gracious!'"

They kept in touch as Murphy continued to appear on TV, talking about *The Apprentice*. In December 2006, when Trump got into a long, protracted public feud with *The View*'s Rosie O'Donnell, after she made fun of his hair and claimed he'd gone bankrupt, the media circus that ensued meant practically every *Apprentice* contestant was asked to chime in. Murphy recalls being in the greenroom of an entertainment show, not

sure what she could say and still stay in Trump's good graces. She asked
the other guest, the power attorney Gloria Allred, who'd later represent
several women who accused Trump of abuse, for advice. "Talk from your
heart—don't compromise," Allred told her.

So Murphy said on TV about Trump's attacks on O'Donnell, "That's
not how I'd handle it." By her own description, it was a tepid response, but
Trump saw the clip and considered it treasonous. When Murphy invited
Trump to the premiere of a short film that she'd starred in, he declined.
"He said, 'You're so disloyal after everything I've done for you,'" Murphy
recalls.

The next time Murphy saw Trump, at the after-party for another season of *The Apprentice*, he was still mad at her. Standing in a group of people, he huffed, "You all see Jennifer right there? After everything I did, she
goes and sides with Rosie O'Donnell."

They stopped talking. In the summer of 2007, after only a year of marriage, Murphy filed for divorce, and she found herself back in New York,
again having lost Trump's phone number. So she walked into the lobby
of Trump Tower and asked a security guard to call his office and let him
know she was downstairs, wanting to see him without an appointment.
Trump said that she could come up in ten minutes.

"So what happened?" he asked her. "Why did you get a divorce?"

He gently ribbed her about the circumstances of her split, and they
became friends again. "We basically reconnected," Murphy says.

When Trump ran for office, Murphy told a reporter that Trump had
kissed her. But she didn't ever see it as abuse or as him taking advantage of
his power. Murphy defended him, unlike at least twenty women who have
come forward to accuse Trump of sexual misconduct or inappropriate behavior. "I think he probably secretly liked it," she says, about her sharing
the story of their kiss. "He was probably like, 'Damn it, now she's helping
add credibility to people who I didn't kiss. Yeah, I kissed Miss Oregon.'"

Murphy sums up the totality of their friendship over the years: "There
is something sexy about a man who takes control and gets things done,"
she says. "And I've always loved when someone is brilliant. I wasn't physi-

cally attracted to him, but I was and am attracted to who he represents—now and then." She says she will support him in the 2024 election. "And I think he always had it in him to help our country."

I ask Murphy if she could have ever seen herself having a romantic relationship with Trump. "I don't think so," she says. "I never would have seen it becoming more than just good friends."

Several months later, on another phone call, Murphy tells me she's putting the finishing touches on an independent film that she's directing and starring in, where she plays a white woman who becomes a ninja and mimics an Asian accent. (She's hoping to ask Trump to shoot a cameo.) Her movie is based on a viral song that she wrote called, "I Want to Be Neenja," which has landed more than eight million views on YouTube. The comments are full of accusations of cultural appropriation and racism.

Sitting down with Trump one afternoon, I'm reminded of something that season 1 contestant Sam Solovey had described to me. As a presidential candidate, Trump had a long list of accusers detailing his alleged abusive and predatory behavior. But when *The Apprentice* began, Trump, in his late fifties, had much younger women hitting on him. Does he remember that?

Trump's face brightens. "I can't say it," Trump says. "But it's true."

CHAPTER 10

Boss of All Celebrities

On January 3, 2008, as Barack Obama declared victory over Hillary Clinton in the Iowa caucuses, Donald Trump was making headlines of his own. That night, he launched *The Celebrity Apprentice*, a reboot that enlisted C-list celebrities instead of civilians as contestants to fill airtime on NBC during a writers' strike. The same night Obama promised a rapturous crowd in Des Moines that "together, ordinary people can do extraordinary things," roughly eleven million viewers watched Trump deploy a smattering of pseudo-stars to sell hot dogs on the streets of Manhattan. By the end of the episode, Trump dismissed the *Playboy* centerfold Tiffany Fallon as the weak link on the women's team—led, of course, by Omarosa Manigault, who'd graduated from would-be business tycoon to demi-celebrity on the strength of her connection to Trump. "You're very beautiful," Trump told Fallon in the boardroom. "But you're very low-key in terms of your beauty compared to Playmates of the Year. I've known a lot of Playmates of the Year."

A new America appeared to be on the horizon, and Trump was undergoing his own metamorphosis. With Ivanka and Don Jr. by his side as judges (elbowing out Carolyn Kepcher and George Ross), Trump was pulling out all the stops to reclaim his mantle as the president of the ratings. The stories in the press that week focused on Obama's mojo, but in the entertainment pages the Trump machine sucked up plenty of oxygen, too. *The Celebrity Apprentice*'s first fired contestant did a round of interviews the next day, answering probing questions, such as this one from *TV Guide*: Could Ivanka cut it as a *Playboy* centerfold? "Oh, definitely!" Fallon said. "You *know* Hef loves blondes."

The Celebrity Apprentice was born not out of creativity or ingenuity but rather out of desperation. When Ben Silverman arrived at NBC as the new chairman in 2007, he was alarmed at how little programming the network had in development. Needing to fill hours of empty airtime as threats of a strike by the Writers Guild of America hung in the air, Silverman came up with the idea of putting celebrities in the boardroom with Trump and having them face off in competitions for charity. (The strike lasted from November 2007 through February 2008, blowing up that TV season.) NBC would start by scheduling *The Celebrity Apprentice* on Thursday nights, eventually moving it to Sunday nights and stretching the show to two hours, the length of a movie. When Silverman shared the idea, Mark Burnett didn't think Trump would go for it, but told him to try.

Silverman was clever in his pitch to Trump. "I say, 'Donald, I have an idea. I want to keep your show going, but I want to make it a celebrity version, and you will be the ultimate celebrity in charge of the other celebrities.'" That's all Trump needed to hear.

One afternoon at Trump Tower, Trump admits to me that he didn't love the name *The Celebrity Apprentice*, indicating that he'd resented the perception that he needed support from a mishmash of vaguely familiar personalities to keep his reality series afloat. After Randal Pinkett's hiring in season 4, which divided the show's fans, and Martha Stewart's failed attempt to mount her own spin-off, Trump saw the ratings for *The Apprentice* continue to plummet in seasons 5 and 6. He'd tried everything he could think of to drum up press—picking fights to coincide with *The*

Apprentice's press cycles, like when he issued a public letter to Stewart in February 2006, right before the start of season 5, that read, "Your performance was terrible in that the show lacked mood, temperament and just about everything a show needs for success."

Later that year, around Christmas 2006, before the start of season 6, Trump had stopped by every media outlet to attack Rosie O'Donnell. She'd delivered a monologue on *The View*, in the midst of his publicly announcing a "second chance" for a Miss USA winner who had entered rehab, that she did not consider him a moral exemplar. The Donald-Rosie war of words eventually led to Trump's longtime friend Barbara Walters condemning him live on *The View*—a hot topic, but not a story that translated into what Trump valued most: ratings.

Bringing in a cast of known quantities was an admission that Trump was no longer carrying the show on his own. But at least he still got to keep top billing as a ringleader of chaos. "I don't even call it *The Celebrity Apprentice*," Trump says. "I never used the term *Celebrity Apprentice*. I just call it *The Apprentice*. I always called it *The Apprentice* purposefully, because it was *The Apprentice*. I thought it was a good name, but I just call it *The Apprentice*." Trump worried the title change would erase the public's memory of his years of success on TV. "I thought it was disrespectful," he says.

As we gather today in a boardroom at Trump Tower, Trump is watching a memorable scene from the second season of *The Celebrity Apprentice*, from April 26, 2009, during which Joan Rivers—perhaps the only media figure as shamelessly canny about leveraging drama to her benefit—storms off the show because her daughter, Melissa, also a competitor, gets fired. "Joan was so angry," Trump says, with excitement in his voice. "I mean, I got the biggest stars to go on that show," he says. "It was so easy. You know, Joan Rivers wouldn't do a show like that normally, right?" In fact, Rivers famously built her career on a willingness to appear anywhere there were cameras, including as a red-carpet host at awards ceremonies. "She went crazy when I fired the daughter."

The mayhem around Melissa's firing was a juicy, dramatic story line that proved just how far *The Apprentice* had drifted from the instructive, aspirational show about business that Burnett had created. To the delight of NBC executives, this boardroom axing spilled into full-on pandemonium. Upon learning about her daughter's fate on a reality TV contest, Joan had exploded in anger at the two contestants who'd outlasted Melissa: the *Playboy* model Brande Roderick and the poker player Annie Duke.

"Your people, you give money with blood on it," Joan yelled at Duke. "I met you people in Vegas for forty years. None of them have last names. None of them! You're a poker player! A poker player. That's beyond white trash. Poker players are trash, darling." But Joan's tantrum wasn't even the biggest meltdown that night. In the waiting room outside the boardroom, Melissa screamed expletives at the crew, refusing to do an exit interview—or to exit the show.

"She was so nasty," Trump says. "I hear Melissa yelling outside. She was yelling at everybody!" As Donald and Ivanka took cover in the boardroom, Melissa carried her wardrobe from the show in both hands and departed Trump Tower with Joan, who hadn't even been fired. For the Rivers family at least, a spot on *The Celebrity Apprentice* was worth fighting for.

"Melissa was—" Trump goes off the record to tell me what he really thinks of this volatile behavior. (In general, Trump looks upon nepo babies—except for his own children—as entitled brats.) "How about this?" Trump continues, more diplomatically, back on the record. "Joan loved Melissa more than anything she's ever loved before. She thought Melissa was the end-all, and she went totally crazy in defense of her daughter. Oh, they were both yelling. It was great TV. But maybe Joan had more of a right to be yelling."

Trump says that Rivers loved him. "I thought she might have been a Republican," he says. "I know one thing: she voted for me, according to what she said." Intriguing—but for the fact that Rivers, who passed away on September 4, 2014, wasn't alive when he ran for president. As part of his election fraud claims in 2020, Trump insisted that thousands of dead people cast ballots in Pennsylvania, Michigan, and Georgia for Joe Biden. Today, though, he's proud to collect the vote of a dead celebrity. "Despite the anger about Melissa, she was a big fan! She said, 'Nobody else that I've met could have done what you did.' She meant it too."

Trump is in an unusually upbeat mood. Revisiting some of his best moments on *The Apprentice* recharges him. I play him the show's opening credits, where a noticeably much younger Trump walks in slow motion with swagger to the song "For the Love of Money" by the O'Jays. (The group later issued a cease and desist, saying that Trump's use of their music at 2016 campaign events was creating the false impression that they supported him politically.) Even though Trump has probably seen this sequence thousands of times, he's as entertained as a child discovering *Star Wars* for the first time. "That's a great opening," Trump says. "It's a really great opening. I haven't seen that in a long time. It's just such a great opening."

But as we speak in August 2021, current events enter his thought bubble, and Trump's narration bounces around between the past and the present. Today, he's monitoring the Taliban's takeover of Afghanistan. With the Delta variant surging through Manhattan, he shows his once notorious germophobic side, telling me, "I think it's easier if you sit there," as he points to a chair across the table and doesn't offer to shake my hand. (Though, once again, neither of us is wearing a mask.) "Make yourself comfortable."

Trump grins as he watches the next clip. After Joan bailed on the show, she returned for the next challenge—intent on regaining Trump's confidence. In this scene that I cue up, Trump names Rivers as the winner on *The Celebrity Apprentice*, choosing her over Duke. For all of Rivers's merits, it was also a perfect made-for-TV ending, because the insult comic triumphed over the subject of her best insults.

Looking back on that night, Trump is ready to heap praise on Rivers. But first he congratulates himself for his acting chops—he faked out the runner-up by making her think she was going to win. "I'd be looking at one, admonishing, and look at the other and say, 'You're fired!'" Trump says proudly, offering a play-by-play of his own performance. "There was no coaching. You understand? You can't coach it!" ("Annie, do you know what I'm going to say?" Trump says in the clip, drawing out the tension, so she raises her hands in a celebratory clasp, before he throws down the gauntlet. "You're fired!") Rivers took home $250,000 for her chosen charity, God's Love We Deliver.

The show's finale, filmed at the American Museum of Natural History in New York, drew a decent 8.7 million viewers. (It still lost its Sunday night time slot to *Desperate Housewives* in its fifth season on ABC.) The year before, even more people—an audience of 12.1 million—had tuned in for the two-hour conclusion of the first round of *The Celebrity Apprentice*, during which the British tabloid editor Piers Morgan clinched victory from a ragtag crew that included the country singer Trace Adkins, the *Taxi* star Marilu Henner, the conservative actor Stephen Baldwin, and Omarosa, always waiting in the wings for another chance to reprise her role as Trumpworld's reigning villain.

Morgan had been a familiar face on the network since he'd been tapped to judge *America's Got Talent*, an *Idol*-like competition that became a surprise summer hit. But appearing in Trump's boardroom brought him an entirely new level of notoriety. "I'm very grateful that I was on," Morgan says. "I'm very grateful that I won. It helped me quadruple my deal on *America's Got Talent*. It helped me land the job on CNN, replacing Larry King; nobody thought a Brit half his age could possibly do it. My whole American career was started by *America's Got Talent*, but absolutely exploded after *The Apprentice*."

One of the few downsides of the competition, for Morgan, was facing off against Omarosa. "She is one of the most appalling human beings I ever met in my entire life," Morgan says, claiming that Omarosa wanted to sleep with him—to put on a "showmance" for the viewers—and then continued to falsely claim he was gay after he shut down her advances. "She would literally do anything if she felt it would keep her on the show and get ratings," Morgan says. "That's her own currency." Asked if he felt any spark with her, Morgan gags. "I think there are something like three billion women on the planet Earth," he says. "She'd be nearly number three billion of women I'd most want to have a romance with."

Trump's decision to embrace the trashier side of reality TV was a survival mechanism, to stay relevant and remain on TV, as the celebrity tabloids fully infiltrated politics, suggesting that future presidents needed to be fluent in the language of pop culture. The two supernovas of that political cycle, Barack Obama and Sarah Palin, saw themselves on entertainment magazine covers and TMZ with the frequency of the Kardashians (whose E! reality show had launched a year earlier). Maybe Obama and Palin were, to quote *Us Weekly*, in some sense "just like us"—more approachable to many than their political predecessors. A Black man had never been nominated by a major party for U.S. president before, and a woman had never been selected for the Republican ticket as vice president. Not only did both candidates stand for previously underrepresented groups, but both talked openly about their relatable family lives.

"I think it was a suggestion made by NBC," Trump says of *The Celebrity Apprentice*. "I said, 'I'm okay with it!' I actually found it a little more exciting, because I'm dealing with people that I've never known that are now celebrities." Trump manages simultaneously to praise and criticize *The Celebrity Apprentice*; he acknowledges that the bar was very low in terms of what the show deemed a celebrity, without quite saying that he lacked the drawing power to bring in bigger names.

Rivers was about as big a famous person as the franchise could nab. (Elsewhere in 2008, *Dancing with the Stars*, the show that had helped kick off the celebrity reality-competition boom, managed to book names including the Olympian Kristi Yamaguchi, the recording artist Toni Braxton, and even Kim Kardashian herself—all figures who were too big for Trump's show.) But Rivers's appearance on the series ended up being a canny choice on her part. Trump recalls how competing on *The Celebrity Apprentice* gave Rivers, at seventy-five, a resurgence in the public eye. "Joan said that Joan's career was over," Trump recalls, before outlining how he helped her make a comeback. In this case, Trump's recollection is not hyperbolic: Rivers had been feeling a professional slump, and showing her mother-hen persona on *The Celebrity Apprentice*—a year before the release of the documentary *Joan Rivers: A Piece of Work*, detailing all the barriers she'd broken in comedy and her workaholic drive—led to more offers. Afterward, E! expanded Rivers's brand with a weekly *Fashion Police* series starting in 2010, and Rivers even entered the Marvel Cinematic Universe, playing herself in 2013's *Iron Man 3*.

Trump pats himself on the back for helping Rivers in the final years of her life. "No. 1, she did very well on *The Apprentice*," Trump says. "But she said it totally reinvigorated her career. She couldn't get a gig. She couldn't get anything. She went on that show, and she was hot until she died."

Trump is still a passionate salesman, at least when he wants to be. And his recap of Rivers's season on *The Celebrity Apprentice* is infectious. It feels in the room as if the show were airing now instead of more than a decade and a half ago and as if it were the hottest thing on TV. "She was funny on that show—a lot!" Trump says. "She was angry on the show—a lot! I don't know, it just made her a much bigger personality than she was. Look, she went out and said she'd sit and wait for the phone to ring—she'd use that expression—and it was ringing! After *The Apprentice*, she didn't have enough nights in the week." Even from across the table, Trump seems somehow close to me as he leans forward to clinch this sale. He's talking about the series with such gusto, and in the present tense, it's as if he were pitching Zucker for another season. "It's a very big show," Trump vows, explaining that's "the reason I'm doing this, and devoting a lot of time to this," referring to our interviews.

Suddenly, in the midst of talking about Rivers, Trump careens off course. "I have to get back up," he says, pointing to his office, "because, you know, I'm doing the whole thing with the Afghanistan." It's not clear if he's talking about conducting another interview, or if he's momentarily forgotten that President Joe Biden has barred him from receiving the customary ex-presidential intelligence briefings. Biden remains on Trump's mind. "Has he blown the Afghanistan?" Trump asks.

I had told Trump that I wasn't there to talk politics today; in our last conversations, he'd spent so much time ranting about how he won the

2020 election that I just needed him to focus on analyzing the show that engineered his rise. But he can't help himself. Trump tells me that if he'd been in charge, the chaotic withdrawal from Afghanistan would have gone a lot differently. "I wanted to get out too," Trump says. "Actually, the Taliban, who I dealt with, was not living up to certain things. But they were getting ready to live up to them." It's strange, but not surprising, to hear Trump suddenly talking about the Taliban like a bad contestant on *The Apprentice* he's about to fire.

With the TV on pause, Trump starts to spitball about global diplomacy done the Trump way: "First thing I was going to do was move all the civilians out. I was going to take all the equipment out. Then I was going to bomb the bases." (Moving American civilians, as well as at-risk Afghan nationals out of Afghanistan before the withdrawal, has been a herculean undertaking for Biden's administration, and the images of those they couldn't move grabbing onto airplanes departing Kabul have dominated the news.) Speaking a mile a minute, Trump faults Biden's strategy as too rushed: "He took the soldiers out before he did anything else. Now they have all our equipment. They have $100 billion worth of equipment. It's the craziest thing I've ever seen! The man's totally incompetent."

He's said his piece for now. Though he claimed he had to get up to "deal with" the situation in Afghanistan, Trump, it seems, has nowhere to be. He looks up at the TV screen, and he's ready to watch another clip of himself as the *Celebrity Apprentice*—or let's just say the *Apprentice*—host.

"Let's go."

Even though he won't admit it, Trump badly needed *The Celebrity Apprentice*. During season 5, which aired in 2006, the team working on *The Apprentice* had resigned themselves to the notion that it was a once-hot show that was sinking fast, far from an unusual predicament in the TV business. As the contestant search was under way, producers were already whispering that this could be the end.

"I was straight up told it was going to be the last season ever, and that's why I should do it," says Andrea Lake, then a thirty-one-year-old serial entrepreneur from San Diego, who asked the show to credit her as a sticker company owner to help boost sales of her latest company. (Since then, she's indeed sold millions of stickers.) "There was minimal promotion, almost none," Lake says. "I knew that was weird." For season 5, NBC had moved *The Apprentice* to Monday nights, giving away its coveted Thursday time slot to the lowbrow comedy *My Name Is Earl*. To many, the writing was on the wall: Trump and *The Apprentice* were no longer a priority for NBC. Even Mark Burnett was slowly backing away, letting Jay Bienstock keep the reins as the show's producer on the ground.

Lake, who didn't own a TV, had never seen *The Apprentice* before, but she says producers had pursued her to join the show because of her success in business: she'd earned her first $1 million at twenty-five. One of her mentors had been Dr. Richard Levak, a renowned psychologist who did the vetting for *Survivor* and *The Apprentice* in the early days of reality TV. On his recommendation, she was put through to the final stage of interviews. Burnett, who still participated in the auditions alongside Trump, simply because he relished messing with the contestants, tried to throw Lake off by saying, "Your friend told us you're actually just really lonely."

"And the way he said it cut into my soul and made me tear up," Lake recalls. "I looked at him and I said, 'You're fucking completely full of shit.' He laughed really hard, and he didn't do that anymore."

At Trump Tower, Lake was expecting to live with some of the most accomplished, up-and-coming entrepreneurs in the country. Instead, when she finally met her cast—whose professions ranged from a medical sales manager to a realtor to multiple attorneys—she was so underwhelmed, she tried to quit. "I felt completely lied to," she says. "I told the producers I was going to walk off the show because it was so very different than what had been described. And they said, 'We are going to follow you around with a camera and make you look like a crazy person if you do that.'"

She was forced to stay. And surprisingly, the person who made her time on *The Apprentice* bearable was someone she thought she was going to hate: Donald Trump. "I had a really bad perception of him going in," Lake says. "I think it should be criminal to file corporate bankruptcy and maintain your private wealth as a strategy and do that multiple times in a row, which he had done. So I didn't expect to like him, because of his lack of ethics in business. But as a person, I found him very funny. We joked around, and I got along really well with him."

Lake was eventually fired over something deeply silly—so much so that it seemed to prove how far *The Apprentice* had slipped into soapy dramatics. Some of the other women on Lake's team, seeing that she was such an overachiever, aligned against her and made up a rumor that she'd tried to poison their food in the apartment. Lake was so paranoid that she'd be portrayed as a murderous villain she remained quiet in the boardroom about these false accusations, and Trump axed her. The day after her episode aired, Trump called her because he'd finally watched all the backstabbing, and he didn't think she should have been fired. "He was like, 'Andrea, I saw the episode. Why didn't you tell me what was going on?'" Lake recalls. "I said, 'I did.' And he said, 'You didn't tell me loud enough.' And I thought, 'That's the most Donald Trump sentence that's ever been spoken.'"

Trump, who had no problem being a squeaky wheel to get what he wanted, was now fully invested in making *The Apprentice* a family business. In this sphere, he actually owed Martha Stewart one thing that he's never acknowledged out loud. If Stewart could hire her daughter, Alexis—who Trump thought lacked even a modicum of star quality—as a judge, then Trump, in season 5, could begin to add Ivanka and Don Jr. as guest judges, rotating out Carolyn Kepcher and George Ross for some episodes so his offspring would have a chance to share the spotlight with him. (Eric would join later, in 2010's season 9. "At first, I was probably a little reluctant, to tell you the truth," he says, adding that he prefers to run things behind the scenes. "I've always operated as an operations person. That's where I like to be.")

"It was my idea," Trump says. "The kids started coming in. The kids all did well. Ivanka was fantastic. Eric and Don did a good job." Ivanka, then only twenty-four, was best known for her friendship with Paris Hilton and involvement in the 2003 documentary *Born Rich*, about the lives of children who'd benefited from generational wealth. A graduate of Choate Rosemary Hall in Connecticut and of the University of Pennsylvania, her father's alma mater, Ivanka was interested in pursuing business and fashion, though she hadn't yet accomplished anything in her career. But her résumé mattered less than her presence.

When given the chance to be her father's sidekick in five episodes, Ivanka rose to the occasion, speaking in calm, quippy soundbites, agreeing with her dad, and seeming to provide a calm, sensible ballast to all of Trump's bluster. Elegantly sycophantic, Ivanka proved she could thrive in his shadow. "It's funny—with show business, once it happens, you like to stay there," Trump says. "They really liked it. They did it naturally, as smart kids."

The live finale that season was shot in Los Angeles, where Trump hired the British businessman Sean Yazbeck as the winner. His apprenticeship would entail working on Trump SoHo, a forty-six-story hotel and condominium project. For the first time, Trump invited the American public to vote on the winner, to help him decide, taking a page out of *American Idol*'s playbook, but this new interactive element didn't rescue *The Apprentice*'s ratings. It was the lowest-rated finale at the time, with 11.2 million viewers, down 13 percent from the previous season.

One of the more troubling legacies of season 5 involves the contestant Summer Zervos, who stayed in touch with Trump after production wrapped to get career advice. Zervos claimed that Trump kissed her in his office at Trump Tower, and alleged that, in 2007, Trump invited her to his bungalow at the Beverly Hills Hotel, where he sexually assaulted her. Trump denied any wrongdoing, claiming, "Every woman lied when they came forward to hurt my campaign." Zervos then sued Trump for defamation in 2017, but eventually dropped the complaint in 2021. She declined to talk to me for this book.

It was clear after season 5 that NBC needed to drastically retool *The Apprentice* or let it die. Burnett suggested a change that ultimately wouldn't be radical enough. He thought they should ship Trump to Los Angeles for season 6, hoping a change of location might brighten up the ratings. As Trump packed his bags, he conducted a real-life firing—axing Kepcher as his adviser. On August 31, 2006, he publicly announced that she'd gotten the pink slip, ousting her from both *The Apprentice* and her job at Trump National Golf Club Westchester. The circumstances around her dismissal were hazy, with an anonymous source inside Trump's camp telling the *New York Post* that "she became a prima donna," writing a best-selling business book, raking in $25,000 speaking fees, while forgetting how much golf supplies cost in the gift shop.

"The problem was she got to a point where she spent time on the show and her own persona rather than do the job that she was hired to do for Trump," George Ross says now. As the show moved to L.A., Ross's time as a boardroom adviser also started to diminish. "There was a chance to get his children involved," Ross says. "I think I got too much fame, if you want to call it that. If it came to a point where I got more publicity than Donald, he didn't like that."

In reality, though, Kepcher's firing had little to do with Kepcher; Trump needed to clear the way for Ivanka's rising star to shine on TV.

And all this time later, Kepcher still won't tell her side of the story. "They were moving the show to California," Kepcher says. "You know what? It was good. I had a good five seasons. It was a great ride, and it was all good."

When pressed for more details, Kepcher stays the straitlaced good soldier America saw in Trump's boardroom—Ivanka before Ivanka, a cool, agreeable right-hand woman who never behaved badly or spoke out against Trump. "I'm not going to get into that. That's TV, right? That's media. I never commented on it. And I'm not going to." She'll only say that she thought the stories written about her, leaked by Trump, weren't a reflection of the truth. "The publicity and all of that around what happened, I can't agree with," Kepcher says. "I think there was nothing that was fair about it. I'm just going to leave it at that. I don't want to rehash it. Sometimes it's best to go with it and move forward."

Kepcher's firing is the one topic that Trump doesn't want to discuss either. For all his well-known grudges, Trump values loyalty, and Kepcher's years of silence, in a universe full of former aides and employees eager to criticize him, is a version of loyalty. As if to return the favor, Trump refuses to go there.

The fifth season was a disappointment. But *The Apprentice*'s sixth season almost ended Trump's television career. Placing the ultimate New Yorker in Los Angeles took whatever still worked about *The Apprentice* and baked it in the sun until it was unrecognizable. It was awkward for everyone, especially the viewers. "We had one season where we went to Hollywood," Trump tells me one afternoon. "Do you know that, right? I didn't want to do it. I said no." Burnett was running out of ideas for how to prolong *The Apprentice*, and so he just started cycling through what he'd learned from *Survivor*, which back then changed its tropical setting with each season.

With his prized TV show at risk, and with his tendency to agree to anything as long as it involved more camera time, Trump left the comforts of Trump Tower. He even lost his necktie during some scenes, to go with the more relaxed West Coast vibe. "I did it," Trump says, of shooting in Los Angeles. "Much tougher for me, because I live in New York and now I have to live in a hotel for a couple of weeks." In the 2000s, Trump's idea of life in L.A. had been defined by short trips, staying at his preferred residency, the Beverly Hills Hotel. (When the *Los Angeles Times* asked him in 1988 if he planned on developing real estate there, Trump replied, "I'm really concerned with the whole earthquake situation in L.A. I am a tremendous believer that someday Las Vegas may be the West Coast.")

Los Angeles, a city where many people waste hours staring at their own reflections, wasn't a good fit for Trump, who needs all eyes on him.

There were only so many times he could visit the Playboy Mansion before missing the sight of his own skyscrapers. "It felt so artificial to me," Trump says. "I was riding down Sunset Boulevard in an open convertible. I don't even know. I think it was a Cadillac. I said, 'This is not good. This is not me!' I didn't like that."

Neither did the viewers. The consensus on season 6 of *The Apprentice* was that the series was trying too hard to clone *Survivor*. Burnett, working behind the scenes, had made some other modifications to the show. Since the contestants were no longer rooming in Trump Tower, the winning team was treated to the perks of a mansion in Beverly Hills, while the losers lived in "Tent City"—a cluster of tents in the backyard without electricity or hot water. (They showered outside.) The winning project manager stayed on as the leader in the following episode, which gave the competition a stale feeling. But regardless of success or failure, everyone was invited to strip down and swim in the communal pool— bringing to mind *Survivor*'s bikinis and briefs.

As for the competitions, Trump could no longer send players racing by foot through Manhattan. Instead, they had to set up their own car wash, strut in a fashion show for Trina Turk swimsuits, and sell Sue Bee honey at Ralphs. Even the contestants missed New York, since they weren't told about the move to the West Coast when they auditioned. "I was disappointed, because it wasn't on my home turf," says Jenn Hoffman, then a twenty-six-year-old publicist who lived in Phoenix and grew up on Long Island. "I also thought the concept took away from Trump's brand. Maybe they were trying to sex up the show a bit."

But being employed by NBC still had its perks for the Trump family. Ivanka finagled a spot as a guest judge on *Project Runway*, then airing on the corporate sibling Bravo. Trump was so pleased with her performance, perched next to Vera Wang, it's all he could talk about on the set of *The Apprentice*. And he bragged that, unlike the show's host Heidi Klum, Ivanka didn't need cue cards or a teleprompter. In Trump's eyes, his daughter was a natural TV star, just like him.

Behind the scenes, however, the situation on *The Apprentice* became so dire that one producer resorted to cheating. In episode 7, the teams were asked to engineer an event to entertain clients of a Lexus dealership, introducing a new car to them. (One of the benefits of filming in L.A. was the opportunity to hit up a new slate of advertisers for product placement money.) As a project manager, Hoffman wanted to organize a round of golf, a steadfast but boring tradition on *The Apprentice*. But a male producer pulled her aside and said, "If you do something wild and make this episode silly, I promise I'll protect you." So she agreed to ambush the Lexus customers with go-kart racing, which she knew made no sense. Hoffman lost the task and ended up in the boardroom, and the producer who'd promised her survival was nowhere to be found. Trump, oblivious to the deal, fired Hoffman in a double elimination.

A few days later, when Hoffman sat down with the show's psychologist for her post-firing medical evaluation, she shared the whole story: "And the psychologist said, 'Wait, that's not supposed to happen!'" Throwing a contest on a competition show could have led to an investigation from the FCC and made *The Apprentice* and NBC vulnerable to lawsuits. (In 2001, a contestant from the first season of *Survivor*, Stacey Stillman, sued Mark Burnett and CBS, claiming that he'd lobbied players to vote her out over the lovably gruff contestant Rudy Boesch.)

To remedy a potentially embarrassing situation, Jay Bienstock called Hoffman about the producer's interference, apologized, and offered to go back and reshoot that task. Doing so would have cost the show a small fortune, but the risk of covering it up was greater. Ultimately, Hoffman told Bienstock it wasn't necessary. "I just felt stupid for believing the producer," she says. "I wasn't as angry as I should have been. So I just said, 'It's fine. We'll just leave it the way it is.' I was so happy to be done that I didn't want to start something all over again." On TV, viewers saw only the manipulated competition, and *The Apprentice* didn't take a hit.

Maybe it didn't even matter, since so few people still cared about the show. The finale, which aired on April 22, 2007, mustered 8 million viewers. Trump's crowning of the second female winner, Stefanie Schaeffer, a thirty-two-year-old attorney from Los Angeles, barely made any news.

When Trump ran for president, Hoffman published an article for *Esquire* the month before the 2016 election, which called out Trump's supposed sexist behavior when dealing with contestants. Hoffman believed Summer Zervos's story about Trump groping her in a hotel room. But she doesn't think the piece—which went through considerable editing and rewriting—was fair, and she wishes she'd never published it. "That *Esquire* article always bothered me," she says. "And I can blame *Esquire*, or I can blame myself. I think it was a little bit manipulative and dishonest for *Esquire* to publish that."

Hoffman says she originally pitched a more fun article about what you didn't see behind the scenes of *The Apprentice*, but an editor suggested beefing up her observations about how Trump treated women instead. In the piece, she describes Trump fixating on the female contestants' looks and making invasive comments about their bodies, but even though she says those things happened during filming, they didn't really bother her. "*Esquire* wanted an article that made him look like a clown, like a bumbling idiot, and that's not who he was or how he behaved," Hoffman says. "Whether I agree with him politically or not, I do not think he's stupid."

In hindsight, Hoffman thinks that Trump's behavior on set was a product of the times. "I do think there was sexism, but I thought that was related to the culture then and the nature of reality television," she says. "Trump was very open about how he likes to talk about beautiful women." And Hoffman didn't think it hurt anyone when it happened on her season. "What are you going to say? 'Fuck you, don't tell me I'm beautiful?' At least, that wasn't how I felt about it. When he said, 'Wow, what a beautiful group of women,' I didn't think, 'You sexist pig.' I thought, 'Well, thanks.'"

After season 6 flopped, NBC was preparing to cancel *The Apprentice*. At the May upfronts, the network left the show off the promotional schedule for the fall 2007 season, which included the reality shows *Deal or No Deal* and *The Biggest Loser*, as well as the lower-rated critical favorites *30 Rock* and *Friday Night Lights*. The network president, Kevin Reilly, who oversaw the shrinking ratings of the post–*Friends, Frasier,* and *Will & Grace* NBC, phoned Trump to fire him.

"I had officially canceled it," Reilly says, revealing this information for the first time. "I will say Donald was incredibly gracious through the whole thing. He didn't do what you'd expect. He didn't go on the attack, make fun of me, leak things negatively. He said, 'Look, you've got a tough job. I understand it. You've been fair to me. It's been fantastic. I get it.'"

But then in late May 2007, shortly after that fall schedule was unveiled, Reilly was fired due to continued clashes with Jeff Zucker. Trump, meanwhile, had issued a series of ominous threats in the press, suggesting that he was both looking to find a new network for *The Apprentice* and that he was ready to move on with a different venture, maybe even hosting his own talk show. He'd taken meetings all over town, and he'd spoken with Rupert Murdoch about doing something on the brand-new Fox Business Network, but nothing solid materialized. "I was made a lot of offers," Trump says now, although he admits he can't remember exactly what they were.

Trump's charisma on TV was specific. Hosting *The Apprentice* played to his strengths, but comically putting people down wasn't a skill that would turn Trump into the next Jim Cramer, let alone the next Oprah Winfrey. Luckily for Trump, Ben Silverman—the wunderkind producer behind such 2000s hits as *The Biggest Loser* and *Ugly Betty* at the height of his career—took over as the co-chairman of NBC Entertainment, succeeding Reilly. And the impending Writers Guild of America strike meant that Silverman needed to quickly stockpile unscripted prime-time programming to fill all those empty hours without *Law & Order* or *Medium*.

"I assumed they had other good things," Silverman says. "But they had *30 Rock* and *Studio 60 on the Sunset Strip*—two shows about one of our other shows." (Both were loosely based on *Saturday Night Live*.) "I was like, 'Are you kidding me, guys? The audience is so confused.'"

One of the successful trends in reality TV at the time was conjuring the audience's nostalgia. At ABC, *Dancing with the Stars* had become one of the biggest TV shows in the country, with its relatively simple premise of inviting fading stars to take a twirl in the ballroom. At Fox, 2006's *Skating with Celebrities* couldn't stick the landing, but tried with the former teen-pop singer Debbie Gibson, *Full House*'s Dave Coulier, and the Olympian Bruce Jenner (as Caitlyn Jenner was then known). Silverman would later say that his first call in his new job was to Trump, but it was actually to Burnett. Silverman outlined the premise of *The Celebrity Apprentice*, telling Burnett that he wouldn't double his fees, even though he needed the show to grow to two hours.

Next, Silverman called Trump. "Donald, you've got to understand," Silverman told him. "Imagine a Donald Trump movie on TV every week, where you will have a two-hour block on the best network in the world, and your first hour—I guarantee!—will grow into the second hour, and it will look like a win every single night." Silverman knew the viewership would naturally jump during the boardroom scenes, starring Trump, as parents tucked their kids into bed and had the night to themselves.

"And he thinks for a minute," Silverman recalls, "and he goes, 'I'm so glad a Jew is running the network again.' And I said, 'Whoa! I could take that in two ways, but somehow coming from you, it's a compliment.' And somehow our friendship was born."

NBC negotiated a new deal where they split the revenue from product placement, helping offset costs and making the show more lucrative. "Now, NBC got smart and said, 'No more of that,'" Trump says, emphasizing just how good of a deal he'd had. "So we ended up splitting it. Because it was ridiculous. It was crazy." Extending *The Apprentice*, even under these more frugal terms, still meant Trump would be lining his pockets with a payday of about $10 million a season, while Burnett—as the show's creator, who'd baked extra bonuses into his contract—could stand to make up to $20 million a season.

In Trump's telling, the stars on *The Celebrity Apprentice* wanted to get close to him, not the other way around. "So many people wanted to be next to me!" Trump says. It's true that in the early seasons of *The Appren-*

tice, before he'd hired his own kids, Trump needed to find judges to fill in for George Ross and Carolyn Kepcher on occasion. But the list wasn't particularly star-driven, nor were the names that he mentions. "Erin Burnett, she'd beg me to be on the show," Trump says, listing the former CNBC journalist who would go on to anchor her own show on CNN. "I think she went on four shows, and look how she is toward me. And another one is Donny Deutsch. This guy used to beg me. I could say, 'Drop to your knees, Donny, and beg!'" (This is a familiar rhetorical flourish from the former president. During the 2016 campaign, he claimed that Mitt Romney had begged for his endorsement four years earlier: "I could have said, 'Mitt, drop to your knees.' He would have dropped to his knees.")

Deutsch was a self-styled branding expert who'd had a talk show on CNBC and seemed always to find himself in the gaze of a camera. "I put him on the show a few times," Trump says, "and he was so thankful, and then right away, 'Could I do another one?' And then I watch him on television on occasion—not much—and he's nasty. He goes with the other point of view. It's a crazy business." (Trump's recollections here require fact-checking: Deutsch appeared on *The Apprentice* to critique advertising campaigns, but he never served as a guest judge. Burnett, during her CNBC days, filled in later as a guest judge on *The Celebrity Apprentice*.)

Trump uses this non sequitur as a bridge to talk about all the celebrities he'd invite on the show as contestants. "And what I did is, I said, 'What if we get a lot of them?' And we did *The Celebrity Apprentice*, and it worked out good. I liked it, because it was celebrities. We got some very good celebrities on the show—amazing celebrities, actually."

At least they really tried to get A-list stars. When the idea of *The Celebrity Apprentice* was announced, Trump claimed that he was in talks with Britney Spears, Lindsay Lohan, and Paris Hilton—three of the biggest tabloid fixtures of the decade. Silverman wanted Rosie O'Donnell, and Trump announced in the press that, given his rocky history with the comedian, he'd make a donation of $2 million to her charity if she joined. But now he's forgotten he ever made her this offer.

"I did?" Trump says. "That must have been done without my consent."

(Trump consented.) "I didn't know that we offered her $2 million," he says. "I did not know that. She's a lowlife. I knew nothing about it. I certainly didn't know about $2 million. I wouldn't have paid her $2 million. I hadn't heard that, I don't think. I don't find her to be a very interesting person."

On *The Celebrity Apprentice*, Donald Trump channeled his own inner Andy Cohen, and not just because NBC—cashing in on some corporate synergy—pulled in several of Bravo's Real Housewives, from NeNe Leakes to Kenya Moore to Brandi Glanville, to shake up the franchise over time. It's true that Trump didn't have to work as hard to manufacture drama on his own. The drama was now all around him, and Trump was simply the bystander and commentator in chief. He knocked this role out of the park; after all, lurking on the outskirts of celebrity culture, even more than dominating the business world, was what came naturally.

Trump still called the shots, but it could be hard to hear him over all the yelling. As Jay Bienstock exited, NBC brought on two showrunners—Page Feldman and Eden Gaha—to steer this new enterprise. Producers no longer needed to waste their time touring the country, trying to scout every state for new contestants. These celebrities were much easier to find. In some cases, Trump would see someone out at a restaurant (such as Kiss's co-lead singer Gene Simmons) and offer him a spot on the show. No wonder the casts, which often comprised figures from yesteryear, felt so random.

The celebrities were all told they'd earn a flat rate of $25,000 a season, no matter how long they lasted during the five weeks of competitions. (For the "all-stars" season, which aired in 2013, the salary jumped to $75,000 for returning players from Dennis Rodman to Omarosa.) The downside of working with famous people was juggling all their handlers and an army of hair and makeup artists. Rather than live in the bunk beds at Trump Tower, the contestants got their own rooms at Trump's hotel in Columbus Circle. And the yellow taxicabs were replaced by black town cars to transport the losers home.

Because of all the egos involved, Feldman and Gaha played a more active role in approving who'd get fired. NBC needed to make sure that the bigger stars, relatively speaking, stayed on through the finale. Trump could see that this would dilute his power, so he doubled down on pretending he made all the hiring decisions on his own. "I never kept anybody because of show business," Trump tells me. "Dennis Rodman, as an example. He was so great. He was so good. People were talking about it. I always did the right thing. I never kept anybody for ratings. That might be important for you to know, that it gave the show credibility."

Brande Roderick recalls going to lunch at the Polo Lounge at the Beverly Hills Hotel with the show's producers, where they vetted her for the first celebrity season. (She also returned for the all-stars edition.) They wanted to know whether she had any celebrity friends she could hit up for charity money during the competitions; any episodes in which the contestants pleaded with their famous pals for money would be an opportunity to get bigger names onto the show, if only as a voice on the other end of the phone. It was a prospect the production took seriously; in Trump's final season, the former *Cosby Show* star Keshia Knight Pulliam, the ex–child actor, would get fired first for not calling her TV dad, Bill Cosby, for money. (Uncomfortably, the dozens of career-ending allegations of sexual assault against Cosby entered widespread public consciousness between filming and air in January 2015, and so the episode left those allegations completely unaddressed.)

Roderick wasn't, perhaps, as widely known as some. But she had connections. "And I kid you not, probably right after they asked me that question, Brett Ratner and Russell Simmons walked in and came right up to the table," Roderick recalls. "And it couldn't have been better timing." (Ratner, the director of films including *Rush Hour* and *Red Dragon*, and Simmons, co-founder of Def Jam Recordings, have both since been accused of sexual misconduct.) Roderick's proximity to other powerful people was enough to get her on *The Celebrity Apprentice*.

Roderick was at the center of Joan's meltdown about Melissa's firing, a day of filming that she'll never forget. "In the end, what's great about it:

Joan and I made up, and Melissa and I made up," Roderick says. "Bygones were bygones, right? But it was a bit intense. You would think, the way reality is, that was all set up, but it was not. I was shocked, because even though I'm a competitive person, I would have left gracefully."

Just how much drama was there on *The Celebrity Apprentice*? NeNe Leakes (season 11) feuded with practically everyone, especially Star Jones and La Toya Jackson, whom she disparagingly referred to as "Casper the Ghost" because of her tendency to disappear during tasks. Gary Busey (seasons 11 and 13), who just a few years earlier had been on *Celebrity Rehab with Dr. Drew*, showed off his maniacal giggle and insane expressions, such as "I'm an angel in an Earth suit." Perhaps the only other celebrity who matched that outer-space energy was Rodman (seasons 8 and 13).

The NBA star struggled with his sobriety when he appeared as a contestant on season 8. "Dennis Rodman, I thought he was great," Trump says, talking about him not as a job candidate but for his ability to create buzz. "He was so bad in terms of tasks. He'd be drunk, and then you'd fire somebody else." Trump acknowledges that this injustice would sometimes frustrate fans. "People asked me a lot, 'Did NBC get involved in the firings?' They wanted to. I'd make my own decision. I had to do that. And they were very good. Look, I can't complain."

I play a clip of the second time Trump fired Rodman, during the all-stars season. In the task, Trump had cleverly leveraged his cast to help create a marketing campaign for Melania's new skin-care line. But Rodman had made a glaring error by misspelling Melania's name as "Milania" on the poster for his team's presentation. "I think I was the person who actually said, 'Melania's name is not spelled right,'" recalls Eric Trump with a smirk. As the cameras zoomed in on the embarrassing typo, Melania, Ivanka, and Eric all looked at each other. "They spelled my name wrong," the future first lady said on TV, in a rare scene where she got to speak. "It's all over the place, and nobody even noticed?"

"It's funny the way she said that," Trump says, giddy at the exchange and the fact that his often-silent wife takes part in the comedy. She's not the natural he is, but she's trying, and that counts for a lot. "I mean, how good is that television? I can't believe it." He turns to his Brooks Brothers–clad handler for affirmation that the scene he's just seen is, in fact, brilliant entertainment.

Trump's entire face lights up from the reflected glow of a faded superstar. At his peak as Michael Jordan's teammate on the dominant Chicago Bulls, Rodman was an icon on the court and off; his living-out-loud persona, replete with piercings, tattoos, a short marriage to Carmen Electra, and large quantities of tabloid ink, made him something more than an athlete. "Dennis was a pretty cool cat in many ways," Trump says. "I'll tell you. He dated Madonna when she was the No. 1 person. You got to have something going." Trump then pulls another name out of his hat to prove Rodman's popularity: Kim Jong Un, the dictator of North Korea, is also a fan. Rodman first visited North Korea during Obama's presidency, before Trump's unusual approach of alternating courtly diplomacy and saber rattling with the leader of the so-called Hermit Kingdom.

"So Kim Jong Un really liked him, legit," Trump says. "And I said, 'You know, I can get these guys out of Harvard, government, central casting, they couldn't do anything with Kim Jong Un. A guy like Dennis Rodman could.'"

Trump admits that he almost asked Rodman for help on foreign diplomacy, preferring his advice over that of the professionals. "I didn't use Dennis for it, but I thought about it a couple times before I got to know Kim Jong Un," says Trump, who flew to Singapore to first meet with Kim in 2018. "Dennis would have done a better job than your traditional Ivy League people that always do that stuff and have no personality." For Trump, being president was all about surrounding himself with star quality—a continuation of the lessons he learned from NBC. "Kim Jong Un liked him," Trump repeats. "You know, he coached their basketball game? I asked him about that. He said he liked Dennis. By the way, Dennis liked him too—a lot. Dennis is a real character, but I always got along with him great."

Trump uses this extra-long boardroom we're sitting in as an excuse to preach about one of his favorite subjects. No, it has nothing to do with his political career. "You know, people really wanted the boardroom. The boardroom became longer and longer because that's what people wanted." And by "people," Trump specifically means one person—himself. "They loved the boardroom," he says.

Trump won't choose between *The Apprentice* and *The Celebrity Apprentice*, in the same way that he won't openly say which of his children did the best on the show. (Ivanka, of course.) But in his answer, you can read between the lines. "If you got the real regular person, it was almost better than a celebrity," Trump says. "A celebrity is harder, because they are trained at how not to make a fool out of yourself."

Perhaps missing the simpler days, in 2010, Trump made one last-ditch attempt to resuscitate his original franchise. In season 10, NBC brought back a version of *The Apprentice* that enlisted regular contestants in economic peril. "Talented, smart people are looking for work," Trump said in the premier episode, just before the midterm elections, in which the Democratic Party under President Obama, still struggling through the aftereffects of the Great Recession, lost dozens of seats in the House. But by then, these non-famous people were no match for Joan Rivers's lungs. Trump's ratings had never been lower, attracting only 4.6 million viewers for its September debut. Trump quickly spun back to the celebrities and turned his attention elsewhere: to politics.

Our time today in the boardroom is up. As Trump leaves, ostensibly as president in exile to tend to the situation in Afghanistan, he asks me if I can send him the reel that he's just watched, not realizing that everything we saw was pulled off YouTube. "That's beautiful," he says, zeroing back in on the Rodman scene. "I wouldn't mind getting a clip of that and show it to my wife." Now, of course, the entire world knows how to spell Melania's name.

CHAPTER 11

He's Running

*T*he *Celebrity Apprentice* provided a second life to a near-dead franchise, and gave Trump a reboot of sorts, too: the businessman who'd spent his career with his nose pressed to the pane of celebrity culture got a group of stars, however dim their wattage, to spend weeks at a time thinking solely of how to please him. These are, for Trump, proud memories, though for others perhaps less so, given the occasional unpleasant moment.

Take the time Vivica A. Fox and Kenya Moore—separated by Geraldo Rivera—attacked each other during a never-ending boardroom in season 14. Their fight had nothing to do with the task at hand. Moore accused Fox of sending an awkwardly phrased and crude tweet about going through menopause, which Fox, protective of her youthful image, denied. "See, that's a dirty-ass bitch right there," Fox said on TV. "You are just a toxic trick." It took a while to unravel just exactly what had happened. But with Don Jr.'s investigative chops, picking up his phone and scrolling through Twitter, Trump and his sons determined that Moore seemed to have stolen Fox's phone and impersonated her on social media. "We've really reached a new low," Trump said, sitting across from them in the boardroom, firing Moore, and never looking more thrilled by bad behavior. (Trump joined Twitter in 2009, as a means to promote the show directly to his fans.)

"Yep, that was a crazy boardroom," Trump recalls. "That was a great one, actually. They still talk about it. You wouldn't think they talk about it, they talk about that—a lot of people!" Trump claims he wasn't prepped by producers to zero in on the stolen phone. "I don't think we knew much either, and it just played out and it was better that way," he says. "We just let it ride."

Eric Trump, who served as the other judge in the boardroom that night, recalls Fox being completely stumped by the menopause tweet that had been sent out from her account. "I remember sitting there thinking, 'She legitimately doesn't know what this other person is talking about,'" Eric says. "There was a lot of confusion. That was pretty dark stuff."

In the epic fight, Rivera was the third contestant on the chopping block, and he sat silently by as a passive observer. Wedged between two strong, outspoken Black women, the Fox News anchor—who'd been a chameleonlike figure in media since first becoming famous in the 1970s— could barely get a word in. And all these years later, while watching the footage, even Donald Trump notices how Rivera slides by unscathed, when maybe he should have been fired—given his lack of participation in this *Real Housewives*–worthy altercation. "Geraldo got lucky," Trump says, soaking in another adrenaline rush from seeing himself in the boardroom. "It is good television," Trump declares. "You know, I'm watching it, I'm saying, 'That's great stuff!'"

"You can't make that up," Trump's handler on this day mutters.

"You couldn't write that!" Trump says, feeding off the faint praise. "There's no writing it."

Trump's performance didn't change on *The Celebrity Apprentice*. But the names around him got slightly bigger—and more unruly. One day, according to a member of the *Apprentice* team, NeNe Leakes stormed off the set after a fight with another celebrity. As the producers gave up on Leakes, Trump chased her out onto the street, persuading her to go back upstairs. Trump was still a pretend ruler, yet his subjects were so difficult that he had to step in to actually govern—something he'd left to producers in the past. And the celebrities responded to his brass-knuckles approach to leadership and to his terse judgments of their business acumen.

The Celebrity Apprentice might have been campy, but it's not an inconsequential chapter in the life story of Donald Trump. Seven of *The Apprentice*'s fourteen seasons were cast with familiar faces, and their ringleader continued to gain admission into millions of living rooms, cracking jokes, acting as a doting father and bragging about his wealth. Even as the audience size was a fraction of what it once was, Trump's having the likes of Sharon Osbourne, Sinbad, Meat Loaf, Kevin Jonas, and Kate Gosselin grovel for his attention only reinforced his image as an all-knowing captain of business. And, as Ben Silverman had predicted when he tried to sell him on the show, it made Trump the king of these other messy celebrities.

"He did a good job," Trump says about Rivera. "He was smart. He was cunning."

Rivera was, in the years after his time on the show (on which he eventually finished in second place), in an unusual position among *Celebrity Apprentice* contenders, as a journalist who would go on to cover Trump as a politician. When I ask Trump whether they're still on good terms, he tells me a story. "After I lost the election . . . ," Trump says. These words come tumbling from his mouth, almost against his own will, and he winces in surprise. It's a moment of candor that catches Trump off guard; even he can't believe he said it.

The spin artist in him takes immediate control, trying to erase this humiliating gaffe of speaking the truth—one that could alienate his base and cost him his pride. "I won the election, but then when they *said* we lost . . . ," Trump corrects himself, looking pleased at his own rapid backtracking. "He called me up three or four times. I didn't take his call, because I was so busy fighting it, with what went on." It's remarkable, then, with "with what went on," Trump remembers with such specificity how frequently Rivera tried to reach him.

"And finally, I had a little time," Trump says. "I called him back. And he went on Fox News, and he started talking about—'The president called me!'"

After they'd hung up, Rivera tweeted about their conversation on November 13, 2020, ten days after the election and six days after Joe Biden was declared the winner: "Just had a heartfelt phone call w friend @realDonaldTrump who said he's a 'realist' who'll do the 'right thing' But he wants to see what 'states do in terms of certification (etc)' He sounded committed to fighting for every vote & if he loses, talking more about all he's accomplished."

Rivera's tweet did not go over well in the White House. On this afternoon, almost a year later, Trump sets the record straight. "I didn't call him," Trump says. "I returned his phone call, and *he* started talking very personally about how I was feeling, how I was doing." By announcing that Trump would "do the right thing," Rivera sent the wrong signal to the public on behalf of Trump, who was still fully focused on staying in charge. "And I said, 'That's a real betrayal,'" Trump says. "I didn't talk about how I was feeling. It was a phone call that lasted very quickly."

The actor in Trump can't resist paraphrasing what he recalls from this exchange. "Just—'Hey, how are you doing, Geraldo? How's it going?' He's not my psychiatrist!" (Trump has never needed one.) "He made it sound like it was such a big deal. It was nothing. All I did was return his call. But he said, 'The president called me,' like I'm reaching out to him. And I haven't spoken to him since."

Bruised feelings aside, Trump doesn't necessarily want to torch this bridge forever. "I like him, though," Trump finally says. "He did a good job on the show." As Rivera later revealed in an interview with *The New York Times*, he tried to call Trump again on November 16, 2020, but he didn't pick up. Maybe Trump sensed he was calling with bad news: Rivera wanted to tell Trump that he couldn't find any evidence of voter fraud with Dominion Voting Systems, which Trump had asked him to investigate.

Rivera has since left Fox News, which means he's no longer obligated to support Trump. After getting axed by the panel show *The Five* in June 2023, Rivera turned on his reality TV boss. "I feel awful that he made me dump him," Rivera would say, making it seem like it was his decision to break up with Trump. In an interview with CNN in October 2023, Rivera said it was "a personal embarrassment" that he had once considered Trump a friend.

But their friendship, as with so many in Trumpworld, had been a transactional exchange. Trump saw every celebrity on his reality show as a prop. And he was always on the go, never lingering long enough to develop meaningful contact with anyone—whether escaping in his chauffeured car or in the Rolls-Royce he'd leave at the curb outside Trump Tower, collecting parking tickets. (Melania once posted a video of Trump driving the car on Facebook, filmed from the backseat, with Barron sitting silently next to his dad—and Taylor Swift's "Blank Space" blasting on the radio.)

The show had been Trump's direct line to the American public, but—never particularly passionate about the fundamentals of making television—Trump was seriously beginning to lose interest around 2010 or 2011. As time went on, he was finicky about having to wait at all on the set of *The Apprentice.* If he arrived and the cameras weren't ready to shoot his scene, he'd storm off and return hours later, just to prove a point. To help track his whereabouts in real time, members of the show's transportation team were instructed to trail Trump when he took his own car.

Easier said than done. As one driver explains, trying to follow Trump as he sped to his golf course at Briarcliff Manor was an occupational hazard. Trump would run red lights, stomping on the gas and leaving other cars in the dust. "They weren't even yellow lights," the driver says. "They were straight up red. So I failed my mission, because I decided to obey the law."

By the time *The Apprentice* pivoted to celebrities, I'd moved on from covering the show—or so I thought. On March 23, 2011, I was reporting a story for *Newsweek*, which sent me to a live taping of *The View*. I had been assigned a profile of Whoopi Goldberg, who'd become the daytime talk show's moderator after the short, turbulent tenure of Rosie O'Donnell. Even as O'Donnell's departure meant that Trump was no longer part of the show's daily fodder, there was no escaping him; he was *The View*'s marquee guest that day as I settled into my seat in the front row of the audience. And he wasn't just there to promote his reality show; he'd lately begun putting the persona he'd cultivated on *The Apprentice* to work in the political arena. While he'd floated the idea of running for president as early as 1988 (which was also the first presidential election in which Joe Biden had sought the Democratic nomination), this time felt different.

There was still something slightly absurd about the idea, of course, but Trump the reality star had the nation following his every word. And, with what fans would call blunt talk and detractors would call a dangerous willingness to outright lie, Trump resurfaced a damaging internet rumor from the 2008 election, treating Barack Obama's nationality as just another boardroom topic on which he could be the judge. As Trump launched his birtherism attacks, he catapulted well ahead of the former Massachusetts governor Mitt Romney (who'd gotten close to the nomination in the previous election cycle) and the former Minnesota governor Tim Pawlenty.

"What I knew was that he was a spectacle, and in the United States of America in 2011, that was a form of power," Obama would later write in his memoir *A Promised Land*, published in 2020. "Trump trafficked in a currency that, however shallow, seemed to gain more purchase with each passing day."

Led by Barbara Walters—a journalist who'd interviewed every president since Richard Nixon—*The View* was going to get to the bottom of Trump's new moves. After all, the hypothetical Trump run existed in the show's sweet spot, at the intersection of pop culture and politics. In the interview, Trump showed a different side of himself, in that he didn't just plug his businesses and promote the star quality of various family members; he suddenly had a great deal to say about politics, particularly foreign affairs. Trump railed against China, OPEC, the Arab League, France, and South Korea. But counting his adversaries was more fun than getting specific—he shrugged off Walters's question about selecting a vice president for now. "I think I'd do a really good job," Trump told her. "I think I'd protect this country like it's not being protected." Trump described his governing style as running the country like "a business with heart," name-dropping a CNN poll that had him "essentially tied," if he ran as the Republican nominee, against Obama.

The co-host Joy Behar, sitting next to him, was among the first members of the media to drill down on Trump's embrace of the canard that Obama was not born in the United States, which would make him ineligible for his office. "Are you a birther, Donald?" she asked. In an answer that seemed to have no end, Trump doubled down. "I was a really good student at the best school," he said. "They make these birthers into the worst idiots. Why doesn't he show his birth certificate?"

"This is bad," Behar said as all the co-hosts started talking over each other.

"I want him to show his birth certificate," Trump went on as the usually left-leaning *View* studio audience applauded this demand as if it were a well-conditioned reflex to cheer for Trump. "There's something on that birth certificate that he doesn't like."

The interview went so off the rails that the co-hosts couldn't even squeeze in any questions about *The Celebrity Apprentice*. (The show was returning for its new season with Leakes and the former *View* co-host Star Jones.) In a moment of bewilderment, Walters extended Trump's time beyond the commercial, adding an extra segment.

Walters knew what she was doing: if Trump the reality star was once good for ratings, Trump the aspiring politician was even better. As he was promoting season 11 of *The Apprentice*, Trump didn't need to rely on picking fights with small fry like Martha Stewart or O'Donnell. Obama, who'd ascended to the highest office in the land with both gravitas and movie-star cool, was the ultimate target. And Trump, in taking him on, could get some of his reflected shine.

Perhaps it was just time to change the narrative. Trump had spent years bragging on TV, including to Meredith Vieira on *Today*, about his "No. 1" ratings for *The Apprentice*, even as the audience for the show had dwindled considerably. This would lead to awkward exchanges between Trump and the Television Critics Association, where journalists would try to hammer Trump and get him to admit to his weaker ratings. But that was easier said than done. Trump remembers one of these encounters.

"Did I tell you about the time I was with Mark Burnett?" Trump asks me one afternoon. "It's actually insightful." In other words, it proves the lengths to which Burnett would go to enable Trump. "I was with the television critics, a whole room full of critics. They knew every ratings point. So I said, 'The Apprentice is the No. 1 show on television.' And this guy stood up, very arrogant, he said, 'The Apprentice is not No. 1.' He looked at Mark Burnett. Mark said, 'Huh. Here's a story: Everything he says turns out to be true. Maybe it's not No. 1, but it will be.' And the next week, it was No. 1! It was sort of a cool answer." Except for the fact that it wasn't true: *The Celebrity Apprentice* was never the No. 1 show on TV; it wasn't even in the Top 30 shows on TV. But if it won the eighteen-to-forty-nine demographic during its Sunday night time slot, Trump took that to mean he triumphed over all of Hollywood.

The 2012 polls that had him at the top gave him something new to fixate on. These numbers weren't invented, and he was actually—to use one of his favorite words—winning at something. Trump might have floated the idea that he was interested in running for president to gain attention, but as the chatter around him grew louder and louder, he felt as if he were reliving his folk hero early years of *The Apprentice* (complete with new data where he was undoubtedly the best at something).

In April 2011, I arranged for Trump to do an interview with Meghan McCain, one of the columnists I edited at *Newsweek* and its website, *The*

Daily Beast. (She'd later become the conservative voice on *The View* from 2017 to 2021.) This was before Trump had turned against John McCain, mocking his personal history as a prisoner of war in Vietnam on the 2016 campaign trail, and Trump was eager to chat with her, confirming the interview immediately. "So are we doing a radio show?" Trump said, ready to spring into action and drum up new headlines. He didn't even know that this phone call was for a print piece. As I listened in, it dawned on me that Trump's sudden popularity in the political arena seemed to be consuming him. Even he wasn't this good of an actor.

"Well, the polls have been very gratifying," Trump said on the call. "One of the pollsters actually said to me that my numbers would be better—and I'm leading in just about every poll—if people thought I was going to run, because a lot of people don't think I'm going to run, and they think it's because of *The Apprentice*. And I say, give me a break! I don't need this to get ratings. It's already the top show on NBC." (For the 2010–11 season, *The Celebrity Apprentice* was the No. 32 show on TV among adults between the ages of eighteen to forty-nine, well behind NBC's own No. 2–ranked *Sunday Night Football* and No. 11–ranked *The Office*, as measured by the Nielsen ratings. Of course, when you factored in the revenue from product placement, it was still making a tidy profit.)

Trump was on a roll that day, barely pausing for questions. He bragged about the crowd size he'd generated at a Tea Party rally in Boca Raton. He quizzed McCain about which advisers he should hire. "Do you have somebody for me in Iowa, New Hampshire, and South Carolina?" He told her that he'd have no problem bunking in ordinary accommodations on the campaign trail. "I wasn't always rich. I used to stay at Holiday Inns all the time!" And he even made her a job offer, inviting her to work on his campaign.

When Tina Brown, then the editor in chief of *Newsweek*, read the interview, I remember her waving sheets of paper in the air as she bellowed in her British accent, "Is Donald Trump running for president?" I looked up from my cubicle, feeling as though I were living in *The Twilight Zone*.

It was only shortly after, on April 30, 2011, that Trump infamously attended the White House Correspondents' Dinner. The annual celebration, at which political figures mingle with celebrities who fly to Washington for the occasion, is traditionally a genial gathering where the president gently roasts himself and others in the room, and it's also a good way for tabloid figures to get some positive press. Obama had just released his birth certificate days before—a mixed blessing for Trump. His flagrantly false claims had finally been proven completely wrong, but on the bright side the president of the United States had been compelled to respond to them, and all attention, particularly from the loftiest office in the land, was good attention.

Or so it might have seemed. The evening's host, Seth Meyers, then a star of *Saturday Night Live*, took a dagger to his target. "Donald Trump has been saying he will run for president as a Republican, which is surprising, since I just assumed he was running as a joke," Meyers said. Trump scowled from his table. "Donald Trump often appears on Fox, which is ironic, because a fox often appears on Donald Trump's head." And another one: "Donald Trump said recently he has a great relationship with the Blacks—though unless the Blacks are a family of white people, I bet he's mistaken."

This turned out to be the perfect follow-up act for Obama. "All kidding aside, we all know about your credentials and breadth of experience," the president had said earlier in the night. "For example, just recently in an episode of *Celebrity Apprentice*, at the steak house the men's cooking team did not impress the judges from Omaha Steaks. And there was a lot of blame to go around. But you, Mr. Trump, recognized the real problem was a lack of leadership. And so ultimately you didn't blame Lil Jon or Meat Loaf—you fired Gary Busey. And these are the kinds of decisions that would keep me up at night. Well handled, sir!"

Trump, who was used to having final say in the boardroom, laughed on TV at Obama's jokes, but he unraveled later. Privately, he told associates that he thought Obama and Meyers had gone out of their way to make a fool out of him, which they surely had.

At NBC, Trump's political activity was causing widespread confusion. What started out as a kind of fun lark had quickly spun out of control. And Trump was suddenly seeing himself as a Kennedy, not a Kardashian. His obsession with his poll numbers was inescapable; he gloated to anyone who would listen every time the Drudge Report linked to another survey that had him leading the Republican pack. All of this chatter was starting to make the network uncomfortable. Against the backdrop of a new season of *The Celebrity Apprentice* due to start filming in the fall, other changes were afoot. Comcast had bought NBC Universal, which had led to Zucker's departure in 2010. Zucker was no longer well liked in Hollywood. But at least for the moment he'd kept Trump as a fan. "You know what? He signed me for *The Apprentice*," says Trump even today. That counted for a lot with him.

The new regime's suits—Steve Burke, the CEO of NBCUniversal; Bob Greenblatt, the chairman of NBC Entertainment; and Paul Telegdy, who oversaw NBC's unscripted programming—thought their star was playing some elaborate mind game with them to negotiate for more money, even though two seasons remained on his contract. If Trump launched a presidential bid, a scenario that NBC brass at the time found hard to say out loud with a straight face, he couldn't continue hosting *The Apprentice*, due to the equal-time rule. (Since 1927, broadcasters have been required to give political candidates equal airtime. If NBC allowed Trump to host *The Apprentice*, theoretically, Mitt Romney and Rick Santorum could have complained that they deserved their own time on national TV firing celebrities.)

In Trump's recollection, NBC deployed full-court pressure to persuade him not to run for president. Mark Burnett was calling him regularly to try to talk him out of politics. Trump says that even Burke personally joined these efforts, which tickled Trump's ego. "So Steve Burke comes along with Paul Telegdy and two other people, sits right in the same chair that you're sitting in," Trump says one afternoon, from his office at Trump Tower. "During the Romney disaster, Romney was running and a poll came out on NBC on *Meet the Press*, and it showed I was beating Romney. And I haven't even thought about running." He switches to the third person. "But if Trump ran, he would get the nomination."

Trump relishes the story about NBC chasing him to keep him in the network's fold; he spins out a version of it almost every time we talk. "I'm telling you, these guys were up in my office," Trump says. "He came up to see me, and Steve was the king." According to Trump, this wasn't the first visit he'd received from Burke. "Steve came to see me with his wife and daughters—beautiful young women, young girls at the time. He asked that he could take pictures with me because he wanted to put it on his Christmas card."

As Trump was deciding on his future, and the fate of *The Celebrity Apprentice*, it was touch and go. He'd drop hints that maybe running for president would be too disruptive to his children's lives, but he'd wake up the next day committed to running. And then he'd be unsure all over again. ("We were young," says Eric Trump, who was entrusted with overseeing aspects of his father's business when he was president. "I'm not sure he would have turned over his entire empire to a twenty-nine-year-old.") Trump's decision making, when he finally made decisions, could often be traced to the last person to whom he'd spoken. But, suddenly in demand again as if it were 2004, Trump was talking to a lot of people and the wires were getting crossed. When I speak to him years later, in the spring of 2021, he once again seems uncertain; it's as if he wants to use a time machine to make a different decision and run for office in 2012 after all. Or at least to spend more time talking about how valuable he was to NBC.

"By the way," Trump says, "just to go forward a little bit, I never thought NBC would treat me so badly. I was so good to them! Other than a couple contract negotiations that were a little rougher than they could have been." Trump shifts to campaign rally mode. "The media is not free, and it's not fair. It's really corrupt. The media is very corrupt."

And yet here he is talking to me. It's a contradiction he doesn't register, because it's more pleasurable to seethe about Biden. "Like now they don't cover the election hoax because they don't want to talk about it, even though it's been caught. Like Arizona—you're watching that? Keep watching! It's going to get more and more interesting." Earlier in our conversation, he'd claimed that "in Arizona, between 10 and 20 percent of the ballots are gone. Do you know why they're gone?" He doesn't wait for an answer. "Because they never existed."

Even with decades of favorable coverage, and then endless broadcasts of his rallies that made it possible for him to become president, Trump feels burned. "It's such dishonesty," he says. "They are writing books about the level of dishonesty, the Russian hoax, all the different things they do."

Back in 2011, the media was salivating over the idea of Trump's potential run, and Trump was captivated by the idea of his name getting even bigger. It ultimately fell on Burnett to keep Trump on *The Celebrity Apprentice*. At the time, Burnett didn't think the future of America hung in the balance; he just wanted to keep the money flowing into his bank account. Burnett once again proved his chops as a showman and salesman, entering Trump's office, where Trump's lawyer and fixer Michael Cohen was waiting. (Cohen was one of the principal people at the time egging on Trump to run.) Burnett made a simple argument to Trump.

"Mark said something that's really amazing," Trump tells me. "That's the one thing—Mark is a really good salesman."

"You don't understand," Burnett had told Trump. "They're offering you millions of dollars to be on a show, to be on prime-time television."

Running for president, Burnett argued, wouldn't match Trump's current standing in American culture as a TV star. Burnett really believed this. And Trump believed him. The two men were bonded by their love of the entertainment industry, VIP access, and standing at the center of fame. Trump paraphrases Burnett's message that has stuck with him all these years later: "Every movie actor wants to be a television star, because when they do a movie, they're on once a year, and if ten million people watch, it's a smash. If ten million people watch a television show, it's just okay, but they watch every week." In other words, with Burnett's prodding, Trump imagined how every season of *The Apprentice* was reaching a cumulative crowd size bigger than the multiplexes packed for the next Tom Cruise movie. Never mind that if he actually left, breaching his contract (and opening himself up to the possibility of a lawsuit from NBC), he'd be walking away from tens of millions of dollars. What was he doing? Why would he risk all of that for something that was the longest of long shots?

Trump is wistful as he considers this information. "And I never thought about it that way. Every movie star wants to be on television." And so how could Trump do something that would dim his star wattage? He chose reality TV over running the country.

On May 16, 2011, the day of the NBC upfronts, Trump finally announced he'd stay host of *The Celebrity Apprentice* and suspend his campaign for president, which he'd never actually launched. "I was building two buildings at the time, and I had a contract with NBC," Trump tells me. "I said, 'I couldn't really do it. I had big jobs.' And I didn't feel the kids were ready yet."

Trump believes if he'd run, he would have certainly clinched the Republican nomination. "I almost did it," Trump says. "Mark talked me out of it. Mark Burnett said nobody quits prime-time television. I was going to run against Romney for the nomination, and I would have beaten him. I wanted to run so badly against Obama."

Since he didn't get to settle his vendetta with Obama in real life, he can only daydream about his landslide victory. "Do you know why?" Trump ponders. "The first time"—meaning in 2008—"would have been hard. The second time was easy because he was a failed president. He was four years in, and the country was doing poorly. I think it would have been easier than beating Hillary Clinton, if you want to know the truth."

In Trump's imagination, he would have pulled in millions more votes than Romney did. "He ran a horrible race," Trump says of Romney. "Do you know why? He was intimidated by African Americans. He was intimidated by Obama. He never fought. I said, 'You know if you fought him like you fought me, you could have won.' He was always saying . . ." Trump makes a gargling sound, as if Romney's campaign speeches were the equivalent of rinsing his throat with a cup of salt water. "He was terrible."

Trump continues. "And he's a total asshole anyway. You can leave that on the record! He's a real schmuck. And now he's resigning because he knows he can't win in Utah because of me. I'm very popular in Utah, and I would never even think about endorsing him. So, anyway, he's out of politics."

In early 2013, back at the Television Critics Association press tour, a group of journalists asked Bob Greenblatt about NBC's efforts to get Trump to curtail his increasingly inflammatory rhetoric. For example, on the night Obama was reelected in 2012, Trump had called for a revolution on Twitter. "We talked him out of running for president," Greenblatt said. "Wasn't that good enough?"

At a certain point, I started to wonder whether I could find an *Apprentice* clip that Trump wouldn't love. Every scene we watch together brings him a tidal wave of enthusiasm and pride, until we get to one particular clip—his firing of the pop singer Aubrey O'Day. This took place during season 12 of *The Apprentice*, which aired in 2012. "Um," Trump says. "She was okay." His eyes barely move as his chin bobs up and down. "She did good. She was well known. I didn't know her. She was fine." Uncharacteristically, his phrases are short and devoid of any meaning; it's like listening to a novelty talking Trump doll, its battery on the fritz.

This edition of *The Apprentice* may not summon fond memories for Trump, because he'd chosen it over the chance to oust Obama from the White House. The latest cast included the former talk show host Arsenio Hall, the comedian Lisa Lampanelli, and the *American Idol* runner-up Clay Aiken. In that crowd, O'Day wasn't among the better-known contestants. In the mid-2000s, she'd made a name for herself on MTV's reality series *Making the Band*. After a few seasons on the show, Sean "Diddy" Combs fired her from Danity Kane, the marginally successful girl group he'd assembled, for her "attitude." But that attitude, viewed another way, was reality TV gold.

O'Day knew how to stir up drama. And she understood she had a job to do: she drove the majority of *The Apprentice*'s conflict that season, picking fights with Hall and crying in front of Trump in the boardroom. But what she did off camera was even more scandalous. For years, O'Day has spoken openly about how she'd had an affair with Don Jr., who was serving as one of that season's boardroom advisers. He was still married to his first wife, Vanessa, at the time, with whom he has five children.

O'Day later recorded a 2013 song about their relationship, titled "DJT." (Sample lyrics: "I hate me for loving you / Hate you for letting our love die.") The song's title—Don Jr.'s initials, which he shares with his father—made plain his identity. It was perhaps the kind of discretion you'd expect from someone who'd go on to date *Jersey Shore*'s Pauly D.

When I ask Trump about O'Day's affair with Don Jr., he takes a long pause. "I had heard that, actually," he says, blinking. "No, I had heard that." Did he know that O'Day had written a song about Don Jr.? "I hadn't heard the song. But I had heard that," Trump says, confirming once again that he's aware of the story about Don Jr. sleeping with one of the contestants on *The Celebrity Apprentice*.

While none of this ever spilled out in the show, there were signs, in retrospect, that something was transpiring between judge and player. "It was not a well-kept secret," Aiken says as he recalls how O'Day was the only contestant with Don Jr.'s personal cell phone number. "There were a few times when I was on Aubrey's team where she either texted or called him to get his advice on something. That was not something anyone else had access to, Don Jr.'s cell phone number."

A reality TV show judge offering special help to a contestant with whom he's romantically involved sounds as if it should have been against the rules. "I don't know," Aiken says. "It probably should have been, frankly. *Idol* had very strict FCC-regulated rules." (Later, when performing at an event together in St. Petersburg, Florida, O'Day revealed to Aiken that she'd been sleeping with the boss's son. "She told me after the show," Aiken says. "Frankly, half of me thought she was full of shit, because she's Aubrey and she tends to exaggerate.")

Aiken can't remember exactly why he agreed to compete on *The Celebrity Apprentice*. It's something his agent brought to him, and he'd seen enough seasons to believe that he could win. Looking back, he's a little embarrassed about how hard everyone clamored for Trump's approval at the time. "When he came in a room, I hate to use the phrase 'alpha,' but he had something about him," Aiken says. "You wanted him to compliment you." Aiken, who ran as a Democrat for a House seat representing North Carolina in 2014, recalls watching Republican members of Congress on TV trample each other for Trump's approval to stay on his good side. "There was always something about him that made him complimenting you feel like a bigger fucking deal than anybody else giving you a compliment," Aiken says. "Please know I'm embarrassed to say that, but I have to be honest."

I can relate to the feeling Aiken is describing. On a phone call once, as we were catching up, Trump said to me, "I have a lot of respect for *Variety*, always have. It's got a great name. So you must be doing a good job. I'm proud of you." He sounded for a moment so genuinely encouraging it was as if I were talking to my own father.

Aiken spent his early adulthood on reality TV as a twenty-four-year-old contestant on *American Idol*, so he could also spot the puppetry behind Trump's decision making. "We all knew who was really cutting people," Aiken says. "Every boardroom, there'd be a tape change and the cameras would shut off. Trump would get up and leave. We'd sit there, waiting for ten minutes or so for this 'tape change'—it was all fucking digital!" Aiken laughs at the sloppiness of this excuse. "As soon as he'd come back, within seconds, he'd go straight to who'd gotten fired."

There was another trick in the boardroom that Aiken uncovered, which unlocks the mystery of how exactly Trump knew what to say. Trump loves to claim that the boardroom scenes were unscripted and that he had an infallible memory. But the secret to Trump's improvisation came in the form of a small device that sat on the table in front of him. On TV, it looks like a telephone. "It's essentially a screen, where they could type him messages, and send him messages from backstage," Aiken says. "And the room is completely mirrored."

Aiken presents additional proof. "I would sit, and my strategy was don't interrupt," he says. "If I had something to say, I would make a face, because I knew some producer in the back would see it and type a message to Trump: 'Ask Clay what he thinks.' He was totally propped up by that prompter. He didn't know shit about what was going on. He had absolutely no idea what was happening."

During his season, NBC had asked Aiken to promote the show on social media, so he watched all the episodes before they aired. "I remember a few times you could see him looking. You could see his eyes glance down to see his message."

That season, *The Celebrity Apprentice* once again featured a face-off between the two most popular contestants: Arsenio Hall and Clay Aiken, a Black man versus a gay man from the South. Behind the scenes, the two rivals actually became pals. "He and I became very close during the process of it," Aiken says. Hall confided in Aiken about his complicated feelings about joining the show in the first place. "Arsenio felt guilty for a while," Aiken says. "He felt bad. I had not understood while it was going on that people thought Trump was racist. And Arsenio explained to me people think he's racist because he's been asking for Obama's birth certificate. I thought he was doing it for attention. I didn't tie those things together."

In the end, Trump crowned Hall as the next winner. And the timing couldn't have been better—Hall was mounting a comeback with the revived *Arsenio Hall Show*, which aired for one season on CBS starting in 2013. It may be that Trump, by picking Hall, wanted to take credit for Hall's success in the late-night landscape. But Aiken recalls Hall offering more suspicious motives. "Arsenio was worried doing the show might make him appear to be tacitly endorsing Trump in some way," he says. "And he told me afterwards he thought Trump probably just chose him to not make himself look racist."

The all-stars edition in 2013 didn't pop in the ratings as NBC had hoped. By then, the network had started to once again realize that Trump's popularity was fading as a reality star, even with the help of a cast of celebrities. Although season 14—with Geraldo Rivera—was filmed in 2014, NBC held the new episodes in favor of multiple nights of *The Voice* and *The Biggest Loser*. The next round of *The Celebrity Apprentice* finally aired in the winter of 2015, with the outdated Bill Cosby references, after many details of the season had already been spoiled due to the long delay. It was time for Trump to try something new. And there was no clear Republican front-runner in the next presidential election cycle.

Trump says that NBC's leadership returned to his office, pleading with him to renew his contract. The ratings for his last season averaged 6.3 million viewers, enough, as viewership continued to fragment, for NBC to want to stay in the Trump business. "We did tremendously well," Trump says.

Burnett once again attempted to block him from entering a crowded Republican primary, which was growing by the day with Jeb Bush, Carly Fiorina, and Ted Cruz. "He said, 'Don't do it!'" Trump recalls. "'You're going to get into a risky field, and chances are, you're not going to win.' By that time, they already had like fifteen announced candidates." Even as Trump didn't seem interested in prolonging his *Apprentice* days, Burnett kept pushing. In Trump's recollection, Burnett told him, "You negotiate. You don't turn down. They'll give you any money you want."

The NBC suits gave it another go, too. "Steve Burke came up to see me with Paul Telegdy, and essentially said the same thing, 'We'll give you anything you want.' I said, 'Steve, I just don't want to do it. I've done it enough. I've done fourteen seasons in twelve years. I don't need the money. I want to do other things.'"

"You want to run for president?" Burke asked him.

"Yeah," Trump said, according to Trump, who is now narrating both sides of the dialogue to me. And then Burke told him, "There are a lot of guys running. Statistically, you can't win, because nobody has done this before. I don't know if you looked, but the only people ever elected president were a politician or a general." (The exception, Herbert Hoover—who was a businessman, not an elected politician, before serving as a cabinet secretary and then president from 1929 to 1933—is nobody's idea of a role model.)

Trump wouldn't budge this time. "Steve, I want to do it." Trump claims he turned down a contract from NBC to host *The Apprentice* for another five seasons. He didn't know what exactly he was getting into, but he was ready for the cameras to follow him on a new endeavor. "And that's when I guess I said I'm running," Trump says. "And then, relatively shortly after that, I went down the escalators."

Trump walked away from *The Apprentice* of his own accord. Yet he still wasn't done tampering with his proudest achievement. As he thought about the future of the franchise, Trump had a clear successor in mind. "I said, 'The best person to hire would be Ivanka Trump,'" he says. "I didn't press it. But I felt Ivanka would have been by far the best person you could hire."

Although Trump hasn't revealed this information before, it's not a surprise that he'd want to keep his reality show in safe hands. *The Apprentice* had benefited Ivanka more than Trump's sons or his wife—more than anyone short of Trump himself. Following her father's zeal for branding, in 2007, Ivanka had launched her own jewelry line, later expanding to shoes and clothing. (It would shutter in 2018, after sales fell off a cliff because customers were offended by her father's policies as president.) In the same way that Fred had handed off the family business to his son, Donald was trying to do the same for Ivanka.

In this incarnation that lived only in Trump's mind, Don Jr. and Eric would permanently take over as the judges of the show, sitting next to their sister. "It was going to be the three of us," Eric says, confirming his father's proposal. "There were talks for a little while about it." In the end, it didn't seem like a practical undertaking. "I think it's pretty hard to say we're going to run with reality TV in a time when you're talking about ending nuclear proliferation around the world," Eric says, remembering one particular aspect of his father's foreign policy platform. "I'm not sure the two could have worked in tandem."

And building a TV show around the children of an already controversial presidential candidate didn't sound like an appealing proposition to those programming the show. "NBC didn't like it, because it became like a family thing," Trump says. "But I said, 'There's nobody you're going to hire that will come even close to Ivanka.' They said, 'Huh . . .' And then they came back with Arnold Schwarzenegger."

It wasn't exactly done in that order. NBC executives had initially thought that Trump's foray into politics would be short-lived—a matter of quickly dipping his toes in before dropping out. So they saved *The Apprentice* on ice for him, figuring he'd return as soon as he got enough of a high from the free press that would be coming his way. But after Trump announced his run on June 16, 2015, he made the likelihood of a quick retreat impossible, with his disparaging remarks about Mexicans. Less than two weeks later, NBC was forced to publicly disavow Trump, issuing a statement that he'd never again host *The Apprentice* and that they wouldn't air his Miss USA and Miss Universe pageants. The campaign had only just begun, and Trump was so radioactive that it looked as if the wheels were coming off before he'd even get to primary season.

Trump says that he has no memory of getting a phone call from NBC telling him it was over. And this period of his life is now foggy to him. "This isn't when they came and begged?" he asks me. Trump thinks it over before turning the narrative on its side. "Okay, are you ready? If I went back to NBC to do something, they would do anything I wanted to do, showbiz-wise. If there's one thing I know about that business, and I learned that business better than anybody else could learn a business in a short period of time, it's all about one thing: ratings. If you have ratings, you can be the meanest, most horrible human being in the world."

Maybe so, but in September 2015, Trump showed a softer side when he took to Twitter to congratulate Schwarzenegger on his new gig, and thanked his fans for watching all those years. "I handed him off a very successful show," Trump says, adding, "He made a big mistake taking that."

Schwarzenegger's edition of *The New Celebrity Apprentice* premiered on January 2, 2017, less than three weeks before Trump's inauguration as the forty-fifth president of the United States of America, with another pack of celebrities that America barely recognized—from *Queer Eye for the Straight Guy*'s Carson Kressley to the UFC fighter Chael Sonnen. But it fared even worse than the Martha Stewart spin-off.

Schwarzenegger had been a movie star before his election as governor of California. Indeed, he could be seen as a bridge figure between Ronald Reagan and Donald Trump; his fame was what got him the job. But, like Stewart, Schwarzenegger didn't relish cutting the contestants down, lacked comedic timing, looked stiff on camera, and couldn't give viewers a reason to watch. "Yeah, I watched it," Trump says. "I watched the beginning. It was not watchable, in my opinion." Trump is thrilled to give me his scathing review. "I said it was terrible. I just felt it had no energy whatsoever."

This is a particularly sweet victory for Trump, because Schwarzenegger headlined some of the biggest movies of his time, from the *Terminator* franchise to *True Lies* and *Total Recall*. The inability of an A-list movie star to carry *The Apprentice* made Trump feel as though his talents as host were unmatched. "Arnold just didn't have what it took," Trump says gleefully. "Arnold Schwarzenegger wanted to be on television, and he was going to do *The Apprentice*, and his friends tried to talk him out of it, saying, 'You can't top it.'" Trump offers a strained metaphor about the son of a golf legend trying to outshine his father on the green, which doesn't make sense in this scenario, since Trump and Schwarzenegger aren't related. "It's, like, you're not going to top it," Trump says. "I don't care who he is. And he just bombed. You know, they have meters. It was dead after the first fifteen minutes, and everybody knew it."

To the dismay of many of Trump's critics, he was still credited as an executive producer on *The Apprentice* due to his original contract with Burnett. Even as he took his oath as president, Trump collected royalties from MGM, which owned the show. "I would have liked to have seen it be successful from an economic standpoint," Trump says. But he admits that his ego preferred for the show to fall apart without him. "I knew if it was successful, they would say Trump gets outdone by Schwarzenegger," he says. "Even if it was a modest success, they try to make it as big as possible." Trump flashes a grin. "He didn't have it. The whole thing was, like, ponderous. And I view that as a great compliment to myself."

Trump claims that Schwarzenegger struggled when he tested out "You're fired!" as a catchphrase. "Arnold couldn't say it properly. Who would think Arnold would be bad? But he was slow. You got to be fast, man." He mocks the catchphrase Schwarzenegger ended up using— "You're terminated!" playing off his biggest role—when axing contestants. "He did say 'Terminator' right, but he was a disaster."

Trump's win against Schwarzenegger seems to give him as much satisfaction as any political victory he's experienced. "I was surprised Arnold failed so badly," Trump says, not sounding surprised at all. "I really was. Who would have thought that Trump gets ratings but Arnold Schwarzenegger doesn't? He's a movie star." Trump is having too much fun to stop now. "I thought he would do okay. He was boring. He was really boring."

As he processes everything he's been through, Trump sounds as if he were ready to take on Schwarzenegger and Stewart all over again. "Here I am, fourteen seasons over a twelve-year period," Trump says. "And these guys bomb out. They are both big names, and they both died like dogs."

Of course, for Trump, Schwarzenegger failing on *The Apprentice* after the high-profile Republican didn't endorse him as a candidate in 2016 is an example of karma in action. "Arnold was a guy, he supported Crooked Hillary, so I didn't give a shit," Trump says. "He was a Kasich supporter too, which made it even worse. So between Kasich and Hillary, I said, 'I hope he bombs like a dog,' and he did."

In the end, *The Apprentice* could make a politician out of a reality star, but it couldn't make a reality star out of a politician.

As the campaign waged on, Donald Trump kept his boardroom TV set intact on the fourteenth floor of Trump Tower for a period of time—like a favorite child's bedroom after they leave for college. "There was a cognizant decision to leave the boardroom, and there was a possibility of it coming back," Eric Trump says. "The boardroom stayed up for maybe six to eight months after *The Apprentice*, until the campaign really started rolling in a meaningful way."

As the beloved room where Donald Trump first uttered the words "You're fired," changing his life forever, was demolished, it evolved into the beating heart of his 2016 presidential run. "The fourteenth floor became the campaign offices for the entire campaign," Eric says. "The presidential election was won through the fourteenth floor of Trump Tower. We didn't have any other office space in the building at that time." And his father felt at home there. "So many pictures on election night, when he's looking up at the TVs as all the results came in, that all took place on the fourteenth floor."

Eric believes that *The Apprentice* deserves its own spotlight in the re-telling of his father's life story. "The show would be a big part of history," he says. "It's going to be a big part of his legacy. I hope it will remain a big part of his legacy. So often, it's easy to forget that—they say, 'Real estate to politics.'"

It's confusing to Eric that MGM, now owned by Amazon, has kept *The Apprentice* in a vault so that old episodes starring Trump aren't available on any streaming platforms. "They also try to write him out of *Home Alone*," Eric says. (Trump's cameo was cut out of the version of *Home Alone 2* broadcast on Canadian TV after he won the presidency.) "It doesn't make a whole lot of sense to me. Right now, it would kill it."

Donald Trump is equally dismayed that it's so hard to find episodes of *The Apprentice*. "Oh, you can't buy them?" he asks me. "They took them down?" Trump frowns as he offers to help me find them. "I have the episodes. I'm sure I have the episodes. I thought you could get them easily. It's very interesting. A lot of people ask me that, 'How do I get the episodes?'"

Through all the ups and downs of Trump's roller-coaster ride into the American presidency, Mark Burnett had been close at hand. But he was just as surprised as the rest of the world by the outcome of the 2016 election. Burnett had kept quiet for most of the duration of Trump's first run for office, smiling through the discomfort as the Emmys host, Jimmy Kimmel, tore into Burnett at the September telecast that year. "Thanks to Mark Burnett, we don't have to watch reality shows anymore, because we're living in one," Kimmel said as the crowd started to boo. "If Donald Trump gets elected, and he builds that wall—the first person we're throwing over it is Mark Burnett. The tribe has spoken."

When the *Access Hollywood* tape leaked on October 7, 2016, Burnett finally issued a statement condemning his TV wingman. "My wife and I reject the hatred, division and misogyny that has been a very unfortunate part of this campaign," it read. Mostly, Burnett just wanted the campaign to be over so Trump could lose. Burnett told his inner circle that he missed his days as a beloved Hollywood producer who didn't get blamed for Trump's untethered proclamations on Twitter and at campaign rallies.

In private, Burnett has always maintained that he voted for Hillary Clinton in 2016. When asked about the election by those in Hollywood, he'd sum up his relationship with Trump by repeating one of his favorite refrains: he was a capitalist, and Trump's partnership made him even richer.

Burnett fell asleep early on the night of the election, thinking—like most of the country—that Clinton would become president. As he came downstairs the next morning, his wife, Roma Downey, was quiet.

"He won," she told him.

"Who won?" Burnett asked.

"Trump."

Burnett laughed, thinking she was joking. And then he turned on the TV and saw the face of America's new president-elect.

Burnett had created the Donald Trump myth, programmed him, fed his ego, and covered up all of his flaws with the magic of Hollywood's best editors. Now Trump was about to permanently exit his reality TV cocoon and try to lead America, with real consequences and access to the nuclear codes. So what did Burnett do? He called Trump to congratulate him.

"Hey, buddy," Burnett said.

Trump, elated, wanted to remind Burnett—a traitor, if only for a matter of weeks—just who was in charge. "Don't call me buddy," Trump said. "It's Mr. President."

"Yes, congratulations—Mr. President," Burnett said. Then Trump asked Burnett to get on a flight to New York. They had much to discuss, starting with the inauguration. Trump needed the producer's help to put on his biggest show yet. And this time, the whole country would be watching.

CHAPTER 12

Apprentice in Wonderland

The gray skies over Palm Beach, Florida, hang mournfully above me on my final visit with Donald Trump. It's November 2023, and Maryanne Trump Barry, Donald's older sister, has died unexpectedly this morning in her Manhattan apartment at the age of eighty-six. Upon hearing the news, I wonder whether Trump might cancel our appointment. He had bad blood with his sister, a former federal judge who'd bitterly disparaged her brother's presidency in an audio recording that leaked in 2020. But, on the other hand, family is family. Trump had a horrible divorce from his first wife, Ivana, and now she's buried on one of his golf clubs in New Jersey, and even though Ivanka has worked hard to distance herself from her dad in recent years, he still loves her. Right?

So I'm a little surprised when his office emails me to say he'll need to push back our interview by only an hour. By the time I pull up to Mar-a-Lago, the Florida sun is shining brightly.

"Are you here to see Mogul?" a member of the Secret Service asks.

It's only fitting that Trump's security code word would be an homage to the smart businessman he played on television. The agent inspects my driver's license, announcing my arrival into a walkie-talkie. "I have some-one here for a meeting with Mogul." I exit the car and bob past a security checkpoint, walking down a long driveway to one of the main entrances of the property.

I'd read for years about Trump's private club, his "Winter White House," but in person it's even more garishly dazzling. It feels like enter-ing a make-believe estate where actors playing members of the royal fam-ily spend holidays on *The Crown*. It's a castle, but one more gaudy than any real European royal other than Ludwig of Bavaria would deign to inhabit. If it hadn't already existed, Trump would have built it, and then given one of his apprentices a fake job overseeing the construction.

At the bottom of the driveway, two stone-engraved lions peer over the guests at the front entrance, with a coat of arms hanging in between them belonging to Joseph Edward Davies, the ambassador who married Mar-a-Lago's original owner, the cereal heiress Marjorie Merriweather Post. (There has been some controversy about Trump doctoring the coat of arms inside the club to add his name without approval from the Davies family.)

In the main building, where I'm meeting Trump, design influences collide and compound upon each other. The floors are carpeted in Persian rugs; the walls are lined with ornate Spanish tiles; the high ceilings evoke a European cathedral; glass chandeliers suggest the old Robin Leach show *Lifestyles of the Rich and Famous*. It's all as well kept, quiet, and spotless as any five-star resort—a far cry from the images splattered online in June 2023, showing what the FBI discovered when it searched Mar-a-Lago for classified documents and found them stacked up in a bathroom, in a ball-room, and in several other rooms that looked like a scene from *Hoarders*. That was just five months before my November visit, and Trump's legal problems have only piled up since.

Margo Martin meets me at the receptionist's desk. Her heels click as she leads me to a couch in the main guest reception area. And then she disappears. The Trump family, busier than ever in defending themselves, can't stop for anything—not even Maryanne's death. Somewhere in a courtroom in downtown Manhattan that same day, Don Jr. is returning to the stand to testify in Trump's $370 million fraud trial that could bar him from any future real estate dealings in New York, defending his father and calling him a "genius."

But all of that is hundreds of miles away. Here at Mar-a-Lago, there's a relaxing calmness on this suddenly beautiful Monday afternoon. The property is mostly empty, except for a TV crew setting up in the room next door. A small sign in my line of sight reads, "Please do not place anything on this 1927 Steinway Baby Grand Piano." As I wait, a woman with the unmistakable task-oriented vibe of a party planner walks past me, inspecting the yellow draperies. "I just talked to Alice to shut these old curtains!" she says to an associate.

Wait, did someone say Alice? I'd been rereading *Alice in Wonderland*, because of a passage in Bob Woodward's *Rage*, his second book about Trump's White House. According to the 2020 exposé, Jared Kushner had told advisers that for them to understand Trump, they simply needed to read Lewis Carroll's fairy tale, because the president embodies the qualities of the Cheshire Cat. But maybe it's the spirit of Wonderland in general that best captures Trump, with the Queen of Hearts yelling "Off with their heads!" instead of "You're fired!" In Carroll's story, for instance, Alice sees a cake that reads, "Eat me," and she consumes it, turning her into a giant, as if she were the biggest and most dominant star in all of Wonderland. She sees a label that reads, "Drink me," and quaffs a potion that shrinks her to the size of a dormouse, like Trump's nightmare version of a life away from the headlines.

Alice wasn't the only one lost in Wonderland. The self-conscious grandeur of the setting—the Steinway, the family crest, the rugs, and chandeliers, all procured by an heiress but now a jerry-rigged tribute to Trump—bring to mind how many *Apprentice* contestants still buy into the made-for-TV narrative. So many people I'd spoken with still worship their former reality TV boss. Stephanie Myers, a contestant from season 3 who campaigned for Trump in 2016 and 2020, said to me, "He's a family-oriented man. He likes to know if you have a family.

'How are your parents?' He's very personable. He really does care about people, as we can see through his leadership as president." Trump's own sister Maryanne, secretly recorded by her niece, Mary, didn't seem particularly convinced: "It's the phoniness of it all," Maryanne once said. "It's the phoniness and this cruelty. Donald is cruel."

On this day, November 13, 2023, Trump suavely makes a grand entrance, dressed in a navy blue suit, white shirt, red tie, his skin glowing with the sheen of a clementine. It had been more than two years since our last meeting, and I wasn't sure how Trump would be doing—given all the grave legal trouble he's in, as he's surging once again in the polls.

His critics have been openly celebrating the possibility that he could be in jail before the next election, but Trump doesn't seem bothered at all. He shakes my hand and looks pleased that I made the trip down to Florida. To prevent me from seeing any of his missed calls or text messages, Trump plops down his phone a few feet away from us, on top of the 1927 Steinway baby grand piano—right next to the sign.

As he settles into his seat, I offer my condolences about his sister. "Awww, thank you very much," Trump says. "I just found out this morning. It's too bad. She was a good woman, actually. Very smart. Very, very smart. Anyway, so good." Trump—who once described himself as "nostalgic" watching old clips of *The Apprentice*—isn't feeling sentimental about Maryanne's passing.

Our conversation picks up right where we left off as Trump summons his surprise at just how much of a disappointment Martha Stewart was as host of *The Apprentice*. At one point, though, sensing that perhaps he hasn't given his sister enough due, he circles back to the night of January 8, 2004, the premiere of the first episode of *The Apprentice*. Trump has told me variations of this story before, about how his phone blew up with so many people breathlessly calling to congratulate him that it overwhelmed him. But there's a new wrinkle to this story today as Maryanne joins his circle of fans. "My sister, who died today, she called me. And she's not that kind," says Trump, still talking about Maryanne in the present tense. "She's very strong, to put it mildly. And very smart. And a judge. And never spoke to the media, which I always said was a mistake. But she does the right thing from the standpoint of a judge. She called up and said, 'That show was unbelievable!'" Trump leans back in his chair, as if he's accepting the compliment all over again. "I've never heard her be that way. It's just not her personality."

Trump pays tribute to his late sister by flattering himself. "And Mary-anne said, 'The show was unbelievable.' She was the first call I got. It was twenty seconds after the show went off. And then I was inundated that night with calls." There's no way for me to check if any of this ever happened, but then, Trump must know that. "It wasn't normal," Trump says about all the phone calls he'd received that night. "It's like our rallies aren't normal. Do you understand?"

I wasn't sure that I'd ever sit down with Trump again. After our talk in August 2021, Trump was so thrilled to be watching clips of *The Apprentice* that he invited me to return to Trump Tower for another meeting. But his office later declined on his behalf. I'm not sure what caused them to reverse course. But my suspicion is that it had to do with the sour expression on his male handler's face when I brought up Don Jr.'s affair with Aubrey O'Day.

Time passed, and Trump receded for a while into the shadows; Biden's presidency, with his popularity collapsing following the American withdrawal from Afghanistan, came to dominate the headlines, while the man who'd preceded him in the presidency faded—no rallies, no tweets, no reason for coverage. It was similar to how his profile diminished in the middle seasons of *The Apprentice*, before the show was reinvented with celebrities. But instead of banking on Piers Morgan or Joan Rivers for attention, Trump simply had to wait for the right circumstances to bring him back into the spotlight.

His media tour first resumed with another cliff-hanger—a series of criminal and civil court cases, which he's called "a witch hunt and a disgrace." For all the criminal allegations and threats of legal penalties that could end him, there was one upside: Trump was back in the news, and in the game.

This time, the drama hanging over his head focused on whether he could escape jail time for trying to manipulate election results in Georgia and mishandling classified material. In New York, Trump had found an adversary in Letitia James, the attorney general, who built a case against him for committing fraud and inflating the value of his real estate dealings. All of this would be terrifying for most human beings, but for Trump it merely unfolded like the next season of his life as Mogul.

I wasn't so sure if even Trump thought that Trump would emerge unscathed this time around. My first email to his office in months had gone unanswered, and that wasn't like Trump, who had practically made a religion out of replying to reporters. As the negative stories piled up, I started to wonder whether Trump's trail of destruction had finally caught up with him. And then, out of the blue, his office had reached out in August 2023 to say he'd get on the phone with me to answer my additional questions.

During Trump's first term as president, I had often wondered how much he'd changed as a person from when, at *Newsweek*, I'd interviewed him at the pinnacle of his reality TV success. It turned out he hadn't changed at all through any of it. Trump presented a conundrum for a reporter: he might have been the sower of chaos all over the globe, and he certainly lacked empathy, but he could also be funny and engaging in conversation. But regardless of what version of Trump I saw in all our time together, it became clear to me in our first post-presidency meeting that there is no way to reasonably interview Trump as a politician. He's not a politician. There's no way to ask him about governing. He's not able to govern. There's no point in trying to pin him down on his hopes for another term. He doesn't care about the specifics of the plot during his time in the White House—he just wants to get renewed for another season.

Sam Solovey, from the first season of *The Apprentice*, was right: Trump conducts himself like an actor playing Trump.

When we speak on the phone in October 2023, Trump had recently appeared on NBC's *Meet the Press*, where the show's new host, Kristen Welker, tried to corner him on his growing list of legal nightmares. Opposite Trump, Welker came across as if she were playing a character, too. "President Trump, welcome back to *Meet the Press*," she said enthusiastically. With a stack of questions in her lap, Welker started the interview by asking why Trump wanted to be president again, which allowed him to vent about "illegal immigrants . . . flooding the countryside . . . they come from prisons, they come from mental institutions, insane asylums." All these years in, the mainstream media still doesn't know how to handle Trump, the reality star whose greatest skill is his resilience in thriving against the odds on TV.

"She did a lot of interrupting," Trump says to me. "They can't allow the truth to come out. She wanted to stop me from doing a lot of things. It was crazy! Actually, it *was* crazy. Did you notice the interruptions?"

On the phone, Trump sighs, offering up a reason why he's so good on TV. "I'm a storyteller, they say. I've never thought of myself as that, but a lot of people say, 'He's the greatest storyteller of all storytellers!' I don't know. I think that's a compliment." It's a no-win situation for any broadcaster to interview Trump. But cutting him off so aggressively only gives Trump an excuse to plant the idea that there's a media conspiracy to silence him. "She'd ask me a question, and I'd go two words into it, and then she'd ask me another question. I'd be like, 'What the hell? Will you let me finish this up?' But she didn't want to hear the answers in some cases because of the political persuasion."

Trump is acutely aware of why he even gets airtime. "She needed the numbers," he says about Welker. "I heard it did phenomenally good." (The episode, Welker's first as the new *Meet the Press* moderator, beat its competition on ABC and CBS.) "That's what I am—a ratings machine! I do these shows, even these political shows, they double and triple and quadruple. That's why they like me doing them." Trump has caught the media in its own hypocrisy. He knows they're inviting him on TV for the spectacle, and so it's a self-fulfilling prophecy where he does his best to deliver so that they keep him coming back. It's the training he got from performing for Jeff Zucker and Mark Burnett on *The Apprentice*, and he was trained all too well.

"Do you know what got high ratings, very high ratings, was that CNN town hall I did?" Trump is referring to a conversation moderated by Kaitlan Collins in May 2023. The cozy chat had been coordinated by Chris Licht, Zucker's successor at CNN, whose own tenure was short-lived. Licht was fired a month later following an embarrassing profile about him in *The Atlantic*, which partly focused on Licht's disastrous decision to give Trump carte blanche at the town hall. But now Trump is taking this media story, distorting all the details, and coming away with a different conclusion. "That got high ratings—so high that they fired the guy that ran CNN because I got my point of view across. They were not happy about that—very political. Usually, in your business, if you get high ratings, you get an increase, right? But anyway, go ahead."

At his prompting, we talk some more about Martha Stewart not measuring up to Trump. "She actually fired people by letter: 'Dear so-and-so, sorry it didn't work out.' I said, 'That's ridiculous!' I didn't know they were going to do that." This is one of the stories on the greatest storyteller of all storytellers' favorite playlists, but then he tells me something I'd never heard him say. Trump believes that the reason NBC News has covered him so critically has nothing to do with the way he's behaved. Instead, he thinks the network wants to get back at him for bailing on *The Apprentice*. For Trump, all roads eventually lead back to his reality TV show.

"You know, NBC wanted to re-sign me so bad," Trump says. "I think it's why they treat me so badly now, if you want to know the truth. The top people came to me, they were begging me not to run for president. They were begging me. I think that's one of the reasons NBC has been so bad."

For Trump, there is no separation between the warm make-believe world on *The Apprentice* and the cold reality of his next job as commander in chief. He starts to wax on, again, about *The Apprentice*'s success. "It was a great experience for me," Trump says on the phone. "It was a very important show. It really was a landmark show. It was a big thing. It was like a meteor went out!"

As he's about to hang up, Trump tries to convince me that it would benefit me to write a positive book about him, because he'll help me promote it. "I hope the book is going to treat it with respect," Trump says. "We'll make that book No. 1. Make it good, we'll make it the biggest book you've ever seen, okay?"

I ask Trump if I can meet with him in person one more time, and he agrees. "You'll come up and see us at Mar-a-Lago."

Dan Brody, a contestant from season 5, recalls having breakfast one morning with George Ross before the live finale. "He told me he was the attorney involved in the Mar-a-Lago purchase," Brody says of Ross. In 1985, Trump had drafted a deal for the property—including all its original furniture and the beachfront land—for the bargain price of $10 million. But there was one problem. "It's all very well-heeled families that own private residences up there," Brody says, "and Trump coming in and trying to turn it into a private club was not received well."

Although this tale of Mar-a-Lago has been told before, Brody got to hear it from the point of view of Trump's attorney. "So George gave me the whole backstory of what he did with that, and it was a very impressive, eye-opening thing," Brody says. "As the attorney, he received all the letters from the families in the area, and they said, 'We're going to stop you.' And then he drafted a letter at Trump's direction letting them know, 'The real reason you don't want us is because, unlike all the clubs that you're part of, this club is going to allow Black people and Spanish people and Jewish people—and that's what you don't want in your neighborhood.' And they all, of course, came back and said, 'No, that's not the reason.'"

Ross told Brody about his next move: "And then they came back with a brilliant idea. 'Okay, well, if that's the truth, you won't mind if we subpoena all of your family memberships. Like, you probably don't belong to any whites-only, men-only clubs, right?' And then quickly those families changed their tunes. And that was Trump's game plan from the beginning."

Brody tells this story as evidence that Trump can't possibly be racist. But, in fact, it just proves that for Trump race—like everything else in the world—matters only when it can be leveraged into an opportunity for Trump.

It's my first trip to Palm Beach, a time capsule from a different era, still frozen in the Reagan 1980s. At the airport, the pictures of the town's board of commissioners look like homogeneous cutouts from small-town U.S.A. My taxicab driver wears a necktie right out of Trump's own dress code. I'm staying at the Colony, a boutique hotel just down the shore from Mar-a-Lago. I've selected it for its proximity and for another, far more superficial reason: one of my colleagues at work, a Gwyneth Paltrow superfan, told me that Paltrow's luxury brand, Goop, had set up a two-bedroom villa at the hotel. I tried to look up the exclusive Goop lodging, but it wasn't even searchable on the hotel's website. So I figured, if this villa was good enough for Gwyneth, a regular room would be fine for me.

On Saturday night, two days before my interview, I received a text from Trump's assistant Natalie Harp. "Looking forward to seeing you on Monday," she wrote. "Sharing the President's New Poll Numbers!" She'd attached a PDF with six pages of data, all of which looked good for Trump. I had the image of him hunkered down alone on a weekend in Mar-a-Lago studying his ratings.

The Colony is a flamingo-pink slab of concrete right off the beach, with green-and-pink rooms and a vibe that feels a bit closer to the present day—maybe the Clinton 1990s instead of the Reagan 1980s. The kitschy pool screams West Hollywood. Gwyneth hadn't failed me.

But on the morning of my interview, I have a rude awakening. As the rain pours hard against my room's windowpanes, the hotel slips a notice under my door: due to some planned repairs, there will be no electricity for most of the day. Hopefully, the letter reads, this wouldn't be too much of an inconvenience.

It is balmy outside—a typical Florida morning, soon to give way to the heat of midday. I start to sweat just thinking about sitting in my dark room for the next few hours without any Wi-Fi, running water, or air-conditioning. I need to go through my questions for the former president. I need to answer work emails. I need to iron my suit. I start to panic. I call the front desk to see if they have a solution for a guest who urgently requires electricity. The woman listens sympathetically to my concerns, hangs up to investigate, and then calls me back to offer me another room. When I go to the lobby, they slip me a new key. "You can stay at the Goop villa tonight."

I cross the street with my luggage in the rain. My room at the hotel had been a small studio. The Goop bungalow is up a flight of stairs, and it's like entering into a miniature Mar-a-Lago, but designed by Gwyneth. As a bellman shows me around, there is enough square footage to house an entire family: two bedrooms, one outfitted with bunk beds; an upstairs office and reading cove; a master bathroom with a full tub; hand-painted wallpaper with palm trees and white rose trees; a full kitchen that even Martha Stewart might deign to cook in; and a living room with white angular furniture that looks as if Gwyneth herself should be lounging across it on the cover of an architecture magazine. One night doesn't seem like long enough to be in this Spanish colonial paradise. The bungalow comes stocked with Paltrow's favorite drink (a carafe of whiskey), her favorite books (including *An Illustrated Catalog of American Fruits & Nuts*), and unlimited Goop beauty supplies (one potion, named Goop Glow, promised "microderm instant glow exfoliation").

I know I have to get dressed. I can't be late for my visit to Mar-a-Lago. But it's tempting to stay in this other, more palatable vision of celebrity adjacency, surrounded by branded merchandise that creates the illusion of comfort and wealth. Times have changed since *The Apprentice*, but the power of a star who doesn't mind lending their name freely as long as it keeps them in the spotlight? That's eternal.

Before I'd even had time to ask a question, Trump wants to know if I finished my required reading. "Have you seen the polls?" he asks. He starts to imagine having the power to move up voting day by a year. "If this were the U.K., I'd say Tuesday is the election," Trump claims. "Or sooner if possible!"

He's riding a high from America's renewed interested in him. "They like me," he says. "They see what's going on in the world with this guy." He makes this assertion without mentioning Biden's name. "What he's doing is unbelievable, whether it's Palestine or Israel, frankly. This would never have happened. It's a shame. Ukraine would have never happened. None of it would happen. China is going to happen too, because they're looking at us now—they're going to go in and do Taiwan, probably. It's pretty amazing."

I suddenly feel bad for Kristen Welker of NBC, because I can't imagine trying to pin down Trump on what exactly he's trying to say about global affairs. But we're moving on rapidly; Trump is at his most coherent when he's in showman mode. And he's beaming, because he has something important that he wants to show me. "Do you have my NFT boards?" he asks his aide, and she returns with a stack of cardboard posters, which look like something MAGA children might hang in their playrooms. These illustrations feature the words "I stand with Trump," with Trump's face in different heroic poses. He holds up one on which the American flag's stars and stripes are transposed over his eyes, chin, and nose.

We're a long way from Trump Ice or Trump University; now Trump is fully on board to conquer blockchain. "You know, I did NFTs!" Trump says. "I did NFTs six months ago. NFT is dead. Not dead, but pretty much dead." Trump wants credit for single-handedly keeping the digital-token fad alive. "It was hot as hell three or four years ago. We sold out in three hours. Forty-five thousand cards! Then we did forty-seven thousand. We sold out in three hours. They projected anywhere from six months to a year. The thing was sold out in hours."

Trump once again dovetails into anecdotes about Lawrence O'Donnell's tears and the time he improvised "You're fired!" in the boardroom. And then, because these cardboard sheets are lying out on the table in front of us, he returns to the topic now close to his heart. "So these are NFTs," he says, looking down at them. "They are good. It's like pop art!

And each one is different. In other words, they make 100,000 of these—each one will be slightly different."

He inspects a sheet that features his face next to a pot of gold at the end of the rainbow. "It may be the color of the gold will be different, but they have to be different. Tiny things. Every one is different in a tiny way. Sometimes, a more major way." Trump starts narrating the different shades of the rainbow. "Sometimes, that will be green, instead of brown. And it's cool. It's cool."

Trump poses a question that I hadn't prepared for as I was quickly thumbing through my notes in the Goop bungalow. "You know what the NFT is?" he asks, not waiting for a response. But he doesn't seem to know either. "It's a form. I put them out, $99. It's an investment." Trump rattles off huge numbers, like an auctioneer trying to collect bids. "One sold for $84,000! Eighty-two thousand dollars! Twenty-seven thousand dollars!" He comes back down to Earth. "But the average is $1,500. And I said, 'That's great. They're my people. They made money.'"

Trump admits that he thought about charging more. But then he decided against it. "I said, 'Do it for $99!' No. 1, it will definitely sell. And that means people make money. I don't need the money." I mention to Trump that Tom Brady—the star quarterback who'd at one time been friendly with Trump before making a joke about election deniers when he visited Biden at the White House following his Super Bowl LV victory—is also in the NFTs business. "He probably did well with it," Trump says. "Does he get liability with his crypto stuff?"

Displaying his unique talents for raising questions about someone else's shadiness is one of Trump's greatest strengths. "Well, he recommended it," Trump says of Brady, who was named in an $8 billion civil action lawsuit for endorsing FTX, the cryptocurrency company founded by convicted felon Sam Bankman-Fried. "And today if you recommend something . . . " Trump gives me an example of how it came back to bite even him, professionally. "I just won the case. I recommended a phone company. They paid me, like, a million bucks to give a speech, so I did four, five speeches, saying wonderful things. Then, all of a sudden, I get sued! They all sued me because I recommended it and their stock didn't go up as much as it should."

Trump is referring to a case in which investors took him to court in 2018, claiming that he duped them for backing a failed "videophone" back in 2008 that proved to not be the next big thing. This led to a deposition in 2022, around the same time he was being sued by the columnist E. Jean Carroll for sexually assaulting her in the 1990s in a dressing room at Bergdorf Goodman in New York. With all his legal problems, I didn't anticipate Trump would be throwing me the curveball of mentioning a less-important lawsuit. "And I said, 'This is a dangerous business!'"

Trump pivots back to Brady. "He recommended crypto. That's bad! Because he lost like $200 million in them. He was friends with this guy, Bankman-Fried, and that's not a good guy to be friends with right now." Trump still keeps the door open a crack, in case Brady ever wants to reconcile. "He's a nice guy, though, Tom!"

Eventually, Trump finds a way to talk about the New York civil case that's dominating the news as we speak. "The judge was a fraud," Trump says, claiming that the trial underestimated his net worth, and therefore, he was being defrauded. "He valued this asset at $18 million," Trump says, meaning the entirety of Mar-a-Lago. Then Trump points to the piano, where he's illegally—by Mar-a-Lago codes—placed his cell phone. "That piano is worth $18 million," he says hyperbolically. "Do you understand?"

The whole time we're talking, Trump's phone has been ringing nonstop on the Steinway. After he's gone another round on Melissa Rivers's bad behavior on *The Celebrity Apprentice*, he answers it in front of me. "I think they should ask for a directive," Trump says, doling out his own legal advice to this mystery caller. "You want me to call? Are they free now? I'll call him."

Trump winks at me. "So they just finished up the trial," he tells me. "We won everything." This isn't true, but Trump thinks he can issue his own verdict as he slams Arthur F. Engoron, the judge overseeing the case. (A former New York City cabdriver and "free-speech absolutist," Engoron quotes Bob Dylan and Shakespeare, as well as the Marx Brothers, in his rulings, according to the Associated Press.) "We have a judge who doesn't want to let it go," Trump says. "He's crazy. I don't know if you're liberal or not, but this guy is a radical-left lunatic! He's a political hack. He's a real hack! When you look at him, he should have never had the case in the first place." The former president is used to disparaging the third branch of government and getting plenty of coverage doing it. "Very dangerous system," he says. "You know what I mean? The good news is, we're killing him. He's getting horrible publicity. Horrible!"

Trump seems to believe that his ability to generate press is more important than any ruling. And who knows, maybe he's right. He references a tabloid media story that has been making the rounds, about Engoron posting a shirtless gym photo of himself in a newsletter for the alumni of a Long Island high school that he edited. "The thing with the weight lifting and shit," Trump says. "He's crazy. He's a fucking lunatic."

Trump picks up his phone and dials Eric, asking me to stop my tape recorder. "Maybe turn your machine off just for a second," he says. On the phone, he sounds like a stage dad, telling Eric to go back into the courtroom and ask for a directed verdict. This turns out to be a more stressful day for Trump than I'd imagined even after hearing his sister had passed away. With so much going on, I'm not sure why he's sitting with me, doing an interview about *The Apprentice*.

He hangs up and travels back to the 2010s. Our conversation touches on everything from Mark Burnett—"I hope he speaks well of me," Trump says—to Jeff Zucker's resignation at CNN in 2022, which Trump says didn't surprise him. "No," he says. "It was time."

Trump still has a bad taste in his mouth from doing Collins's CNN town hall. "With crazy Kaitlan, where they went crazy," he says. "I thought it was going to be a friendly show, because they don't do well with ratings. And if they came more toward the middle, they'd do much better. So I thought, like a schmuck, this was a start of them doing good television."

Trump recoils at the mention of CNN. "Fake television! Fake news! One of the great terms ever," he says, mischievously. "Do I get credit for it?"

Trump proudly tells me about how he's found a new acronym for MSNBC. "I watch MSDNC, which is the worst!" He asks me if I understand what the letters stand for: "MS-Democratic-National-Convention!" Trump says. "I'm good with names. There's nobody better. You know what's funny?" He mentions the current GOP debates—all of which he's skipped—when another candidate tried to pin a nickname on him. "Chris Christie took a shot. He said, 'Uh, Donald Duck.' It was so bad." To give credit where it's due, Trump's aptitude for coming up with taunts is singular. "It's actually an art," he tells me.

For 2024, he has decided to retire Biden's "Sleepy Joe" moniker in favor of "Crooked Joe." That, of course, was how he smeared Hillary Clinton in 2016. But it makes sense from a Hollywood branding perspective: if the sequel fails, for the third movie, go back to what worked in the original. "I changed Biden's name from Sleepy Joe to Crooked Joe because I think it's more effective," Trump explains.

This reminds me of something I've been wanting to ask Trump. If his campaign for president had quickly fallen apart in 2016, and NBC hadn't been forced to cut ties with him because of his disparaging comments, had he always planned on returning to the show? Trump speaks about *The Apprentice* with so much affection, it's hard to imagine he'd ever willingly let it go.

"No," Trump says. "When you go back to something, it never works out." He gives me a comparison. "It's like when you go back to a marriage—you see plenty of them—it tends not to work out. To go back to it, to have failed at something, I don't think I would have done it."

Remembering the image of the *Apprentice* boardroom remaining untouched for months after the show ended, I point out that Trump is attempting to return to the White House after it didn't work out last time. "That's different because I won twice!" Trump says, shuffling in his chair. "I got more votes than any sitting president ever got. It's a fucking crooked deal. If I lost—let's say I lost—I wouldn't be running again. They rigged it and robbed it." Trump's storytelling is stuck on the same track. But it's a storytelling track that millions seem to love.

Our show-and-tell that afternoon doesn't end with the NFTs. Trump takes me for a stroll to the receptionist's desk of Mar-a-Lago so that we can look at a copy of the *Variety* ratings chart from the spring of 2004 hanging in the entryway. This is the first activity we did together at Trump Tower when I started writing my book. It's the same chart—we've come full circle.

"I think I have a *Variety* over there," he says, pointing to the front door. "C'mon! I had the record—forty-two million people saw the finale of number one." Trump looks at the framed artifact. "Look at it, look at it there!" He's momentarily puzzled at seeing the prized chart hanging too close to the floor, below a bevy of other accolades and magazine covers. "I should lift it up higher. I mean, you can't see the damn thing. You see?" He turns to Margo Martin. "Do you have a light on your phone? Give him a light. Light it up!"

And here we are again, playing his favorite game: I read Trump the ratings. The numbers haven't changed since the last time we looked at this sheet together, and it's still not true that forty-two million viewers watched the finale for season 1. This time I say the real number a little louder than last time: forty million viewers.

"That's a big hit, isn't it?" He raises up his hands as if he's about to accept a trophy—maybe the Emmy that he'd always wanted, or an Oscar. "I think I beat the Academy Awards." No, that's not right either. I tell Trump that the Oscars still had a bigger viewership that year. "Okay, maybe," but he's already ahead of me. "You know when the Academy Awards went bad? When they started criticizing me. I don't want to take credit for it, but I should!" He looks at the chart. "Who's No. 2?"

Trump is pleased to have it confirmed, all these years later, that in 2004 for one week he defeated *CSI*, *American Idol*, and *Survivor*. He looks around at the other magazine covers that adorn the wall of Mar-a-Lago, including *Time*, which selected him as "Person of the Year" in 2016. "I was on the cover fifty-six times, the record," Trump says about *Time*. "I shouldn't brag about it, because of the fifty-six, I'd say twelve are doable to put up!" (*Time*'s covers during his presidency were often deeply critical, and even his "Person of the Year" cover features him sitting in a chair with torn and tattered upholstery and a headline that calls him "President of the Divided States of America.") He starts to crack himself up as he looks back at the ratings chart. "It's cool that I put that up. That's been up there from the beginning."

When we sit back down, Trump marvels at how far he's come. When I hadn't heard from him over the summer, I imagined him cowering in the corner, a cranky shell of himself. But, in fact, Trump is ebullient today. Once again, he has risen from the ashes. He's not the least bit ashamed that newspapers are publishing charts that summarize his different alleged crimes. Reality TV made Trump into one of the most powerful men in the world, and he's a big believer in one of its most common tropes: the opportunity for redemption and revenge. Who cares what people are whispering—at least they're still talking about him. "I would certainly say I have a good chance," he says about his 2024 odds. "I don't want to be foolish. And we have a man that's mentally incapacitated, if he gets there. I don't know if he gets there—he wants to get there."

It's up to the listener to decide the identity of this man. Trump portrays Biden in language that Trump's critics often use to deride Trump. "Let's put it this way: he's the worst president in the history of our country, and he's the most corrupt president in the history of our country," Trump says. "Other than that, he's wonderful."

As our time is ending—the camera crew next door is setting up for Lou Dobbs, now the host of a streaming show on the My Pillow founder Mike Lindell's fringe-right media website—Trump wants to make sure that we have an understanding. He offers to help sell my book at his rallies. He says that vendors with trailers will usually follow him around the country, peddling Trump memorabilia to his fans. "You'll sell ten thousand books at one rally," Trump assures me. "We can sell thousands of thousands of books if we do this. Let's see how this works out."

The energy of interviewing Trump is so all consuming I have a history of losing my belongings on my way to see him. The first time I visited him in Trump Tower, back in 2005, I left my then au courant flip phone in the backseat of a cab. On my first visit back for this book, in 2021, I lost the keys to my apartment in an Uber. On this afternoon, something has come tumbling out of my pocket.

"Is that your phone?" Trump asks, pointing to the couch. "I should have kept it!"

I suddenly imagine Trump, taking a page from the Vivica A. Fox boardroom of *The Celebrity Apprentice*, sending ruinous tweets from my phone.

Trump motions for me to come stand next to him by the window. He wants us to snap a photo together, and asks Martin to do it. She takes a round. He asks to see the pictures. He makes a face. "The light's a little—" He wants to do another take. So I stand next to America's first reality TV president, and we try again.

Back in the Goop suite, I sip on the Gwyneth whiskey as I lounge on a couch that costs more than the average person spends on groceries in a year. I think about the American dream. Celebrity culture has taken a great deal from our country and our world, but the upside—at least in theory—is that it allows people to dream big. The idea goes that if Paltrow or Trump or even Omarosa exists as a living depiction of following your dreams, then, who knows, maybe you, too, can achieve the highest pinnacle of success. (And if not, you can always live vicariously through them.) But having been around famous people as a journalist for twenty years, I know that celebrity is a fantasy and that stardom isn't all that it's cracked up to be. The disconnect between who the star is and who they pretend to be—the grinding, relentless work that goes into maintaining a persona, however fraudulent—is one of the oldest tales of show business.

Trump's vanity, his preening ego, and his love of attention—qualities that other politicians keep out of public view—have always been part of his identity. But somehow, through the course of American history, a portal was unlocked, and people thought that this man—this reality star—should be our leader, and rather than having Trump transform into a person he couldn't be, we all became players in his boardroom, waiting to see what would happen after the next commercial break.

I feel as comfortable as I've been in months sitting here in the Goop suite. Is it so harmful to have a lifestyle brand with endless paths for the average person to buy into? Maybe not, unless the brand swallows the world.

I've been chronicling Trump for twenty years. By now, I've seen him up close more than any other famous figure I've ever interviewed. I've laughed at his jokes to curry favor and patiently sat in front of him as he's spun out fabricated stories. I've waited for him to invent new ways to dis Omarosa and Arnold Schwarzenegger. Sitting in his presence, I feel certain that Trump can be as charismatic as any politician. That's not the problem. The problem is he can deliver his lines, but can't inhabit the part outside a Hollywood set.

Donald Trump should not have been president of the United States; even he, on some level, probably knows this. And it's not true that he could learn the job, in the same way that I could never look like Gwyneth Paltrow, no matter how many of her Goop creams I rub into my face. But in part due to trends in the culture that were percolating way before Trump, we've reached a threshold in our twenty-four-hour-news-cycle, pop-culture-obsessed society where politics and celebrity have merged so closely there's no going back. We've gone down the rabbit hole with Trump. He's eaten up everything, and grown massive in the process, all while we've shrunk into his playthings. And, unlike Alice, we can't easily wake up from this nightmare.

I fly home the next day, trading the Florida heat of Palm Beach for the crisp chill of winter in New York. On the night before Thanksgiving, I'm walking on the Upper West Side, running some errands, when my phone rings. It's from a number that I don't recognize, and I almost don't pick up. As I press the receiver to my ear, I hear a familiar voice: "Hello—it's Donald Trump." I say his name out loud ("Oh, hi, President Trump"), and a man walking nearby gives me a dirty look. I wonder what he'd think if he knew I was actually talking to the real former president.

Trump is calling me at dinnertime to see if I can help a friend of his by trying to place a positive story somewhere, and he asks me to call this friend as a favor. Do I know him? Can I call him? I race for a pen in my bag as he rattles off the number. Then Trump is off, rambling about his own genes—"the best genes"—and once again brings up his ability to captivate the biggest possible audience through his ratings. This is a performance that I've witnessed many times before, but I feel especially empty listening to it on this night. It's at this preholiday moment—when most of the country is unplugging from work and spending time with their loved ones—that Trump has reached out to me. Doesn't he have anything better to do? "I hope you have a happy Thanksgiving," I tell him. There's a pause on the other end of line. "Have a happy Thanksgiving," he finally says, and I hang up.

At Mar-a-Lago, one of the last questions I ask Trump is about the *Alice in Wonderland* reference in *Rage*. It's the part of the book where Bob Woodward reports that Jared Kushner believed the secret to unlocking Trump is seeing him as a real-life Cheshire Cat—that Trump is always appearing and disappearing, confusing people for the sake of confusion. "I don't know what he means by that," Trump says. "You'd have to ask him."

Fair enough. But does he know the story of *Alice in Wonderland*? "Well," Trump says. "It was like a fairy tale." He repeats it with more conviction. "Look! It was a fairy tale. The first night in the White House, I end up standing outside the Lincoln Bedroom. It's so iconic. I call people. I said, 'I'm standing in the Lincoln Bedroom right now.' He had pictures of his son who died—it's tragic. But it was Lincoln. What can I do? It was like," Trump tries to find the right word, "amazing."

Trump seems pleased with himself. "It takes you a while to get over it. It was a dream, yeah. There's nothing like it." It was a dream from which he has yet to wake up—and neither have any of us. He looks up at me, desperate to keep the shared delusion of his time in public office going, to get renewed for another season. "I'm leading!" he says, bringing up the polls again. "Look, I won twice, and I'm better now than I ever did on one or two." He has that gleam of TV-ready optimism about him once more. Trump seems to sense, even to know, that the ratings are going to keep going up until once again, in the greatest and most attention-getting season finale yet, he's hired.

Acknowledgments

I first want to thank my parents. After they came to the United States from Iran as young immigrants in the 1970s, they were determined to build a better life for me and my sister, Sheila. And although they hoped that I'd pursue a career as a doctor, they've been almost as enthusiastic about my writing a book as they would be if I were performing surgery.

Donald Trump called me on Thanksgiving Eve 2023, while I was putting the finishing touches on this book. In the middle of our conversation, he asked me a question that I'm used to answering: *What's the difference between* Variety *and* Variety's *competitors?* I rattled off a fact that I've always been proud to tell anyone, whether it be a stranger or the former (and possibly future) occupant of the Oval Office: Under my editorship, *Variety* has been the No. 1 publication covering the business of Hollywood.

That was speaking in Trump's language of superlatives and bests, but it happens to be true, and I'm proud of all the hard work that's made it so. I'm so honored to be the co-editor-in-chief of *Variety*, and so grateful for our newsroom of thoughtful, creative, energetic, inspired journalists. It's been the privilege of my lifetime to work with all of them.

Michael Lovito, my former journalism student at NYU, is a dogged, thoughtful, and tireless researcher and fact-checker. He helped me find and interview former contestants and producers who worked on *The Apprentice*—and even interview some of them. Michael's reporting is featured throughout this book, and I'm indebted to him for all his hard work, great interviewing skills, and careful research.

I'm appreciative to all the contestants, producers, and sources who co-operated with me for this book, allowing me to find a greater understanding of the man beyond the Trump mythology. Margo Martin, Trump's deputy director of communications, is one of the most organized people I've ever met, so quick in returning emails and helpful with everything I needed. Kimberly Benza in Eric Trump's office was similarly accommodating.

Daniel D'Addario's eyes were the first to look over each chapter, as he offered constructive notes on telling this story and encouraged me to keep writing—and when I'd get stuck, he'd tell me to imagine I was just sending an email to him. Dan is a star, as I like to call him, and his eternal light was a guide to me in completing this book.

Kate Aurthur, who worked on my first book, about *The View*, has said that she was born to be my editor, which may be the nicest way anyone has ever described my work. All writers deserve an editor like Kate. She tirelessly read through early pages of my manuscript, helping me every step of the way.

The extraordinary Trish Deitch had me over to her apartment for a week, to the point where I practically moved in, as we went through this book word by word. She came in with fresh eyes as someone who has never seen an episode of *The Apprentice* in her life, and her notes made my final manuscript shine.

Matt Latimer at Javelin helped me develop this idea, after brilliantly convincing me there'd be no better subject than *The Apprentice* for my second book. He was right about this—and about almost everything as the world's best book agent.

Noah Eaker, an executive editor at HarperCollins, has been a champion of this book from day one, and believed in it and me, for which I'm eternally grateful. The rest of the team at HarperCollins—Jonathan

Burnham, Tina Andreadis, Kate D'Esmond, Edie Astley, Hayley Silverman, and Frieda Duggan—took perfect care of this book. Thank you to Ingrid Sterner for deft copyediting.

The city of New York has loomed large in my life and has made me the writer I am today. And writing about *The Apprentice* reminded me of what it felt like to set foot here as a twenty-year-old intern, trying to build a career at a weekly magazine. It's hard to recall a day where I haven't thought of all the great journalists and editors who inspired me at *Newsweek*, starting with Marcus Mabry, Marc Peyser, David Jefferson, Mark Whitaker, and Alexis Gelber. And Sam Register, from the *Newsweek* library, served as another researcher on this project, helping me find old newspaper and magazine articles about Trump.

I want to thank all my friends who have supported me throughout the years, especially Robert Drury, Melissa Durliat, Meghan McCain, Daniel Pearle, Helen Hoehne, Sam Skey, Jessica Bennett, Susie Banikarim, Marlow Stern, Jeremy O. Harris, Brian Stelter, Michelle Sobrino-Stearns, Cynthia Littleton, Gerry Byrne, Cindi Berger, Evelyn Karamanos, Linda Duncombe, ZZ Packer, Tobias Wolff, Pam Rakis, Deborah Ledford, Karen Kyer, Kathy Brandes, Katherine Barna, John Ross, Brent Lang, Matt Donnelly, Jennifer Dorn, Nicholas Stango, Elsa Keslassy, Tatiana Siegel, Owen Gleiberman, Elizabeth Wagmeister, Rebecca Rubin, Sylvia Tan, William Earl, Angelique Jackson, Chris Willman, Meg Zukin, Selome Hailu, Jem Aswad, Mary Corbet, Jazz Tangcay, Donna Pennestri, Dea Lawrence, Haley Kluge, Lauren Utecht, and Brooke Jaffe.

Finally, a major thank-you to Danica Tersigni at the Colony Hotel in Palm Beach, for upgrading to the Goop suite during my stay in November. When I told her I needed electricity to prepare for an important meeting, I'm sure she didn't know just how important that day was to me, but she was gracious and excellent at her job. I hope her bosses see this and give her a huge raise.

Notes on Sources

This book is based largely on new interviews, including six conversations I had with Donald Trump—four of which took place in person—between May 2021 and November 2023. In total, I interviewed more than fifty people for this book. Many of them spoke on the record, while others, fearing reprisal, spoke on background or not for attribution. I also relied on some of my prior experiences reporting on Trump and *The Apprentice* for *Newsweek*, where I worked from 2004 to 2013.

Index

About the Author

RAMIN SETOODEH is *Variety's* co–editor in chief, the executive producer of *Actors on Actors*, and the author of the *New York Times* best-selling book *Ladies Who Punch: The Explosive Inside Story of "The View."* In 2018, Setoodeh was named entertainment journalist of the year by the Los Angeles Press Club. He previously worked as a senior writer for *Newsweek* and *The Daily Beast*. He lives in New York.